James D. Hardy, M.D

THE
ACADEMIC SURGEON

An Autobiography

by

James Daniel Hardy

Magnolia Mansions Press

Copyright ©2002 by James Daniel Hardy

Library of Congress Catalog Card Number 2002100738
ISBN 0-9665175-5-5

Printed in the United States of America

Design and production, Carolyn Mayson Miller

Magnolia Mansions Press
4661 Pinewood Drive East
Mobile, Alabama 36618
www.magnoliamansions.com

For —
Weezie, my wife —
who is a part
of all that there is.
— and with all my love.
    Jim
September 5, 1998

Ihr bringt mit euch die Bilder froher
Tage, und manche liebe Schatten
steigen auf.

(You bring with you the pictures of earlier days,
and many dear memories come to mind.)
—Goethe, Dedication of Faust

CONTENTS

Preface

ACKNOWLEDGEMENTS

First, my parents, my wife and my children have all contributed to my inner growth. Teachers at all levels also showed the way and many of these are acknowledged in the appendix.

A special pleasure has been the association with my oldest daughter Dr. Louise Roeska-Hardy, who helped with the editing. But all four have made significant contributions.

The work of Mrs. Mary Ruth Ruffin, typist-"producer," has been exemplary. As indeed has been that of Mrs. Virginia W. Keith, research-library assistant.

Appreciation is expressed to the University of Pennsylvania Press for allowing me to draw on my Memoirs, written in 1984 and published in 1986.

The excellent Department of Illustration of the University of Mississippi Medical Center has been outstanding.

Lastly, the efficiency, editing and accuracy of Mrs. Margaret B. Ellis and the Magnolia Mansions Press.

PREFACE

The academic surgeon is a specialist within the specialty of surgery. His or her chief responsibility is to teach medical students about surgery and to train surgery residents how to do surgery. Hopefully, he will perform and publish meritorious research. He commonly has substantial administrative responsibilities within his medical school department and with assignments in the associated teaching hospital. He populates committees of national importance such as the National Institutes of Health (N.I.H.), Board examinations for medical students and for surgery residents, and he interfaces with other academic surgeons throughout the world, bringing new ideas and new surgical procedures to his own medical school and teaching hospital promptly.

He carries on a private practice but the amount is limited by time and university policy. His income is often much less than were he to be in pure private practice, but the other compensations are substantial. His income and a certain level of retirement are secure and his laboratory is provided free of charge by the university. And he is constantly learning new things from the surrounding academic milieu.

There is one other special reward. It is to see the more than one hundred new doctors and, in thought, the new surgeons cross the stage at graduation. And to know that one had a part.

The Table of Contents reflects the experiences of one academic surgeon, but they were typical of the activities of most academic surgeons and teaching centers throughout the United States, the fountainheads of virtually all American surgeons.

In founding a new four-year medical school and University Hospital, this writer and his host of colleagues throughout the University Medical Center revolutionized medical care in Mississippi. For as higher standards of medical care were achieved in Jackson, this achievement was to be seen in ever widening circles throughout the state.

As for the appendix, one requests from the reader a special indulgence. It contains three sections: Teachers that I had over the years, the curricula vitae of the four female Doctors Hardy, and a list of surgeons who had a major part of their training at the University of Mississippi while I was in the chair. The relation between a resident and his chief is very special. We have spent countless hours across the operating table from each other in all sorts of circumstances. We have fought together to save lives when the outlook was bleak. This was one of the most significant life periods for the resident, and the Chief comes to include each one as a "member" of his family.

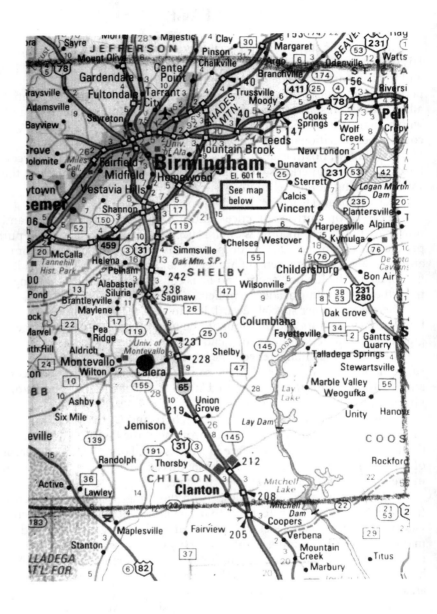

The large dot identifies Newala, AL

CHAPTER ONE

‿

The Way We Were

THE MOLDING OF A PERSONALITY

"I believe there's another one, Mrs. Hardy," the nurse exclaimed. And indeed, James Daniel Hardy followed Julian Patterson Hardy by sixteen minutes in St. Vincent's Hospital in Birmingham on May 14, 1918. Though she lived at Newala, about thirty-five miles south, she had been sent to the hospital by her physician because she looked too large for a normal pregnancy. A Latin teacher at the nearby Montevallo College for Women, she had married Fred Henry Hardy when he was fifty years old and she thirty-five. Father had attended the University of Tennessee and Maryville College, both in Knoxville. His ancestors were of Scottish extraction and Presbyterian. Mother, whose family was of English ancestry and Episcopalian, was from Mt. Hebron, Alabama. Her father, Captain Diggs Poynor, had graduated from the Virginia Military Institute and had taught military science and tactics at the University of Alabama at Tuscaloosa from 1861 to 1865. After the Civil War he had bought a plantation at Mt. Hebron, about fifty miles away, and

1

Fred Henry Hardy and Julia Poynor Hardy (James D. Hardy's parents). From: Hardy, J.D.: The World of Surgery, 1945-1985, Memoirs of One Particiapnt. Philadelphia: University of Pennsylvania Press, 1986.

founded a one-room school which emphasized Latin, Greek, mathematics and English. He also "read law." Mother and her sisters were expected to learn to sew, play the piano and cook—though there always were black cooks in the kitchen. Mother graduated Phi Beta Kappa from the University of Alabama and later took an advanced degree in Latin from Columbia University in New York City. (Coincidentally, many years later one of our secretaries, Suzanne Rau Wolfe, who had occupied our "marriage desk," surfaced as the editor of the splendid *Pictorial History of the University of Alabama*. Sending me a copy she wrote, "Dr. Hardy, if I'd known you had gone to the University of Alabama I would have contrived in some way to include you in this volume." I replied, "Have no concern. That Captain Diggs Poynor shown on page 41 is my maternal grandfather.")

Left: James Daniel Hardy (curly hair) Right: Julian Patterson Hardy

My father's first wife had died from the complications of an ectopic pregnancy, leaving him with four children to be cared for. These, plus the twins and one additional boy to be born a year later, comprised the Hardy family. Mother set out immediately to gain the love and confidence of her four stepchildren. We thus grew up a closely knit group, and this closeness was to last all our lives. Our home was adjacent to the Newala Lime Plant, which had been founded by my father. His father, for whom I was named, owned and operated a lime plant in Calera (see map). The string of lime plants were along a rich vein of virtually pure limestone that ran through Shelby County.

Our father was a forceful disciplinarian and a memorable whipping could result from a serious infraction of the rules. If one of us boys was slow in getting started on some errand, Father would simply glance up at a sign on his office wall that said DO IT NOW. However, we never doubted his love and affection for us. From him we learned discipline, fairness, honesty, the puritan ethic of hard work, and relationships with the outside world. And I learned from him moral courage. Once during the depression, he had seventeen splendid Poland China male shoats as his readily available "cash crop." He hired a veterinarian to castrate them, but their wounds got infected and all seventeen of them died. But not once did I ever hear him voice the question, why me?

Another time, again during the depression, he had men search neighboring counties far and wide for a very large used water tank that supplied the process by which rock lime (sold in barrels and boxcars) was converted to the white powder sold in heavy-duty paper bags. A suitable tank was found at a considerable distance and transported safely to Newala. But the workmen had just managed to get the tank on top of the tall supporting platform and sat down to eat dinner out of their lard buckets when a noise came from above and the tank was seen to be falling to the ground. Mercifully, no one was killed or seriously injured, but the tank was now a twisted mass of iron and useless for its original purpose. Again, my father never questioned, why me?

Mother "switched" us more often than Father, always for obvious cause, but we could often delay the switching, or talk her out of it, or select a fragile switch from a peach tree that broke promptly—or we would simply yell so loudly that she was afraid she was damaging our legs and quit. We really did not mind Mother's occasional switching too much, for we would rather she switched us than to "talk shame" on us. Mother voiced many proverbs, such as "nothing succeeds like success," "never put off until tomorrow what you can do today," "waste not want not," "early to bed and early to rise," "penny wise pound foolish," "an ounce of prevention——," and still others.

Our house was a drafty dwelling, but it was home and a solid refuge. The name Newala was selected to recognize the fact that Father had been brought to Alabama from New York State as a child and Mother was a native Alabamian. Open fireplaces and wood burning stoves provided heating in the winter, but summers were very hot and humid. Kerosene (coal oil) lamps and candles provided lighting until we were able to buy a small Delco electricity generator. The frame house was poorly heated in winter and colds and lobar pneumonia were common. The lobar pneumonia was a very serious disease, this long before sulfonamides became available in the late 1930's. (Gerhard Domagk, Germany, Nobel prize, medicine,1939.)

When a member of our family contracted pneumonia, "Miz." Sarah Crim would be sent for at her home in Thorsby, about eleven miles away. She would put on her white uniform, pack her suitcase, and move into our home at Newala. She applied the mustard plasters to the patient's chest, carried out the doctor's other orders, relieved Mother at the bedside and was always optimistic. People in hospitals do not realize the respect and authority accorded the registered nurse in a rural community. Dr. C.O.(?) Lawrence would come out from Calera as often as he could as the "crisis" approached, sipping coffee far into the night before he had to leave for

5

his early morning office patients. Fortunately, Dr. Lawrence believed in feeding a fever, whereas the other physicians believed in starving a fever. Some years later he was accused of using a controlled sedative, but no accusations could have impaired his reputation in our minds and hearts.

In our farming community, the four seasons were distinct and each had its special charms. Mother had resigned from teaching to be with her small children, but her continuous teaching had been transferred from college students to her young children. For example, once I was supposed to have said to her, "Mamma, I'm tired." "Why, James," she replied. "You've just had your nap and bath. How can you be tired?"

"Mamma, you know all dose tings you tell us? Well, I know so many of dose that it makes me tired."

She usually fed Julian, Taylor and me on the kitchen steps at night before the older family members gathered around the long oval table in the dining room. As the sun set in the west we would say, "Goodnight, Mr. Sun."

There were three solid meals each day. The cook would prepare supper before leaving, to be heated about six or seven o'clock.

EDUCATION. Mother was not satisfied with the local first to six-grade school, for which Father had given the land, so she bought two school desks for Julian and me, and we "went to school" in our parlor through the fourth grade. Taylor would lie on the floor, having no one to play with, and he would often chirp up with the answer before Julian and I could.

In the afternoon in the spring and summer months, Mother would often take her small brood berry picking:

blackberries, huckleberries, plums, and wild grapes (muscadines). We learned to identify different tree species and a good many flowers. With caution, snakes posed no problem, but the ubiquitous chiggers ("red bugs") often diminished considerably the fun of the outing. I do not recall that ticks posed a major problem but wasps and yellow jackets were to be avoided.

In the fall we gathered hickory nuts, wild pecans, hazelnuts, and walnuts.

After going to school with Mother for the first four years, we moved to the local Newala grade school. I remember only four things: the spelling bees, the auctions for the ladies' box suppers, basketball in the gym, and the fact that our young home room teacher had difficulty in keeping discipline amongst the older boys.

JOBS FOR BOYS. The jobs available to boys all derived from my father's enterprises, mostly on the farm but for older teenagers down at the limestone quarry. The entry position was to serve as water boy, carrying water from our deep well out to workers in the fields.

"Water boy, water jack, you orta done been there, and half-ways back!"

Everyone drank from the same two and one-half gallon bucket but my oldest brother, John, had instructed me how to drink without catching germs. You leaned over to the middle of the bucket and slurped from there.

The next job level, for early teenage boys, was to hoe corn from sunup to sundown, for fifty cents a day. (Grown men with families got only a dollar a day or perhaps a dollar and a quarter.)

The third level was to graduate to having one's own mule to plough.

The fourth level was to advance to the quarry where the boy with his mule or horse helped scrape dirt off the surface overlying the limestone, which would then be dynamited and the split rocks hauled to the kilns.

Boys were not allowed to work in or around the lime plant, because of exposed machinery. But injuries were remarkably few.

"HAINTS" (SPIRITS, GHOSTS) AND "PANTERS" (PANTHERS). Many black people believed firmly in nocturnal "panters" and in "haints." It made no difference that no panther had ever been seen (though, actually, bobcats did exist).

But "haints" were also real. Such creatures had no bodies but could be seen.

I, of course, had never really believed in such ghosts until one night I saw one myself. It was down in the barn and I was with Negro boy Herman Hawkins, who was milking a cow by the light of a lantern. All of a sudden he grabbed my shoulder, "shushed" me, and whispered, "There's a haint in the hayloft."

And sure enough there was! It was a light beam, about the size of a two and one-half gallon water bucket, shining against the hay. He took my hand and when he said, "Now," we hurtled out of the barn and toward home.

Explanation. We soon saw that a car with powerful headlights had parked on a slight rise and its lights had passed through the air and through an old pigeonhole in the loft of the barn. That's the last "haint" I ever saw.

THE 4-H CLUB (HEAD, HEART, HEALTH, HAND). This was a popular activity supported by the county farm agent. To go to the summer camp, one had to have underway a project. I listed a calf. The first camp I attended was beside Spring Creek near Montevallo. Every

8

boy had to bring specific food items and something else. We slept on the ground on a blanket. Well, during the night some of the larger boys threw several smaller ones into the creek. They also threw Irish potatoes up into the air, fall where they might. I walked home four miles the next morning.

The only other 4-H Club Camp that I attended was held at Shelby Springs, near the county seat, Columbiana. My memory of it is the boxing match. I had come out of a building and walked over to see what was going on. A rather small boy was in the ring, wearing boxing gloves and challenging anyone who would come forward. My friends "egged" me on and I thought I could at least hold my own. Wrong! That little "ole" boy beat the "stuffin" out of me.

CHRISTMAS IN ALABAMA. Mother made much of the holidays, especially Thanksgiving, Christmas, and Easter and their music. But, in fact, she played the piano almost daily and in church when needed. Christmas was always a very special time. We children believed firmly in Santa Claus.

The holiday season began with a trip down into the woods with Mother to select a Christmas tree—always a cedar. When we found one that was tall enough but not too tall, which had sufficient and symmetrical foliage, we cut it down and dragged it home. We all took turns at decorating the tree. Next, a Saturday in early December was selected for the annual Christmas gift buying trip to Birmingham in the Model-T Ford. We smallest children were given two dollars each, with which we were to buy presents for our immediate family members plus one or more of Mother's siblings. Then at noon we would all reassemble at a popular cafeteria before returning home over the mountains.

Then the wonderful cakes arrived from Aunt Mattie at Pleasant Ridge. She had no money but she baked delicious cakes. Incidentally, she warned us that bubble gum would cause "curvature of the spine," as she bent over backwards to an astonishing degree. She also believed that children should have a dose of castor oil every Saturday morning.

Finally Christmas Eve arrived, when Santa was to visit while we ate supper. Basically, Father didn't want to get up at dawn to pass out the presents from beneath the tree, but Mother held back some presents until morning. And after Christmas day, we drove 120 miles to visit our maternal grandmother near Eutaw, who of course had additional presents for us. It was a sad day when I had to admit, finally, that my parents were Santa Claus.

For the seventh grade we were bussed four miles to the consolidated high school in Montevallo, where first-class teaching prevailed in the courses that were taught. However, virtually no science was offered and mathematics was limited to plane geometry and perhaps a smattering of algebra. This weak math program was to prove a serious omission when we reached college.

My Pneumonia. It was in 1927 that it came my turn to have pneumonia (Fred, John, Taylor and Father would have had it before then or afterward.) I remember mine because I remained in bed the night Santa Claus came. My gifts consisted largely of books, while Julian and Taylor got firecrackers, Roman candles and sizzlers. I broke into tears and Father asked, "Son, what's the matter?" When I told him, he told John to jump in the car, go to Montevallo and ask Joe Klotzman to open his store and sell him some fireworks.

But the new year found me listless and Dr. Lawrence advised that I be taken to a specialist in Montgomery, a pediatrician. In brief, he recommended that I be taken out of school for three months. My parents agreed.

At home alone (with Julian and Taylor away at school) I gradually improved and was able to start a small garden. My father had the workmen build a chicken house in the middle of a large chicken pen, and I hatched out and raised chickens. (My brothers teased that I was so stingy that I would not feed a rooster, that I just ran one of my father's roosters into my enclosure for a visit with the hens and then ran him out again.) But it was spring: young pigs, calves, and chickens. And I shot my first rabbit with my .22 rifle. I also developed the habit of reading, which was to last for the rest of my life.

I tried to keep up with the lessons Julian brought home and near the end of the year I was given a special examination and passed (without distinction) and was allowed to go on into the eighth grade the next year.

When we reached high school age the major outdoor non-scholastic sports available were swimming, ball of various types, and hunting. We had learned to swim in a very primitive way. There were two adjacent abandoned "quarry holes" which were separated by a cow path crossing in dry weather. But in the rainy season, that path was submerged to a depth of from three to four feet. We eight or nine year olds would follow behind a "colored" boy, Herman Hawkins, who was much larger, being about eleven or twelve, as we crossed. Then, in time, we learned to dog-paddle behind him and thereafter without his assistance.

Then, one fine day, we invited Mother and Father down to a long abandoned quarry hole, now filled with water for many years. It was about fifty yards across and with a known depth of about seventy-five feet.

Well, when we suddenly stripped and dived in, Mother almost fainted. (Father had known we'd learned to swim.)

Many years later, during the integration struggle, a surgical friend asked if he might ask me a personal question. "What is it?", I asked.

"Have you ever been in swimming with a Negro?"

"Of course," I replied, "As has just about every farm boy in the South."

He replied, "Yes, but if we admitted it today, we would be ostracized or run out on a rail."

Ball games consisted of a mixture of white boys and black boys. The word "nigger" was never countenanced by my parents. A black man, Cliff Gilmore, had snatched me from the track in front of a locomotive when I was two. I had managed to squeeze under a closed gate.

On Sunday afternoon boys would come from far and wide to play ball. Later, Mother would read to all on the veranda, usually a story from the American Boy.

Dogs. It was at Grandma's on a Christmas trip that my Uncle Dudley gave me a lifelong interest. He had graduated from the University of Alabama, but then returned to Mt. Hebron to help run the family plantation and associated enterprises. One day he asked, "James, do you hunt?"

"Yes," I replied, "I hunt."

"What do you hunt?"

"Rabbits and squirrels."

Quail hunting. Tennessee II on point.

"Son," he intoned, wearing a pained expression, "Gentlemen hunt birds (quail). Would you like for me to give you a dog?"

He gave me a well-trained pointer bitch, and I never looked back. Many years later, Tennessee was most outstanding. During weekdays, after our school bus returned us to Newala, I would take my shotgun and dog and hunt the known haunts of one or more coveys. But on Saturday I would hunt far and wide, to discover the location of new coveys of quail. I can still remember the dog and I leaving home for the day, as Julian kicked the football from one end of our yard to the other and then went down and kicked it back. At noon the dog and I would snuggle into the dead pine straw in a pine thicket, eat our sandwiches, and listen to the murmur as the wind blew through the tops of the evergreen pine trees.

COWS: LITTLE ROSE AND OTHERS. Cows and cattle were a prominent daily consideration. Basically, the herd was composed of milk cows and beef cattle. The latter, out of Texas, had been bought from a boxcar load in nearby Calera and were completely wild and had never known a barbed wire fence. When frightened, the whole herd would stampede right through the fences and have to be quickly retrieved from neighbors' property. Eventually it became prudent to sell this herd. The man who bought them came with a large bulldog. As the dog ran along beside the cow, she or he would turn down to defend itself. The dog then hooked onto the cow's nose and squatted down, causing the cow to somersault. At this, the men would rush up and rope the animal.

The milk cows, in contrast, were reasonably docile and were brought home from the pasture late in the afternoon to be milked and to feed their calves. One front teat was usually reserved for her calf, and to prompt her to "give down" her milk. A large Holstein cow had torn off the end of one front teat in a barbed wire fence, and one had to place the milk bucket beneath her bag quickly or the milk from the injured teat would simply fall on the ground. But if she was angry, she would not give down (the milk) until put with her calf. Later when in medical school we studied the posterior lobe of the pituitary gland, we found the "let down" phenomenon explained.

Little Rose was a young Jersey heifer which Father had bought at the stockyards in Birmingham. He said that Julian, Taylor and I could have her calves if we learned to milk her. Sadly, one of us threw a rock at her which cut her right eye and the clear jelly-like insides ran down her face, causing blindness. It was my first realization of what careless stoning could do to animals, and I regret what we did to Little Rose to this day. All that she'd ever done was to give us lots of milk, calves, and be a friend.

THE LAMB. We had a few sheep and some goats. Just at daylight the night watchman down at the quarry, about half a mile from the lime plant, saw a pack of wild dogs chasing a ewe. Taking his shotgun and surveying the scene, he found that the dogs had killed the mother but had spared the nearby lamb. The watchman brought the lamb to my father and he gave it to me. But I just could not get the lamb to drink (cow's) milk. At this, Father told one of his workmen to go out there and find a way to feed that lamb. Through trial and error, the workman found that placing a cloth wick down into a vanilla flavoring bottle filled with milk enabled the lamb to mouth the milk-soaked wick and swallow the milk. And within a week or so, the lamb was able to drink straight from the bottle.

He became a pet and followed me everywhere. Sadly, however, he developed an intense dislike for my younger brother, Taylor, and would charge him immediately if he caught Taylor out in the yard. Finally, now a large ram, he caught Taylor as he tried desperately to pass through a screen door on the veranda. At this, Father said, "Jim, we can't have Taylor threatened every time he goes outdoors. The ram has to go." So, I sold him to a butcher in Montevallo for $3.00.

I went out for football my junior year in high school. I was a rather inept ball handler and I knew that my only hope was to make the team in the line. But I weighed only 120 pounds and could make only the scrubs, while Julian played quarterback. My mother sought to console me: "But James, you are doing the noble part."

I replied that I did not want to do the noble part, that I wanted to play on the varsity. The next year I weighed 130 pounds and made the team at right guard. We had two and one-half sets of twins on the team. We had a winning season (5-4), and thereafter lost our coach, who was said to have gone to some Millsaps College in

The arrow indicates JDH at right guard. Montevallo High School football team. 1934

Mississippi.

I have always valued the high school football—the Friday afternoon camaraderie, the relished competition, the knowledge that hard physical contact between men may smart considerably but won't prove fatal, that you win some/you lose some, and that victory may loom just one last thrust ahead so never quit—not a bad motto for a surgeon.

I did not play the other competitive sports. During winter I was hunting and in the spring I was putting in my crop, to sell in the commissary and to buy shotgun shells for the fall and winter.

THE DEPRESSION. Meanwhile, the Depression had been upon us. I remember a particular vignette. On Christmas day the little son of a black neighborhood workman came over to our house. "Buck," I asked, "Did you have a good Christmas?" "Yeah, I'se had a good Christmas." "What did Santa Claus bring you?" "A orange," he replied.

The use of lime by farmers, or for water purification or for cement for construction work had virtually dried up. Our "place" was advertised in the county newspaper for non-payment of taxes. Father was over sixty. What could he do? Where would we go?

Blessed be his name, a Mr. Aaron of Meridian, Mississippi, took a five thousand dollar mortgage on the lime plant, the home, and the approximately twelve hundred acres of land. This permitted us to pay the taxes, repair the machinery, and get lime business as President Roosevelt got public building under way. And my personal finances also improved. Before, our weekly allowance was 35 cents each and the movie was 25 cents. Therefore, one had to let the girl go in first on her own finances. Then the boy would go in, happen to see her there, and slide into the conveniently empty seat. Later on we would each have a 5-cent coke. But we did have the car to drive around in and that was a lot.

Also, each spring I would select about an acre in the middle of what I considered my father's best field. He would then have his tractor man "turn over" the vetch-laden soil. From there on I myself hoed and ploughed whenever necessary to raise my crop, consisting largely of tomatoes, watermelons, cantaloupes, cucumbers and corn. I sold the produce in the commissary. I also raised chickens and worked for my father in the fields.

Next, three Mahaffeys formed a dance orchestra, The Bama Skippers. They used Taylor's trumpet and singing and Julian's saxophone. They did not need my clarinet but they did need a trombone. So, I bought one for twenty dollars at a pawnshop in Birmingham and, with Mother to strike the notes on the piano, I gradually taught myself.

The Bama Skippers Front row: (left to right) Clifford Fulford (sax and clarinet), Julian Hardy (sax), Eddie Mahoney (sax and clarinet), Mack Vinson (drums) Back row: (left to right) Taylor Hardy (trumpet and singer), Charles Mahaffey (trumpet and musical director), James Hardy (trombone), John May (large horn), Mary Lee Mahaffey (piano)

My senior year in high school was filled with classes, football, playing trombone with the Bama Skippers, and a lead in the senior play. In the spring the principal called John and me to his office. He said we were tied for grades and that the final six weeks would decide who led the class. Well, John got an A in French and I a B, with the result that at graduation he gave the valedictory address and I the salutatorian address.

Meanwhile, Julian and I had been interviewed by a representative of the University of Alabama. When we said we were thinking of pre-med, he said that the medical training would take too long and was too expensive, with Taylor to come the following year. But Father said that he could always sell a load of cattle to pay the tuition and Mother applied successfully to teach Latin at "the college."

As I departed the home environment, I announced that I had milked my last cow and taken my last dose of castor oil. That has stood.

MEDICAL LESSONS LEARNED IN CHILDHOOD.
Each of a number of disease conditions taught me
a lasting lesson.

SUMMER DIARRHEA AT AGE FOUR. I had developed diarrhea and finally had to be sent to the hospital in Birmingham. Big, black Aunt Eppie cried and kept saying, "I ain't never gonna see my chile no mo'." And she had considerable justification for her opinion of hospitals. All too often the patient went up to Birmingham in Rogan's ambulance and returned in Rogan's hearse—the "same vehicle" but with the curtains reversed. There was no specific treatment in those days. My parents could visit only once a week and the loneliness I felt is a vivid memory today. When in medical practice, I tried to have the mother stay with her child in the hospital whenever possible.

HEAT STROKE. A number of feral pigs were sighted down in the swamp, and Father said that we could have any that we managed to catch. Well, a number of us boys spread out in the swamp and located the herd. It was August and very hot, but we pursued our quarry as fast as we could. I had singled one out and, when cornered, he jumped into the creek to swim across. But I jumped in on top of him and managed to tie him up. I took him home but he died that afternoon, as did most of the others

19

caught. They died from overheating.

APOPLEXY. Late midafternoon in intense heat the elderly black man hoeing corn with me said, "Mr. James, I'se have a bad headache." He had just finished telling me how a policeman could detect a thief on the train when the thief was disguised in a woman's clothing: He said the policeman would drop a 50 cent piece in the person's lap; that a woman would automatically spread her skirt, while the man would slap his knees together. I told him that he'd better knock off for the day.

He did. But he died that night.

CONSERVATISM WITH LEG AMPUTATION. One of the workmen was shot with a .30.30 rifle as he fled another man's home. It blew a two-inch section out of his tibia and it of course became infected. Immediate amputation was recommended but he steadfastly refused, going back and forth to Selma for months on end. Perhaps his opinion was influenced by our blacksmith, who walked on his amputated leg by means of a strapped on hickory fork. His "prosthesis" was a miserable fit, but he did manage to stamp about the blacksmith shop well enough to do his work.

But eventually, the injured leg healed, though about two inches shorter than the opposite leg. But he was fitted with a raised shoe, and got back his prestigious job of running the boiler which furnished the power to run the lime plant. (If serviceable at all, the patient's own leg is usually superior to an artificial one.)

THE SECURE LABORATORY DIAGNOSIS. For almost a year I had been passing a parasite that we later learned was contracted by eating inadequately cooked pork. Our family doctor had prescribed nostrum after nostrum to no avail. One day Father saw me deeply dejected, and asked, "Son, what's the matter?" I replied that all the "treatments" I'd taken had done no good. He then told me to jump into the car and go see Dr. Lawrence who had moved from Calera to, I think, Thorsby. He said at once that the only way to be sure was to send a stool specimen to the state laboratory in Montgomery. The diagnosis was returned in days, I took a single dose of the correct medicine, and was completely cured.

WORKMAN'S COMPENSATION. A tram car loaded with limerock from the quarry was hauled up the inclined track to the top of the tallest kiln. The man stationed there used a long iron bar to release the latch and drop the tram car's rock down into the white hot hopper to be "cooked" for 48 hours into white lime. He was always yelling down to friends, but silence this time had gone on too long and he could not be seen from below. It was found that he had been overcome by fumes and had fallen into the kiln himself. He was literally cooked, but was lifted out by the wide and thick leather belt he always wore.

He left his wife and three small children. She was given $100 and a job, but nothing was required by law. Nowadays, Workman's Compensation is often abused, but I understand its need.

THE DAY SLAVERY ENDED. It was perhaps my last year in high school and I was again visiting Uncle Dudley. "James," he said, "Let's go turkey hunting. We'll have to go over and get Uncle Joe. He's a good turkey caller."

Well, we got into the car and drove over to Uncle Joe's. He was there in his side yard forking hay into a two-horse wagon.

"Uncle Joe, let's go turkey hunting. It's a good afternoon for it."

"I'm sorry, Mister Dud, but I just can't go today. I done promised Mr. Jones this hay today and he needs it."

"Oh, come on, Uncle Joe, you can take that hay tomorrow morning."

"No, Sir, Mister Dud, I done promised and I have to take it today." And he stood his ground.

As Uncle Dudley and I were walking away, he said, "I don't know what this country is coming to when you have a nigger turn you down like that." (The screw had turned. Ten years previously Uncle Joe would have gone turkey hunting regardless.)

GREAT EXPECTATIONS ENDING IN HUMILIATION. The freshman year at Alabama was to prove a watershed in my life. It involved classes, fraternities, football and military bands, concert orchestra, and travel with the glee club. Upper classmen advised us to not let classes interfere with our college education. At the end of the first semester, in January, my report card reflected an A in English composition and German, and B's in chemistry and biology. However, Julian and I got a D in math. I was vaguely unhappy at being pulled in so many directions but I felt confident that by "cramming" I could get a decent grade in math. But unfortunately, the weak math in high school plus inadequate serious studying resulted in an F in trigonometry.

It was a colossal humiliation, and it had probably cost me Phi Beta Kappa. Julian and I went to summer school at Montevallo College for Women. The courses were psychology, taught by Dr. Helen Vickery, and sociology by Dr. Alice Keliher. Both were fine teachers, but Dr. Keliher, down from the University of Chicago for just the summer session, clearly considered herself on safari there in

Alabama. We assured her that we had never seen a lynching and knew of none in Shelby County. I got straight A's in both courses. These were fully transferable to the University of Alabama, giving me a solid "B" average there.

From then on I sharply limited my bridge playing and dug in. The result was that during my second (middle) year, I had achieved solid standing as an able pre-medical student.

I was invited to take a doctorate in German and remain on the faculty thereafter, this in part because of my thesis "The Life of Goethe as Reflected in *Faust*," but my parents agreed with me that I should go on to medical school and the invitation by the German faculty was respectfully declined.

Meanwhile, a classmate had told me that although I had the required grade point average, I had missed Phi Beta Kappa because there was a longstanding rule that failure in a course precluded election. (Incidentally, many years later I was elected an Honorary Member, and the following year I gave the principal address.)

Three particular courses especially prepared me for later years: astronomy (which Mother had also taken), atomic structure, and genetics.

But the most important chemistry course was organic chemistry. Dr. Jack Montgomery was the professor and also Chairman of the Premedical Advisors for medical school applications. I knew that the first two years of medical school, offered at the University, were solid, but I wanted to go to a four-year university, preferably in the northeast. And here Dr. Montgomery was most helpful. For the final examination in his course, he had said more than once that if a student knew all the chemical steps required to convert an aldehyde to a ketone, then that student would make 100 on the final examination. The night before the test a friend of mine called and suggested that we go over to the Education Building and write on the blackboards the sequence of the steps in the conversion. The next day the sole question on the examination was the aldehyde to ketone conversion, and I made the 100.

At about this time I had been appointed by the faculty to arrange speakers and other programs for the pre-medical students for the coming year. In addition, I was appointed a paid teaching assistant. The principal requirements were that I serve as a prosector for mammalian (cat) anatomy for the premedical students and conduct the exercises for liberal arts students who were required to take six hours of laboratory science, usually general biology. Dissection of the fetal pig was conducted amidst squeals. I'd had no botany and did not know a pistil (the female element) from a stamen (the male element). I was just a jump ahead of the students, largely girls, who delighted in teasing me, but we had good sessions.

The medical school aptitude test was given for the first time in the spring of that year. We were told that it was a trial run and that it would not count in our medical school application. But to my considerable surprise, one of the secretaries in the dean's office at Pennsylvania later asked me if I would like to see my grades on the aptitude test.

In the fall I had applied to the University of Pennsylvania's medical school but not to Alabama's two

24

years in Tuscaloosa. Penn replied that no decision would be made until the following March. Meanwhile I was being pressed to pay $50 and sign up at Alabama. Dr. Jack said, "James, hold out for Penn if you want to go there. If Penn turns you down, I will see to it that you are accepted by Alabama, no matter how late."

I wrote to Penn, explained the situation, and urged an earlier decision—that if I was forced to deposit the non-refundable $50 at Alabama I would have to go there. Whereupon Penn accepted me by telegram in late October.

This would mean that Julian and I would be separated for the first time, for he had elected to stay at Alabama to be near the girl he eventually married.

Julian and I graduated in the very hot football stadium late on the afternoon of May 24, 1938.

Chapter 2

〜

Medical School at The University of Pennsylvania

One day in early September, 1938, my parents drove me to Birmingham. If I recall correctly, the train bore the name "The Southerner". It left Birmingham in the early evening and arrived at 30th Street Station in Philadelphia the following afternoon. Stifling heat in the coach forced us to raise the window, through which cinders from the locomotive peppered my white shirt. Never one to sleep well sitting up, I was awake when we passed the heavily laden apple trees in Virginia, red in some orchards but green in others.

On arrival in Philadelphia, I found two Alabama "transfers" waiting for me. One was James Donald, who was from a medical family in Alabama and had recommended Pennsylvania to me. His father had been a physician in Pine Apple, Alabama, located not far north of Mobile. The second student was Henry Hodo. Both entered surgery and in the years to come I would be their guest speaker when each was president of the Alabama Chapter of the American College of Surgeons.

We three piled into a taxi, with my trunk and suitcase, and rode out to Pennsylvania's graduate dormitory, Morris Hall. My room, reserved from Alabama, was on the fourth floor, just beneath the sloping roof and with an attic window that looked out upon the interior of the dormitory "quadrangle." It would be ideal for studying, if the steam heat got all the way up to my room. And, to my surprise, Tom Magruder, the son of a Birmingham surgeon, had the room directly across the narrow hall. A veterinary student lived next door and I came to respect that he had to learn the anatomy of a variety of creatures. He studied very hard.

After getting settled in, I went down to the campus post office to get a mail box. I found waiting there a poignant letter from my mother, imagining what I should expect about the campus. It was a memorable document and I always wanted to do this for my own children but, alas, I never got around to it in time.

During the next several days I had been "rushed" by several medical fraternities. These were important social centers in those days when only several of the 120 students were married. The Phi Chi group took some of us over to the University Hospital to watch an operation. A Dr. Ravdin was performing a cholecystectomy, assisted by Jonathan Rhoads who, he said, had come up from Johns Hopkins. The fairly short, rotund professor stepped back from the operation, preserved the sterility of his hands, and gave a bit of the patient's history. Little did I dream what a huge role these two men would one day play in my career.

I remember, as if yesterday, my first day in medical school. We freshman students gathered in the long circular rising rows, and the august Dean of the Medical School, Dr. William Pepper, entered by a side door down in front, to address us. Tall, with a mustache, he looked the very picture of a dean. He told us that each of us was the chosen one in the ten that had applied. He said we were to wear a jacket at all times, that slovenliness could not be tolerated. He told us to begin studying immediately, lest we fall too far behind to catch up. And he wished us well.

He did not need to urge *me* to study, for I had learned my lesson with the trigonometry failure in college. I went to medical school with unabashed idealism and with a respect for my teachers that was not all that far from reverence. I had learned the hard way Carlyle's Dictum that "it is less important to see what lies dimly in the distance than it is to *do* what lies clearly at hand."

Anatomy, gross and microscopic, occupied the first half of the year. The class was divided into sections in the gross anatomy laboratory, with four students assigned to each cadaver. We would dissect one region of the body, then move to another. (Confidentially, I never did get to the foot.) Our body was that of an elderly black male. We named him Caleb the Cadaver. We respected the bodies, seldom wondered who they had been, and sepulchral formality was not observed. Tom Magruder was one of our foursome. Our section instructor was Henry Lee Spangler, a young physician of recent vintage. He often gave pop quizzes on the dissected part of the cadaver, and he noted that I usually did well. One day, he abruptly announced that he would predict right then that Hardy would intern at the University Hospital, the pinnacle of achievement in his mind and in ours. I did not tell him that I had taught mammalian anatomy at Alabama the year before: He did not ask me.

The smell of the gross anatomy lab permeated our hair and clothing. We freshmen were always discernible to experienced nostrils. Also, the grease seeped into the covers of the dissection manuals. Noting this, Jack Lafferty wrote the publisher and suggested that impermeable covers be substituted. And to everyone's surprise, the publisher did that and made Lafferty a present of a handsome new set of the dissection guide.

The first afternoon in histology (microscopic anatomy) after the formal lecture, Dr. Mary Hogue, our section teacher, came along the row as we were getting out our microscopes and opening the large box of slides that we would be studying for the semester. She asked the man on my left, Lincoln Godfrey (years later to be my co-chief medical resident), where he had gone to college: "Harvard, madam," he replied. She expressed much admiration for Harvard and moved to me. When I answered "The University of Alabama," she asked where the school was located. She then moved on to the man on my right. He too was from Harvard, and thus received warm congratulations. My two neighbors, who of course knew each other well, began to tease me about my college and the backward South in general. They said that the teacher should not be blamed for not knowing where the University of Alabama was located, since few people even knew where the state of Alabama was. They joked that Southerners were all so anemic from hookworm disease that when they became amorously aroused they fainted from blood loss. I listened to all this, as I looked through the slides in the box, which we would be studying for the semester. Then I said, "I'll make you fellows a bet," as I placed two fifty-cent pieces on the table. "I'll bet each of you that I will identify correctly seven out of any ten you select from these slides that we will be studying." They promptly placed their bets, and I identified eight of the ten. After that they subsided. I did, however, acknowledge to them the obvious, that I'd had histology at Alabama the previous year.

BIOCHEMISTRY began after Christmas. Quizzes were given in rapid succession to assess our knowledge of inorganic, organic and physical chemistry. The only strong chemistry courses I'd had in college were organic chemistry and quantitative analysis. Well organized lectures were accompanied by solid laboratory supervision. I was woefully weak in physical chemistry, barely passing, while a friend, a University of Pennsylvania graduate, made in the high nineties. But then an elective unknown was offered for extra credit. Here came my quantitative analysis from college, where I had made A's. The distributed substance was to be identified and then quantitated. My analyses were so close to the "unknown" that my section instructor, Dr. Smythe, came over to my laboratory unit and asked, "Hardy, where did you say you went to college?" He then asked who had taught quantitative analysis at the University of Alabama. I would have written Dr. Kassner about this, but he had been such a stern and reserved man that I doubted he would appreciate my letter. With the special credit I got from identifying and quantifying the "unknown" substance, I made 85 on biochemistry. Meanwhile, I had learned to be ever more efficient in the laboratory and had come to know Dr. David L. Drabkin, a laboratory instructor who held court at the window while our various experiments were "cooking." He said that loss of key faculty at a great medical school was taken in stride but when a lesser school lost its two or three major faculty members it could be years before that school regained its previous stature.

PHYSIOLOGY was different. I liked it from the start, for physiology is the science of bodily function, of how the body works. If one knows how it works normally, one can usually figure out when it is working abnormally.

We were offered electives in research and four of us, including Robert Mayock and Robert Helm, took up work with Dr. Joseph Doupe, a laboratory instructor who had come down from Canada that year. We studied the inhibiting role of fat (olive oil) introduced into the

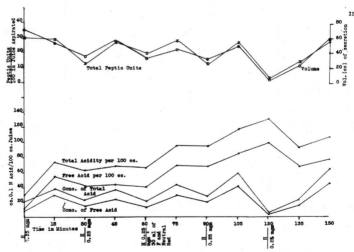

My first laboratory research (with Robert Mayock and Robert Helm). An elective research project in freshman physiology: The effect of olive oil introduced into the duodenum by nasogastric tube on the quantitative and qualitative aspects of gastric secretion. Experimental subjects: ourselves.

duodenum by stomach tube upon the quantitative and the qualitative aspects of the secretion of gastric acid and gastric digestive enzymes. Using ourselves as experimental subjects, we proved the point well. At the end of the year we were called upon to present our research work to the assembled class and faculty in one of the large lecture halls, and my group insisted that I give the report. Later Dr. Henry C. Bassett, the chairman of the department, called me in. He asked what my future plans were and, regarding research, that to make a discovery one must have a new idea or a better method; and that, above all, one should not use a method inferior to the best one currently available.

On Saturday mornings, from time to time, we had a "clinical correlation" hour in the medical auditorium of the University Hospital. It was intended to show us the relationship of the basic science courses to the treatment of patients. After a number of poor speakers, resulting in a massive dwindling of student attendance, Dr. Bernard Comroe, an arthritis specialist, was assigned to restore interest. This charismatic physician brought in things to see and feel—patients with knobby hands, swollen knees and twisted feet, who came right along between the rows of students. Student attendance rose meteorically. This experience taught me the value of showing patients and of laying on hands. We were told that the physician should always touch the patient, but should be careful with women lest the gesture be misinterpreted. Incidentally, one might consider the foot safe enough, but some people cannot bear to have their feet touched. When in doubt, one is wise simply to shake hands.

In May I received my birthday check from my father.

He had promised Julian, Taylor and me one hundred dollars if we did not smoke before we were twenty-one. The check was for only twenty-one cents, but with Julian also in medical school and Taylor in law school back in Alabama, I understood and still have it. The important motivation had been the challenge, not the money.

THE FIRST YEAR: LOOKING BACK. The courses in my first year were largely an extension of courses I'd had in college.

While studies were ninety to ninety-five percent of our focus, there was life outside the classroom and laboratories. I had pledged to the Phi Chi medical fraternity. We either played tennis on the university courts down by the Schuylkill River or went downtown to look and shop, or took in a movie or sometimes the risqué Faye's Burlesque show on Market Street. We occasionally visited the Philadelphia Museum of Art; if memory serves, the large painting Prometheus Bound, in which vultures ate away Prometheus's liver as fast as it regenerated, was hung at the first landing of the stairs. Later on, when Dr. Ravdin talked about "the irresistible urge of the liver to regenerate," I wondered if the ancients had been aware of the remarkable biological phenomenon that, when a portion of the liver is removed, the organ will regenerate to a size approximately equal to its previous volume.

We also had Friday evening upper-balcony student tickets to the Philadelphia Orchestra. Leopold Stokowski was initially the conductor. With his snow white mane, he made a striking appearance. Highly volatile, he once halted the concert when someone was allowed to enter late, noisily. Eugene Ormandy followed and I recall that he once had emergency treatment at the University Hospital for subdeltoid bursitis, before the afternoon concert—a painful affliction for a great orchestra conductor. The Philadelphia Music Appreciation Committee distributed classical music albums at a cost of only $1.50. Numerous friends and I began our music libraries in this way. If memory serves, the performers were not divulged, but the music sounded very much like that of the Philadelphia Orchestra. I always felt that Philadelphia liked students.

Saturday evening was sometimes passed at the Phi Chi house or around the corner at Smokey Joe's, a poorly lit beer joint. Two Saturdays a month, however, I worked from noon until midnight at an NYA (National Youth Administration) job in the bacteriology preparation room in the basement of the medical school (wonderful solitude!). Sunday morning was devoted to the *Philadelphia Inquirer* and the *New York Times* section "The Week in Review," plus church irregularly.

But Sunday afternoon was a time of loneliness. It was hard to meet congenial girls as a stranger in Philadelphia.

Very rarely we treated ourselves to a seafood dinner at the old original Bookbinder's restaurant, way down on Walnut Street near the Front Street wharves. One night we found that the check was more than we had calculated, and we had to leave a minimal tip for the waiter. Disgusted, he held the coin between his thumb and forefinger and asked us loudly and repeatedly if we could spare it. We were mortified.

More often we went to a spaghetti place, Victor di Stephano's on Broad Street, where selections were played on request from a huge collection of classical recordings as the patrons sipped Chianti at red checkered tablecloths by candlelight.

My one sortie out of Philadelphia was at Thanksgiving with a fellow freshman medical student whose father practiced medicine at Pocono Lake in the Pocono Mountains.

Finally the freshman year was over. My grades were 90 in gross anatomy, 97 in microscopic anatomy (histology), 88 in physiology and 85 in physiological chemistry. I didn't know where I'd ranked in the class but, all things considered, I was satisfied.

That summer I got a job as "doctor," teacher and director of athletics in an NYA camp in rural Alabama, where two groups of penniless unemployed teenage boys were rotated on a two-week basis building a schoolhouse near Weogufka. One half the current group would depart in the morning to work on the schoolhouse and the other half would remain in camp (in old CCC [Civilian Conservation Corps] buildings). I would teach improved English and current events that were moving us toward war, and play baseball.

The manager was a Mr. Smith, whose claim to fame was that he had been (Claude) Pepper's campaign manager at the University of Alabama when Pepper ran for president of the student body. He later became a U.S. Senator from Florida. I was Mr. Smith's deputy, and there was an elderly cook.

Before crossing the Coosa River to take up our responsibilities at Weogufka, Mr. Smith and I were called to Montgomery. We were told that we were to reopen the camp that had previously been closed because some of the boys would get drunk and terrorize neighboring families in the woods. The NYA officials in Montgomery said that they were trying again but if there was a single report of alcohol in the camp, it would be closed permanently.

Well, things went along smoothly for several weeks and we had formed a little band (theme song, "Wabash Cannon Ball"). So, Mr. Smith took the weekend to visit his wife, and I was left in charge. As always on Saturday morning, I took the government car and drove to Sylacauga to buy the food provisions for the coming week.

When I returned to camp, one of the boys whispered to me that "Wormy" had been drinking. He said that he had not been drinking. So I told him to come out to the grassy and uneven baseball diamond, that I would take the bat and knock him some "skinners." Poor fellow, he staggered around trying to catch the balls that hit him in the face. It was cruel to persist so I said, "Wormy, I've got to take you home now. You know the rules. No alcohol."

He of course protested, as did two of his cousins. I backed the government car out and faced the dirt road. At this point Vance, one of the boys, clearly a leader, furtively motioned me to one side, as all the other boys sat around waiting to see what was going to happen. Vance said that the two of Wormy's cousins, who wanted to go along, were known to be knife fighters. It would be dangerous to let them ride with me to take Wormy home, that they would just as soon stab me as not.

Here I was sorely tested. We had been warned in Montgomery that a report of alcohol would close the camp permanently. Mr. Smith was depending upon me, as were all the boys who got at least a little money every two weeks. After thinking for a few moments, I asked Vance if he would sit on the back seat between the two threatening cousins, while Wormy sat in front beside me in the passenger's seat. Vance replied that he would, but he added that the ferry we had to cross was run by even more of Wormy's relatives. But I reflected that it might be safer to have them with me than to leave them back at camp. It was by now pouring rain, and when we put Wormy out he trudged over the ploughed ground to his home, a truly pitiable shack.

I was sorry I'd had to do it, but I had faced down a situation that had required considerable courage, and there were no further disciplinary problems for the rest of the summer.

The inner hardening of this experience served me well when I had to "bust" a very popular sergeant down to a buck private in Germany five years later.

THE SOPHOMORE YEAR

The second year began smoothly, as we were all seasoned veterans. A few classmates were no longer to be seen. With the sophomore year came the realization that we were finally studying medicine. I lived in the fraternity house. Bacteriology and pathology, the fall disciplines, were both solid courses that required a great deal of laboratory time. In the former, we noted that bacteria did not grow immediately adjacent to some molds on old culture plates, but unlike Nobel prize winning Sir Alexander Fleming, we did not perceive the significance of this phenomenon. "To see the world in a grain of sand...."

Virtually no virology or genetics was presented and rather little immunology.

38

Pathology was not so different from what it is today, with lectures, gross pathology and microscopic pathology, and the autopsy service. But from pathology I developed a lasting pedagogical conviction that the grade for a truly major course should not rest on a single examination. At mid-term I took the examination when I had the flu. It was announced that students whose grade was above a certain level would not be required (indeed, allowed) to take the examination at the end of the course. I felt I knew more pathology than I had displayed at mid-term and requested that I be allowed to take the final examination, but my request was denied.

During the fall my twin applied to Pennsylvania as he was finishing the two years of medicine offered back at Alabama. When he did not get a positive reply, I made an appointment with Dean Pepper, who sent for my own grades the freshman year. He looked it over while puffing on his pipe. He then spun back to face me and said, "If Dean Graves at Alabama backs your brother, we'll take him." Julian was accepted for the junior class the following fall.

Pharmacology, physical diagnosis and neurology occupied the second semester of the sophomore year. Physical diagnosis included what is now called introduction to clinical medicine with physical examinations performed on ourselves and on an occasional patient, under supervision. Neurology was a weak and poorly organized course. It had been announced that the course was to be completely reorganized, I think by Dr. Detlev Bronk. However, he was called to war work in Washington so often that we rarely saw him.

Pharmacology was perhaps the best course we had in medical school, taught by six very able physician scientists. Emphatically each week revolved around the Friday afternoon quiz in pharmacology. After the final weekly test, I was called in by one of the instructors, Dr. Robert Dripps. He showed me that I had misread one of the three questions and had gone in the wrong direction—but accurately. I was stunned. *Anybody* knew better than that! He went on to say, however, that since my overall average had been the best in the class, the faculty had met. He then smiled and showed me the front of the bluebook. The grade was 100.

During the spring an "ethics committee," consisting of one representative from each class plus a faculty chairman, was appointed through the Dean's office to look into medical school cheating. I found the way of the reformer an uncomfortable one. Two students in our sophomore class were caught and expelled, but I had not reported them personally. Actually, cheating was not widespread, but the worst one was never caught. We were under the Honor Code, but it was no more effective than it is now insofar as student reporting of cheating was concerned. (The University of Mississippi School of Medicine abandoned the Honor system years ago in favor of effective proctoring.)

I casually elected to take ROTC in medical school for no better reason than that I could go to camp Carlisle Barracks in the summer after the sophomore year and would be commissioned a first lieutenant on graduation from medical school. This fateful decision was ultimately to determine my marriage and my medical career.

When at Carlisle Barracks out from Harrisburg,

Pennsylvania, I received a letter from Assistant Dean Edward Thorpe asking me to state honestly whether or not I had answered all four questions on the neurology examination. He said that I had done well on the other three questions and would pass, but that my grade would have been much higher if the other question had been turned in. With the commandant's permission, I took the train down to Philadelphia and went straight to neurophysiologist McCooch's office. He was away but there I saw a profusion of examination bluebooks piled in disorder on his desk. I soon found my missing question and took it to Dean Thorpe's office to be graded.

Then one day, when we were drilling on the parade ground, there came over the loudspeaker system the order for everyone in the command to assemble in the grandstand for an announcement. I shall never forget the moment, for here fate again intervened in my future. The commandant said, very simply, "Gentlemen, France fell this morning."

How could this be? There was the French Marshal Gamelin, who *Life* magazine said was the greatest general of his time. And the impregnable Maginot line. And the vaunted French army, supposedly the best in the world. But France had fallen in almost a matter of days after the German onslaught.

The Commandant went on to say that, inevitably, we would be in the war very soon. It was still 1940, a year before the Japanese bombed Pearl Harbor, but I knew in my bones that the colonel was right.

UNIVERSITY OF PENNSYLVANIA
PHILADELPHIA

THE SCHOOL OF MEDICINE

June 19, 1940

Mr. James D. Hardy
Pennsylvania Unit of R. O. T. C.
Carlisle Barracks
Carlisle, Pennsylvania

Dear Hardy:

In examining the paper which
you turned in for the course in Neurology,
the answer to one question was omitted
or was not found to be with the rest of
your paper.

In order to relieve your mind of
any anxiety about passing the course, I
can tell you now that the other answers
were good but you would get a very much
better grade if you had finished the
examination.

Because of the good record which
you have made in other courses, it occurred
to me that perhaps the answer to the missing
question was lost.

I should appreciate it very much
if you would tell me honestly what happened
and whether you answered all the questions
in the examination.

Yours cordially

Edward S. Thorpe, Jr., M. D.
Assistant to the Dean

THE JUNIOR YEAR

For the medical student, the first and the third years are the worst. Survival is the first-year objective, for few students are dropped thereafter. But the third year is a key one, for an enormous volume of information must be assimilated in internal medicine with its numerous subdivisions, plus surgery, pediatrics, obstetrics and gynecology, psychiatry, ophthalmology, neurosurgery, orthopedics, urology, otolaryngology and public health. Furthermore, this book learning must be achieved at the same time the student is learning how to work with sick patients. Each specialty had its own textbook which supplemented lectures, small conferences, clinics, and individual patient work-ups. We did not go on the hospital floors until our senior year. My personal error was that I tried to learn too much detail, sometimes not perceiving the major points.

Thus, we rotated through the various clinics during the third year, with a lecture each afternoon to the whole class by a faculty member in one of the various clinical specialties. The quality of the lecture varied considerably, but was generally good.

Julian and I were on medicine clinic first. And here we first, also, became familiar with the patient stratum that is more likely to address the physician as "Doc" rather than the more dignified "Doctor." I remember particularly a considerably obese lady whose chart was inches thick, signifying many, many visits to the University Hospital in the past. There was no major scientific problem, but she did have mild-to-moderate osteoarthritis in her knees, not uncommon in seriously overweight patients. But she wanted some medicine. But having been taught in pharmacology not to prescribe drugs except for specific indications, Julian and I refused. We then sought out Dr. Arthur Phillips, our chief, who had to review our case and see the patient with us. He listened to us and then said, "Boys, this happens again each year. You are not in pure science now, you are treating a patient. This lady is going to get herself some medicine somehow, perhaps by coming back tomorrow with the chance that she will be seen by someone else, or by going to the emergency room, or even to another hospital. The psychological effect of taking medicine is very important to her. Let's give her a prescription that has a bright color, tastes good, won't harm, and doesn't cost much. She'll be satisfied and, believe it or not, she'll feel better too." She got the medicine and we got the message.

With experience, it became increasingly clear that to make a correct diagnosis one could readily discard numerous possibilities and then concentrate, with tests as indicated, on the remaining and most likely choices.

Easily the most spectacular professor we had the third year was Dr. John Stokes, who taught dermatology and syphilology. He was a world authority on syphilis and his textbook *Dermatology and Syphilology* was a virtual bible in the field. Dr. Stokes kept all of us nervous at the two-hour session in the amphitheater each Thursday morning from nine to eleven. He would come in with his entire staff in their white jackets and about six patients who were placed behind blinds. Two students would be assigned to each patient to take the history, do a physical examination and come up with a diagnosis to be presented to the class about thirty minutes later. The students had never seen the patient before and we were sorely under the gun.

44

Meanwhile, Stokes had the seating arrangement of the class before him on the lecturn, and he fired questions on the reading assignment. (When he called "Hardy" I would always ask which one and he would usually name Julian.) And he would say the most shocking things, for sex, venereal disease, and such intimate relationships were simply not discussed openly in those days. For example, he asked one student what people did after intercourse. When the student made some lame reply, Stokes said, "I can tell you're a virgin. They sleep." Or, "Don't ask the man if he's had gonorrhea. Ask him *how often* he's had gonorrhea. Asked in this way, he'll usually admit to at least one dose." On another occasion he told us, "One positive test for syphilis will convict a day laborer. Two positives will convict a white-collar worker. Three positives will convict a bank president. But, gentlemen, sometimes four positive Wassermanns will not convict a clergyman!" We were commanded to remain forever vigilant, always with a "high index of suspicion." I don't know how much dermatology I learned in that course, but I came out suspecting almost anyone of harboring syphilis.

Dr. Richard Kern was another very effective lecturer, in infectious diseases and allergy. He was later to be the editor of "The American Journal of Medical Sciences" for many years. Tall and imposing, he had a dramatic way of wagging his long index finger at the class and making his points emphatically. For example, he stressed that not all that wheezes is asthma—meaning that partial obstruction of a bronchus by a tumor might be responsible, a point that led me to diagnose lung malignancy in my mother. "To control rabies, *muzzle the dog*," this became a byword with the students. Regarding a serious and dangerous upper respiratory tract infection, he demanded bed rest ("When you have a fire in the attic, put it out before it spreads below [to the lungs]"). He said that any doctor could make at least enough money to get along, that the commodity most important in life was *time*.

Surgery lectures were given by Drs. Isidor Ravdin and Eldridge Eliason. Good lectures in Gynecology and Obstetrics were given by Drs. Franklin Payne and Carl Bachman, respectively.

Clinical Pharmacology was a small course conducted by Dr. Isaac Starr. I cite it particularly because it was my first introduction to the fact that there was another James Daniel Hardy, a physiologist with a "dolorimeter" with which he compared the pain-relief capacities of morphine, codeine, and perhaps aspirin. It developed that both he and I were members of the American Physiological Society, and often requests for reprints were directed to the wrong Hardy. Even worse, his college in Texas offered me an honorary "Doctor of Science" degree. When I wrote that the offer had been directed to the wrong James Daniel Hardy, the college president answered with a delightful reply. We two James Daniel Hardys later met and found that we might be distant relatives.

In October Julian and I were called home urgently. Father was critically and probably terminally ill. Always substantially obese, he had had diabetes for some years, requiring insulin daily. He hated to inject himself but did so stoically, except for brief periods when he would feel so well that he would skip the injection and promptly get into trouble.

Father, at 74, died of heart failure secondary to the atherosclerotic complications of obesity, diabetes, hypertension and advanced age. In addition to the sadness of losing a parent, I regretted not having been closer to him after I was grown. After I'd gone to college, we'd rarely had the long talks on the side porch during the summer evenings that we'd had when I was a boy.

One particular problem, especially from Mother's standpoint, was that no will could be found, though I had been present some years before when Father made a will as he faced emergency gallbladder surgery. The probate court moved at a snail's pace, and the importance of a current will was all too apparent.

Then on December 7, 1941, came the Japanese attack on Pearl Harbor.

In the spring I received a letter from Geneva ("Gene") Ziegler, secretary of Alpha Omega Alpha (AOA), the medical school scholarship society, telling me that I had been elected to membership. It meant that I ranked among the top five in my class. At the subsequent business meeting Franklin Murphy, the current president, abruptly nominated me for president and the nomination carried into election, since no one else was nominated. I felt embarrassed, for I wondered whether the four other junior members might have preferred someone else. I wrote Mother that I hoped Father would have felt I'd done my part, for my education had indeed been a joint venture with my parents as major participants.

After all the final examinations were finished I returned to Alabama where I served as an externe at the Alabama (Brice) State Mental Hospital in Tuscaloosa.

THE SENIOR YEAR

The senior year was the best of any school year so far. The pressure was off, for outside the Dean's office had been posted the ranking of the entire class at the end of the third year, the only ranking that counted because senior grades were irrelevant. From these rankings would come our internships, the next step in front of us. Reid Bahnson of Winston Salem, North Carolina, was first and, to my best memory, I was third.

This freedom allowed me to read widely as I had not done for years, other than to study the textbooks. Each weekend I took home a load of current medical periodicals. Four of us did a research project to determine in dogs whether placing sulfonamide powder in new wounds retarded healing. We found that it did not. When we gave our results on the Undergraduate Medical Association Day we won a prize, and with our money we presented our surgery resident supervisor Harold Zintel with a new briefcase.

Then Dr. Ravdin called us into his research office and asked where we wanted to publish our results. We were surprised and delighted, and our paper was published in *Surgery*, my first publication.

Another project was competition for the Medical History Prize. Inasmuch as the United States was now in the war, I chose the topic "The History and Importance of Military Field Hygiene." After I had turned my dissertation into the Dean's office, I was confidentially told by his imposing Miss Gallagher that I would receive the Medical History Prize at graduation. However, when I saw the program someone else's name appeared in the Medical History Prize slot. Julian had seen it first and characteristically touched my elbow and said, "James, don't let it bother you." It was learned that the winner had turned in his manuscript at the very last moment.

Another arbeit was my effort to determine from slides in the Sir William Osler Museum at Philadelphia General Hospital just when the "hard" tubercle of sarcoidosis began to be distinguished from the "soft" tubercle of tuberculosis. Despite many hours of poring through the microscope, I was not able to reach a conclusion.

But the major concern of the senior year was to find an internship. I knew I wanted to stay at the Hospital of the University of Pennsylvania. The policy there was to accept fifteen students from the upper 25 percent of our senior class and five from the other universities.

My first internship interview at Penn was with Dr. T. Grier Miller, Chief of Gastroenterology and co-developer of the Miller-Abbott tube. He greeted me pleasantly and then handed me a sheet of paper on which I was to list in preferred order the fifteen students in my class that I would most like to intern with. This was not an easy task, for I liked practically everyone in the class, but I focused on intelligence, integrity, industry, dependability, compatibility with others and stamina. He looked over my list and remarked that my name had appeared on every list handed in so far.

Next I went to see Dr. Eldridge Eliason, Chairman of the Department of Surgery. Everyone knew that being appropriately dressed in a suit and tie, with a recent haircut and clean fingernails, was important to him, for he was the embodiment of the suave, wavy gray-haired, well-dressed, and immaculately clean bachelor. Having looked me over, he asked where all I was applying. I answered, "Just this hospital, Dr. Eliason."

To this he raised an eyebrow, looked at me narrowly and asked, "What if you don't get it?" I replied that I'd rush over and see the dean, at which he broke out laughing and said, "That's an honest answer if I ever heard one. Well, that's all."

What I did not tell him was that I had already been over to ask the dean to write me a letter for an internship at the University of Michigan, as a backup. He had asked, "Hardy, do you really want to go to Michigan?"

"No, sir, I'd rather intern here."

"Then I'm not going to waste my time writing to Michigan."

At graduation, I was commissioned 1st Lieutenant 0-448702 and Julian 0-448703.

Left: Dr. Julian Patterson Hardy
Right: Dr. James Daniel Hardy

Reproduced by permission of the University of Pennsylvania Press. (Memoirs)

CHAPTER 3

Housestaff: The Internship and Medical Residency

NO DOCTOR WILL EVER FORGET HIS INTERNSHIP.

Owing to a massive loss of personnel to the war effort, the University Hospital had asked for volunteers to begin their internship early and so Lincoln Godfrey and I had begun in April. We began on the **laboratory service**. There were no technicians at night, and Godfrey and I supported each other doing urinalyses, blood counts, plating out pus for bacterial growth or sputum for possible tuberculosis, typed pneumococci to permit selection of the appropriate antiserum and ran chemistries for blood sugar levels in diabetes and blood urea nitrogen levels to exclude uremia. It was frequently an all night job, and I was uneasy over the responsibility for crossmatching blood during the night lest an error result in transfusion of mismatched blood causing major illness or even death of the patient. In fact, I was aware of an instance in which two hospitalized patients had had identical names, and one had received the blood intended for the other, though not with fatal outcome. (Later, all hospitals used consecutive numbers for hospital

51

admissions instead of depending solely on names.) After Godfrey and I had supported each other for a few nights, each of us covered the laboratory service every other night. During the day we worked in the lab along with the regular technicians.

My first clinical service was **neurosurgery**. Neurosurgery was a severe service. Previously it had had two interns, one of which was a second-year man. Now it had only one intern who was on his first clinical service. I got only about three or four hours of sleep a night, never saw my roommate awake except perhaps in the dining room, and did not go out of the hospital even once during the six weeks I was on the service. And to make matters even worse, the tension was such that everyone was afraid

Interns. Back row: Dr. Broen, Dr. Shenkin, Dr. Fisher, Dr. Lace, Dr. Clark, Dr. Freeborn. Second row: Dr. Fletcher, Dr. Tompkins, Dr. Walker, Dr. Hardy, Dr. Bahnson, Dr. Morgan. Front row: Dr. Gislason, Dr. Bills, Dr. Kirklin, Dr. Freshwater, Dr. Lafferty, Dr. Longley

that a minor matter could suddenly become a federal offence. The chief resident, a competent and confident man, was nice to me and the first assistant was as nice to me to the degree that he could risk. But the second assistant resident, Roger Cheney, was a terror and I virtually despised him. Even so, things were going along fairly well until an anesthesiologist poked his head through a crack in the operating door to say that the child in a crib outside was hardly breathing. The surgeon quickly asked me how much morphine had I given him. I said that I had waked the intern on Pediatrics about three o'clock to ask the dosage. He had said 1/12 grain of morphine, followed by another 1/12 in three hours would be adequate and safe. George Markley, the chief resident said, "That's a good bit for his size. Drop out and see about him."

I at first thought he was dead but I "stirred" him up to make him breathe. I sent a nurse to get an anesthesiologist. To be brief, he was fully narcotized and the anesthesiologists "bagged" him through an endotracheal tube for hours on end. That the little boy's mother said a special sensitivity to morphine ran in her family was scant comfort.

I was sitting in the corner of the little patient's room dreading that he might have suffered brain damage. Here I was, on my first clinical service and I may have killed a patient. Just then Cheney came in from the completed operation and I hunkered down for (this time) his deserved abuse. But instead, he put his arm around my shoulders and said quietly, "Jim, we're going to save this kid. We have cancelled the rest of the operative schedule for today so that we can all be here to help. We're going to save him and don't you worry."

The boy recovered completely, but now after 57 years, I still choke up a bit in memory.

After neurosursgery, which I now knew I did not want to specialize in, no other service was nearly as stressful.

Two patients on **ward medicine** during internship. The first was a white woman in her mid-thirties who had been admitted for partial small bowel obstruction. In routine stool examinations, it was found that she harbored a tapeworm. Meanwhile a Miller-Abbott tube (a long tube with a balloon on the end) had been passed to relieve the intestinal obstruction. Then, one morning she asked me to draw the curtains around her bed. She then whispered to me that the tapeworm's head had come out and that she had him by the neck! (Until then it had not been well appreciated that the ten-foot Miller-Abbott tube, taped to the nose, could pass through the stomach, the small bowel, the colon and appear at the anus.)

The other patient was a middle-aged female dying from metastatic cancer. She was screaming with pain on the open ward, and truly huge doses of morphine provided no relief. Thus, I told the nurse to fill a syringe with morphine and I would sit by her bed giving small but repeated doses intravenously until she got relief. Finally, she said, "Thank God," and she went to sleep— never to wake up again. Once the morphine provided relief, the large amounts of morphine in her body caused respiratory arrest.

THE PIANO. In fact, I began to take piano lessons, for I had learned that my trombone was not really a solo instrument and gained few friends in close quarters. I called the University's School of Music, not far across

Spruce Street which ran beside the Hospital, and stated my requirements: I would have to come at night, that I would practice one hour each night no matter how late, that I wanted to start with classical music and not scales, and that when my hospital duties prevented my coming I would of course pay anyway. I already knew the base clef from my trombone and the treble clef from my clarinet. My challenge was accepted and a member of the music faculty took me on as a student. But, alas, he was drafted within the week. A young man, Bill Smith, who had "a spot on his lung" and was classified as 4F, took me on and I worked with him for the approximately 18 months I had before I was called up by the Army ground forces.

Pediatrics was a busy time in the winter months. Many of the little patients presented with "strep throat" and all too often they transferred streptococci to my throat. We did a lot of good for sick children on that service but it was not for me.

The **ophthalmology** suite was the private domain of the chairman, Dr. Francis Adler. His hospital section was said to have been given by one of his wealthy patients. It was a world to itself and the rest of the hospital might as well have been on Mars. I liked the eye service and was offered a residency but it was too narrow for me.

The **otolaryngology** service consisted particularly of tonsillectomies, sinus pathology and the extraction of ear wax. It was important to the patients who had such problems but it too was not for me.

General Surgery cared for all the acute bone fractures, as well as breast and abdominal visceral lesions. There was virtually no chest surgery at that time. Dr. Jonathan Rhoads was chief and the two residents were Harold

Zintel and C. Everett ("Chick") Koop.

Obstetrics and Gynecology were generally happy services and there were very few deaths. I was offered a residency but Julian was to take a residency in that specialty in Birmingham, and one in the family was enough. Too, I had become increasingly interested in the heart and circulation, and cardiology was my tentative ultimate specialty goal.

And it was on my **private internal medicine** rotation that I had a lot of luck, for by this stage of the internship I knew I wanted to apply for a residency in Medicine. One morning Dr. Charles Wolferth, Chief of Cardiology, called me to say that he was admitting a lady who ran a "cat house" up in Scranton but that she was a jolly soul and that she paid her bills. I was to examine her and that he would see her again on his afternoon rounds. Well, she wore a lot of expensive looking jewelry and was indeed jolly—but she was short of breath. I believed I had found a substantial collection of fluid in her left chest, so I called Dr. Wolferth and suggested that we try to aspirate this heart failure fluid and thus improve her respiration. But he said, no, that he had just examined her himself. Whereupon, I brashly told him that I would bet him fifty cents that I could remove at least a liter of fluid from her left chest. "You are on," he replied. I removed 1200 cc. and simply wrote that on the chart.

When he came down for his afternoon rounds, he found my note on the chart and laughed. The next day the lady wanted him to come down during his office hours, but he replied that Dr. Hardy was his intern and that he would not come down unless Dr. Hardy thought it necessary.

Another fortunate occurrence involved the management of a patient of Dr. Edward Rose's, Chief of **Endocrinology**. He had admitted her on a Sunday because of fever and malaise. I examined her and thought I'd heard a patch of pneumonia in her left lung. I called Dr. Rose at home to report this finding. However, he said that he had already examined her with his "experienced" stethoscope and that he'd found her lungs to be clear. At this, I asked permission to get a chest X-ray. He was reluctant but, since it was after all a teaching hospital, he agreed. The film revealed a patch of pneumonia at the precise site of my finding, and thus it was justified to begin sulfonamide therapy. When Dr. Rose came in Monday morning, the patient was much improved. He said nothing but after that he treated me differently.

A third fortunate episode involved the passing of a Miller-Abbott tube for high-grade small bowel obstruction in our august Chief of Pediatrics, Dr. Joseph Stokes. I assumed that Dr. Miller would want to pass the M-A tube himself on this special patient, and I had it already iced down in a bowl of isotonic saline solution. But, try as he would, Dr. Miller simply could not pass the tube and it became embarrassing. Abruptly he motioned me to follow him out of the room and, once we were outside, he said "Hardy, go back in there and pass that tube." I returned to the bedside and said, "Dr. Stokes, the passing of a tube requires a mutual forbearance on the part of both the patient and the physician. You will gag and your eyes will water, but keep swallowing." It passed.

At the end of this rotation on private medicine, Dr. Miller asked, "Jim, what are you going to do next year?"

I replied that I was going to apply for a residency in

Medicine but that, since I already had a commission, I probably would not be allowed by the Army to serve as a medical resident.

"We'll see," he replied.

Finally, rumors surfaced that the medical resident selection committee had begun meeting. A number of us interns had applied. Then one morning as we sat briefly in the doctors' lounge after breakfast Freshwater, later a nationally prominent neurosurgeon, picked up the ringing telephone, listened a moment and then said, "Hardy, it's for you."

I immediately realized that it was Dr. Pepper himself, Chairman of the Department of Medicine. He asked, "Hardy, did you apply for the medical residency? If so, we seem to have lost your application."

My heart sank and Freshwater exclaimed "Hardy, that fixes you." And I knew he was right. But Dr. Pepper continued, "How old are you? Do you hold a commission? Are you single?"

I answered, "Twenty-five, and yes and yes."

I went on down to the EMERGENCY room. But soon Dr. Pepper's imposing secretary called to say that Dr. Pepper wanted to see me. I pulled myself together. I knew that he always called in also those applicants who had not been chosen, to say that he appreciated their applying and wished there were more positions available.

I entered Dr. Pepper's suite and was ushered all the way back to his inner sanctum. I was determined to show no emotion but I felt plenty inside.

He bade me sit down and offered me a cigarette, which I declined.

"Hardy," he said, "The selection committee has only

Dr. O.H. Perry Pepper
Reproduced by permission
of the University
of Pennsylvania Press.
(Memoirs)

one concern about you. It's whether or not you can support all your women on a resident's pay."

"Dr. Pepper," I exulted, "I'll certainly try."

"Then you've got it" and he reached across the desk to shake my hand.

The world was my oyster! I had the best job, in the specialty of my choice, with teachers that I respected enormously.

THE MEDICAL RESIDENCY AT PENN

The medical residency "year" was a most rewarding nine months, truncated by events to be told. The responsibilities of the resident were not dissimilar to those of the intern, but the resident stayed in one specialty (Medicine) all year whereas the intern rotated through other services as well. Furthermore, the resident had far more authority, prerogatives, extensive responsibilities, and time to carry on research, interspersed among new patient admissions, ward rounds, and conferences.

My daily duties began with rounds on the wards at about 6:00 or 6:30; after breakfast and a glance at the newspaper, I was back on the ward for staff-resident-intern-student rounds at 8:00 a.m. Anyone who has been on a medical service is well aware of how stylized this minuet can be. Moving from bed to bed down the aisle, the intern would give the history and physical examination from memory. The resident would be asked by the staff man (the "attending") what he thought about the situation. And then the attending would pontificate for the benefit of all present, which usually included the head nurse on the ward. The "work rounds" usually lasted about two hours. When the attending staff changed every three months, Dr. Pepper would caution me not to let the superspecialist fill the ward with too many patients within his specialty—arthritis, vascular, metabolic and so forth; this precaution was sometimes important to preserve the ward as a balanced laboratory for student and housestaff learning.

Three days a week the chiefs of the various specialties (heart, gastrointestinal, metabolic, etc.) made separate teaching rounds. In this exercise, Dr. Pepper himself was masterful. He often made "look" rounds. He would allow no history while he looked silently at the patient. Then he would announce what he thought was wrong with the patient. And he was often astonishingly accurate. Such demonstrations were not lost on me and in later years I did the same with students myself. Dr. Pepper was very good but one does not have to be a genius. The answer lies in experience: The value of seeing a great many patients or doing large numbers of operations cannot be overemphasized.

With experience the physician learns to note a host of things as he sees the patient. He notes the general appearance. (Cancer, which Leonardo da Vinci could put in the face), the walk (limp? staggering? or stiff.) Each suggests a different disease. Virtually everything about a patient can suggest a present disease. Poor teeth suggest financial and social status. Tattoos suggest occupation, perhaps periods of intoxication and potential exposure to venereal disease.

After the morning rounds were over and we had set in motion all the needs of each patient, I was free, between conferences, to do research.

RESEARCH DURING THE MEDICAL RESIDENCY. Shortly after the beginning of the year, I went to Dr. John Lockwood who was running the Harrison Department of Surgical Research for Dr. Ravdin during the war. I asked him to suggest a jumping-off place for research in the management of surgical infections. (It was interesting that, though a resident in Medicine, I had turned first to

*ISAAC STARR
Reproduced by
permission of the
University
of Pennsylvania Press.
(Memoirs)*

61

surgery for guidance.) "Hardy," he said, "infections are a dead issue. Penicillin is going to make surgical infections research irrelevant. I advise you to enter some other field." But looking back at all that has transpired since then, it is apparent that his position was premature.

Lincoln Godfrey and I then asked Dr. Isaac Starr, who had developed the "ballistocardiograph" and later received the Lasker Award (the medical Nobel prize of the United States), to recommend a research project. The ballistocardiograph permitted fairly accurate estimation of the cardiac output per minute. Have you ever lain in bed, worrying about some serious problem, and had the sensation that the bed moved up and down, if only slightly, with each beat of the heart? Well, you do move ever so slightly as the blood from the left ventricle hits the curving arch of the aorta. Thus, with the patient lying on a light weight table suspended from the ceiling by piano wires, this tiny excursion can be magnified with mirrors to produce a strip resembling an electrocardiogram. Then, by measuring the area beneath several complexes, the cardiac output per minute can be calculated.

Dr. Starr suggested that we study the effect of intravenous fluids in dehydrated patients awaiting operation for intestinal obstruction, as compared with normal individuals (we ourselves plus several other housestaff volunteers). We found that intravenous fluids did increase the previously low cardiac output in the dehydrated patients but had little or no effect on cardiac output in the normal volunteers. Of course, this outcome might have been expected, but at that time the methods for measuring cardiac output were in their infancy. Dr. Starr looked at our results and said, "Boys, you've got a

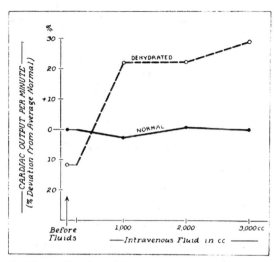

The cardiac output of the normal subjects has been averaged and is compared graphically with the average of the dehydrated patients, before and after intravenous fluid administration.

HARDY and GODFREY, J.A.M.A., 126:23, 1944

Effect of intravenous fluid on cardiac output in dehydrated patients as compared with normal subjects (ourselves and other interns and residents). The intravenous fluid caused no change in the cardiac output of normal individuals but a marked increase in dehydrated patients.

find!" We published in the Journal of the American Medical Association.

Another study, which I worked on alone and published after the war, had to do with whether patients with low serum protein levels absorbed amino acids at a normal rate. First, a tube with four lumens or conduits was constructed, being actually a long Miller-Abbott tube with two small tubes tied along it. Through each of the small tubes a balloon was inflated to block off a sixty-centimeter segment of the small intestine selected at fluoroscopy. Then, a known concentration of amino acid solution was instilled at a fixed rate into the intestine just below the first balloon; the solution not absorbed was sucked out when it reached the second balloon, below. Using a timed interval and rate of infusion, it was possible to calculate how much nitrogen had been absorbed. The normal controls were myself and my fellow interns and residents, but such was the discomfort of swallowing and then tolerating the large (four-lumened) tube for the required eighteen hours on the hard fluoroscopic table, that I never got anyone to volunteer twice. I had no technician and ran every chemical analysis myself. It was time consuming, yes, but research is never quite the same as when the investigator himself does every analysis and calculation himself: He knows his data cold, something that is deeply satisfying.

I had learned by now that it is not necessary to be a genius or have some primordial insight in order to do useful research. One simply has to work at it hard and intelligently as one otherwise would be doing with patients on the floors. Research became a vital part of my professional life during my medical residency and was to remain so thereafter.

Another project arose from the great need, in 1943, for further studies of the effects of blood loss in wounded soldiers. A massive search was mounted for "plasma expanders" that could be stored on the battlefield and then used to support a patient's blood pressure until blood itself became available for transfusing. In the University's blood substitute research program, I gave gelatin intravenously to myself, housestaff and to a large number of patient volunteers in order to exclude any reactions or sensitivities to the gelatin itself. Its circulatory effects were studied on the ballistocardiograph table. And from this study I learned something not measurable in grams or centimeters about research policies and politics. One day I was sitting over in the corner of Dr. Starr's laboratory calculating ballisto tracings with a slide rule, when Dr. Starr came in and said, "Jim, I've just monitored reports from different groups doing research in the medical school, and I heard something that disturbed me. The gelatin project was presented, but your name was not mentioned as a participant who would share in publications. What is your arrangement?" I replied that I had been assured that my name would appear on any paper in which my data were used. He then said, "Well, I'm concerned about it. I've seen too many young men soured on research by some unhappy early experience. I want you to go to John Lockwood, and let me know what you find out."

But I first called Dr. Archibald Fletcher, a resident in surgery who had enlisted my very considerable collaboration. He said that my recollection was of course correct, and he went at once to Dr. C. Everett ("Chick") Koop, resident in surgery and the executive for the gelatin project. Possibly inadequately informed of the informal arrangement with me, Dr. Koop took the position that to include my name on publications would require acknowledgement of the fact that I was in another department, thus giving undue credit to the Department of Medicine, as opposed to the Department of Surgery. However, Dr. Lockwood took a different tack and my name was included. The affair led to somewhat bruised feelings, though, and thereafter the interdepartmental collaboration was terminated by mutual agreement.

After the dust had settled, Dr. Starr advised, "Now, Jim, in the future, when you participate with others in a research project, draw up a memorandum of understanding at the outset, before any substantial amount of work has been done. Lay out who is to do what, and list a tentative order for the authors' names to appear on any papers—first author, second author, last author, and so forth. Like a will, it can always be changed later, in the light of subsequent events and personnel changes, but it preserves a written record of the original agreement."

I followed this advice in all significant activities thereafter. It startled colleagues occasionally, appearing to the novice that I did not have complete trust. But with appropriate attention to verbal explanations, it preserved friendships and gave credit where credit was due.

One day in the early spring Dr. Pepper called me to his office to meet with Dr. Robert Loeb of Columbia-Presbyterian Medical Center in New York, a very influential figure in the world of internal medicine. He had been charged with the responsibility of assembling at the University of Chicago a research team to find some way to control the ravages of malaria among our troops in the South Pacific, where this disease was often causing more casualties than did the Japanese. Dr. Pepper had recommended Franklin Murphy (later president of U.C.L.A.) and me, and he urged that we take the assignment because it would keep us in touch with the laboratory and with at least some element of clinical medicine while we were in the military service. Certainly there would be few such opportunities in the army ground forces, so I accepted. Dr. Pepper and the University Hospital released me from the essential list immediately. But to my dismay, while Murphy was approved, the War Department said that I had a commission, had been trained in the army ground forces (in the ROTC), and that was where I would be assigned.

The staff at Penn remonstrated to the Army but to no avail, and about a month later I was on my way to Carlisle Barracks in Pennsylvania, about fifteen miles out from Harrisburg. This assignment was ultimately to determine the girl I would marry and my shift from internal medicine to surgery after the war.

When I went by to say goodbye to the women in the dean's office, Miss Gallagher, his major assistant and who had known me since my freshman year asked, "Dr. Hardy, what have you lined up in the military?"

"Why, nothing, Miss Gallagher," and I recounted my research assignment failure.

"I'll be in touch with you," she said.

My last full day at the University Hospital was one of the most memorable. A major military project measuring the effects of blood loss in man was being conducted in Dr. Starr's laboratory. Some large men were bled almost a liter of blood, to be stored in the blood bank for a sick relative. I volunteered as an experimental subject and was bled almost 1100 ml. As this blood loss approached this level my vision became blurred and I had to take deep breaths and keep flexing my arms and legs to avoid blacking out. My blood pressure fell to 70 mm. Hg. and my cardiac output fell by almost 50 percent. When blood loss ceased, however, my vision gradually cleared over the next few minutes and, although I remained very weak and somewhat breathless and with a rapid pulse, I did not decompensate again. My blood pressure gradually rose to between 80 and 90 mm. Hg. but it did not return to the pre-bleeding level throughout the night. For several hours I could not sit up without passing out, but later on I could sit up with my feet on the floor. By morning I could stand weakly but to observers I "looked and acted like a sick man." This was my last full day in Philadelphia, and I had to go downtown to buy an army footlocker to take to camp at Carlisle Barracks. I made it down and got it, but it was just about all I could do to pick up the empty footlocker and get it back to the University Hospital. At this point, I had my stored blood transfused back, and cardiac output promptly returned to normal. I felt like a new man and departed for vacation in Alabama.

On April 22, Lincoln Godfrey and I took the train to Harrisburg, where an army truck would ferry us out to Carlisle Barracks. On the way up, Linc, who had celebrated considerably the night before, suddenly asked me very soberly, "Are you nervous?" It was extremely unusual for him to ask any personal question—he was so reserved, so Harvard de rigueur.

"Why, no, Linc, I'm not nervous. After all, we are doctors. We won't exactly be in a foxhole, though since we're headed for the infantry we may well be in a battalion aid station."

He said, "Well, whenever I have to change from one place to another, or from one job to another, I get all nervous inside."

I did not think too much about this exchange at the time, but some years later, upon learning of his untimely death, I was to recall with sadness his then apparently trivial question and comment. And when subsequently I met one of our classmates, George Austin, and expressed my sadness over Linc, George said, "Jim, you never know what's in another man's heart."

CHAPTER 4

⌒

Military Service: The Army in WWII

CARLISLE BARRACKS. (1944). Upon arriving at the post, Godfrey and I went to learn our quarters. There we found that, since we were late on arrival, we would be billeted on the second floor of a long wooden frame building. And upon climbing the stairs, we found that almost every bed was occupied by black dentists who had just graduated from Howard University in Washington, D.C. Godfrey was incensed and uttered some clearly audible remarks to that effect. But as we were leaving five weeks later he said, "You know, this is the first time I have ever had social contact with Negroes on an equal level. They're really very nice guys." Unlike our ROTC Camp at Carlisle in the summer of 1940, this time Carlisle was all business.

The next morning a full colonel addressed us in the rain. We were still in dress uniform, for we had yet to get our fatigues. Apparently, the Army was not deterred by rain.

We were then drilled by the officers who would command our 53rd Officers Training Battalion.

We went to the supply building and drew our fatigue clothing. Then that night, ignoring the continuing rain, we were trucked into the woods and ordered to put up our pup tents. With the ground soaking wet, I had elected to stand beneath a thick pine tree, but I did not get away with it. The captain came over, saw me, and said, "Hardy, put up that pup tent and get in it! The Army does not require that you like it, but it does require that you do it."

I got the message.

Then we were given five weeks of the best course in my experience. The instruction included physical conditioning, logistics (including the duties of a train commander), field hygiene and emergency wound management. And for the first time I learned the great value of movies as instructional aids. I recall that one movie dealt with the detection of booby traps. A British soldier thought he'd checked every possible hiding place, but when he pulled the chain on the commode it blew him sky high.

Another film emphasized the importance of rifle maintenance. As a German soldier closed in for the kill, the British soldier's dirty rifle failed to fire.

Meanwhile, the army shoes issued me by the supply officer hurt my feet, and I took them back and asked to exchange them for another pair. But the sergeant said, "Lieutenant, take this hatchet and go behind the building and chop them up. Then I can 'survey' them as unfit for further use."

I remonstrated that I'd worn them only once; but he told me again to whack the shoes, and so I did.

One day I was paged for a telephone call from Philadelphia. It was from Miss Gallagher, the dean's secretary. "Dr. Hardy, how would you like to join Sarge Pepper at the McGuire General Hospital just completed near Richmond? He will be Chief of Medicine."

"I would!"

STARK GENERAL HOSPITAL. Charleston, S.C., June 2, 1944. Orders directed me to this first "permanent" post. It functioned as a Medical Officers Replacement pool (MDRP). When I reported in and made my best snappy salute, the adjutant almost fell out of his chair. He then returned a very casual salute. Clearly, military formalities were relaxed "in the field."

I was assigned to Captain Hoffman's cardiology ward. He was a Pennsylvania graduate.

I was billeted in the torrid "Green Mansions" barracks, where I had three different roommates in three days.

Stark GH was a debarkation station which received wounded soldiers from the ETO (European Theater of Operations).

Shortly after my arrival, Lieutenant Archibald Fletcher, my Penn research colleague, arranged a blind date for me through the Scottish Presbyterian Church. He, the son of Presbyterian missionaries, had been in the 52nd OTB at Carlisle and thus had preceded me by several weeks.

Well, he had done such a good job with securing me a blind date that I knew I'd met the girl I could happily marry—Louise Scott Sams of Decatur, Georgia. Her father, an official with the Atlantic Coast Railway, had been transferred to Charleston for the duration of the war, to handle the large volume of war shipping going through the port at Charleston.

I encountered Major Sergeant Pepper in the officers' chow line and he recognized me. He discreetly confirmed

Letter to Mother: Julia Ann Hardy on meeting the girl I would
▪ *eventually marry.*

that I would get orders to join him at McGuire GH at Richmond.

Meanwhile, I was ordered as train commander to accompany a train load of wounded soldiers to Cushing GH at Framingham, Massachusetts. I scrambled around looking for my notes of the logistics instruction at Carlisle but I certainly did not feel very confident in this assignment. But fortunately, one of the sergeants was an old hand at hospital train service, and he was just what a good sergeant can be.

At Cushing GH the efficiency exhibited was truly astonishing. We backed in, delivered the patients, turned over valuables, unloaded baggage, made property exchange, had men's records signed for, sent telegram advising Stark GH and the War Department of our arrival, and backed out again—all in 15 minutes.

Incidentally, the railroads were invariably most considerate of the needs and comfort of wounded soldiers.

On return to Charleston, we found four blankets missing. We reported them on survey—"fault of no one concerned."

I was told that a new batch of orders had been posted at headquarters during my absence. I sped over and found confirmed that I was ordered to proceed to McGuire GH at Richmond, Virginia.

McGuire GH. No patients had yet been admitted to the brand new McGuire General. Major Pepper assigned me to the Isolation Section. There I collaborated with Lieutenant Foster (ANC [Army Nurse Corps]) of Baltimore. I was surprised at all the details that the nurses at Penn had dealt with, but which I had scarcely noticed. My principal new duties were to help train technicians. Although this was not exactly what I had expected my role in the Army would be, it afforded me experience in speaking and I had nothing else to do. The subject was isolation techniques with demonstrations.

Private flying license:
"Single engine land based airplane. Must wear Glasses."

A group of us went to a lake to swim one Sunday afternoon, and a small plane came spinning down, apparently out of control. But at the last moment it pulled up and flew away.

LEARNING TO FLY. With a lot of free time, without patients, I decided to learn to fly. Next day I called the Hermitage Airport, and one A.B. Lowery answered my call. He said that he could teach me how to fly an airplane, but that the army cadet flying program had just been discontinued. He doubted that I could achieve the book learning necessary to pass the CAA (Civil Aeronautics Authority) examinations. I told him that I would buy the books and adopt medical school study discipline; that I thought I could pass the examination in navigation (with the compass), meteorology, CAA flight regulations and aircraft maintenance.

The only time I could get to the airfield outside Richmond was after duty hours at five o'clock. And then the laborious trek by trolley and bus plus a final ten-minute walk. This whole process took over an hour, but it was summer and adequate light persisted until about eight-thirty. Lowery, true to his word, did teach me to fly a Cub (single engined) plane. There were "spins," power turns, many take-off and landings, many "force landings," stalls, and the rest. The sudden forced landing command was accompanied by Lowery's shutting off the power, and I had to survey the terrain quickly for a possible landing spot. As I glided downward toward an open field, at an altitude of about 500 to 1000 feet he would suddenly restore the power and we would fly away. Fortunately, I never had occasion to meet "force landing" in subsequent years, but Lowery's drilling me in the management of such an event had steeled me against panic should it have occurred.

One fine day, Lowery and I went up and he said to circle the field and land. Back on the ground, he got out and said, "Hardy, she's all yours. Take off and land a few times and I will write you up as qualified for solo flight."

Meanwhile, I had served as medical train officer to a train load of patients to Schick GH at Camden, Iowa. Before I left Richmond I had reminded Major Pepper of how heavy the train traffic would be on the way back through Chicago. Looking at him carefully, I remarked that it might require a two-day layover. He grinned and said, "Hardy, it had better not take more than three days!"

First time to cross the Mississippi River.

And I fell in love with Chicago: The University of Chicago, Professor A.J. Carlson's physiology laboratory, Grant Park, the wonderful field museum, the arts museum, the aquarium, and Lake Michigan. As I was leaving the officers club where I was billeted, I encountered Walter Martin of my 53rd OTB at Carlisle Barracks. We would eventually go overseas together.

My other train trip from Richmond was to serve as medical officer for the transport of about five hundred German prisoners, most of them from General Rommel's Afrika korps, from Newport News to Rupert, Idaho. The train was filthy and the men were forced to sit two by two, facing each other, twenty-four hours a day. One by one, they were allowed to go to the latrine. From this 24-hour posture, 8.5% developed ankle edema. I was struck by the wide range of ages. One late teenage boy went raging insane and was put off the train in Illinois. They were to dig sugar beets in Idaho.

My other sortie from Richmond was an assignment to Swift Creek Maneuver Area as medical officer to a battalion of quartermaster Negro troops. We were in tents and were often wet and uncomfortable, but for some army regulation I got paid per diem and got a chance to fire a machine gun.

Meanwhile, I went to Richmond and took the CAA written examination and passed. Later, my flying was assessed by a federal inspector and I got my private flying license, limited to a single engine land based airplane and "must wear glasses."

The flying license achieved, I asked Major Pepper to send me to Camp Ellis in Illinois, where a large number of general hospitals, station hospitals, and field hospitals were being developed for overseas duty. I wanted to get "over there" before the war ended. Lieutenant Harold Barker, a fellow house officer from Penn, had been assigned to McGuire GH, and we asked Major Pepper to send us to Camp Ellis together. We obtained a letter from Colonel Percy, Commandant of McGuire, to the commanding officer at Camp Ellis requesting that Barker and I be assigned to the same unit, whatever it proved to be. I certainly hoped it would go to Europe, where I would have a chance to use my college German and high school French.

At Camp Ellis, Barker and I took our letter from Colonel Percy to the commandant, I believe a brigadier general. We requested again that we be assigned to the same unit. He replied that we must surely know that special treatment was not permissible in times of war, and we left his office disappointed.

The next morning several hundred medical officers gathered in a large lecture hall and, in alphabetical order, ten or so names would be called over the sound system as assigned to a specific hospital. Well, when B (Barker) was called out, the name of Hardy came next before returning to the alphabetical order. Everyone looked around but

U.S. ARMY FIELD HOSPITAL 81
MAJOR GERALD F BANKS M C Commanding
DEC 1944 IMMEDIATELY PRIOR TO EMBARKING FOR OVERSEAS

Reproduced by permission of the University of Pennsylvania Press. (Memoirs)

Barker and I studied the floor. Several days later when the General came through our bivouac camp in the field, Barker and I tried to thank him. But he brushed us off as if he'd never seen us before in his life!

We'd met the other members of our 81st Field Hospital which had been activated September 21, 1944. Major Gerald Banks, Commander, was fairly short, wiry, sun-bleached, with close cropped blond hair and a neat mustache. Regular army, he was the soul of spit and polish. The adjutant was Arthur Hurand, a swarthy young lawyer from Flint, Michigan. He worked tirelessly and though administratively second in command, never was I to see him exercise this authority unfairly. The First Sergeant was Harold Williams. Tall, stocky and sporting a black mustache, he was already a favorite of both the officers and the men. Leadership is where you find it and he was a natural leader of men. Lieutenant Russell Lewis was supply officer. Having been in the army eleven years and come up through the ranks, he was the most accomplished "borrower" of my experience. For example, he had acquired literally truckloads of furniture for the 81st's offices without ever signing a single receipt. Such a man would prove invaluable.

The TO (table of organization) called for 22 officers, 18 nurses (officers themselves) and 182 enlisted men (EM). The field Hospital was divided into three units, A, B and C. It could function as a whole as a station hospital, or it could function as three independent, self-contained, units. It was to function in both these capacities overseas. When three units were combined, the hospital could handle 400 patients.

At out first staff meeting, Major Banks gave us a general survey of the purposes of a field hospital and made officer assignments to each of the three units (A, B, and C). I was assigned to C-Unit, Major Corley commanding, and Barker to A-Unit, Captain Bounds commanding. The nurses were similarly divided. Major Corley was a radiologist, Ben Smith the surgeon, I the chief of medicine and laboratory. At the end of his introductory remarks, Major Banks asked if there were any questions. I held my hand up and asked, "Major, is this outfit going to Europe or the Pacific?"

At this he replied, "Lieutenant, surely you must realize that what you ask is restricted information. However, I will say one thing. I've just spent two years at the Pentagon and I was assured that I would not go to the Pacific!"

As the tons of hospital equipment were being assembled, Major Banks directed me, with Barker, to lay out a night compass and map-reading exercise—this on the strength of my flight navigation using the compass. All officers, non-commissioned officers and vehicle drivers would be required to complete this laid-out course at night under black-out conditions.

When a surprise visit by the IG (inspector general) disclosed specific deficiencies, I was ordered to lecture the enlisted men on mines and booby traps. My presentations were embellished considerably by explosions set off suddenly in the back of the lecture hall by Sergeant Shaw, previously with the infantry.

The nearest "watering hole" was Peoria, Illinois. One evening several of us were sitting around a table in the bar of the Pierre Marquette Hotel and the talk turned as to how one could begin conversation with a stranger. Adjutant Hurand (a lawyer) said it was no problem. At this, someone bet him five dollars that he could not begin a conversation with a lone man sitting on a stool at the counter. Whereupon Hurand went up, ordered a beer, and sat two seats down from the lonely drinker. Then he presently moved to a stool beside the lonely drinker. Then he told the drinker that he looked familiar and asked where he was from. Next, he asked if he lived near a hardware store. He did. Then Hurand said that his uncle was a broker for nails. Did the stranger's hardware store carry 20-penny nails? And from there on they were talking like magpies!

The 81st was transported by train from Camp Ellis in Illinois to Camp Lee in Virginia. Here our nurses and medical corpsmen worked side by side in the station hospital, and mutual respect was developed. On this ride, I joined three officers in a compartment to play bridge. To my best memory, it was the last time I played bridge until my retirement in 1990.

We again bivouacked at Swift Creek maneuver area.

The second visit by the IG found the 81st in readiness and it was rumored that we would be overseas by Christmas. We went to Swift Creek Maneuver area again briefly for a final shakedown, with full equipment. Then back to Camp Lee, from which we were ordered to the POE (Port of Embarcation).

CAMP KILMER (N.J.) 18 Dec. 44. There was activity in all directions as hordes of soldiers in all ranks and units prepared to ship out. Long lines of men marched in cadence, often to risqué chants such as:

"I used to work in Chicago,
In a department store.
I used to work in Chicago

> *but I don't work there anymore.*
> *A lady came in and asked for a goose*
> *So goose her I promptly did,*
> *I used to work in Chicago*
> *But I don't work there anymore."*

There were passes to New York, abandon ship drill, test gas masks and endless meetings ("sharp!") It was extremely cold, with deep snow.

Then on December 23, 1944, we were transported in trucks in the early morning darkness to the New Jersey wharves where we boarded the HMS (His Majesty's Ship)—The Vollendam. I was the advance officer for the 81st and found the ship to be much smaller than we had expected: Probably does not carry more than 500 troops.

But to my great surprise, three thousand men were packed into the lower compartments. Officers quarters held 15 men *going overseas*, while in peacetime only two persons occupied the compartment *going abroad*. Still, I was glad I was an officer. Below, the enlisted men slept three deep vertically: one in a hammock, one on the dining table and one on the floor.

The ship was manned by British and Dutch seamen. It was said to be quite seaworthy. The latter was to be greatly appreciated as we weathered a storm in the Atlantic, while the accompanying destroyers were tossed about like toys in a bathtub. Many of our personnel were miserably seasick. There would be two meals a day, at approximately six a.m. and six p.m. There was a canteen where Spam and Nabisco wafers could be purchased: It was to be many years after the war before I could gaze at cans of Spam and boxes of Nabisco wafers without a mild revulsion.

Dec. 25, 1944. Merry Christmas! In the late afternoon came the voice over the speaker system: "Fill canteens before retiring; carry life belts at all times; no more smoking on the open decks."

Dec. 26. Got up and looked all around. We were now well out to sea and there were ships in all directions. It was said later that this was the largest convoy of the war.

At night, in a calm sea, the scent of soft sea breeze, full moon, soft fleecy clouds, luminescent creatures in the water below, and the silhouettes of the ships on the horizon combined to paint a scene of breathtaking beauty. And all my life thereafter the scent of a fresh sea breeze reminded me of those nights on the ocean.

In brief, we went straight to the almost totally destroyed port of Le Havre, France, and put off the infantry in the snowy weather to assist in defending against the Germans in the Battle of the Bulge. Then back across the channel to England and finally, after several detours to escape wolf packs of German submarines, debarked at Gourock on heavy rope nets and entrained on the narrow gauge track for Oulton Park staging area, about 35 miles from Liverpool. (Incidentally, my twin brother Julian's ship had been sunk in the English Channel and he had been rescued by a French fishing vessel.)

At Oulton Park Staging Area, I was appointed to run the post's medical dispensary. And here the air mattress and sleeping bag that I'd bought in Chicago (from Camp Ellis) proved to be one of the best investments of my career.

The daily sick call: pediculosis, pharyngitis, poison ivy, hoarseness for one month referred to 109th GH for ENT consultation, insurance exams, examination of food handlers, anterior dislocation of the shoulder in touch football, and painful feet. Engineers marched out at dark to practice building Bailey bridges over a stream. Ice and snow.

Chaplain Norris and Lieutenants Barker, Cummings and I were given a 3-day pass to London. There Red Cross found us quarters and we saw the usual sights: 10 Downing Street, the War Ministry, the Tower of London, Madame Tussaud's exhibits, the Admiralty, St. James Palace, Westminster Abbey, Fleet Street, Reuters, Lloyds, Old Curiosity Shop of Dickens fame from which I sent Mother a card and many other places of lore. Barker and I looked in vain for Sherlock Holmes' Baker Street.

Westminster Abbey was the most impressive, with enshrined on the walls the immortals of England. A performance of Rigoletto was good but not outstanding. And the hordes of prostitutes on the streets after dark was daunting. (It has been rumored mischievously that after the war many of these business ladies retired to the countryside and had tea with the Vicar each Tuesday.)

On February 20, 1945, it was clear that I had developed pneumonia: Severe productive cough with hemoptysis, fever ranging from 99 to 103 degrees F, anorexia, severely tender gums, and intermittent abdominal pains not unlike those of peptic ulcer. Major Harvey, post surgeon and C.O. of dispensary No. 1, came by and found me still abed. He auscultated my lungs, diagnosed atypical pneumonia, and sent me to the 109th GH. How pleasant to have bed linen and an attractive diet. Tonsillitis and sinusitis diagnosed.

After several days on isolation in a private room, on the officers' ward, I was moved to the open ward. On my left was a 1st Lieutenant who'd been wounded in the foot during the Battle of the Bulge. He'd run about a mile and dived into a foxhole to return fire before he'd realized he'd been shot. He said that the carbine rifle issued to officers might fail to stop a charging German but that the Garand rifle issued to enlisted men would.

On my right was a lieutenant who had been wounded seven times and was admitted for combat fatigue. He told that once, in a forward evacuation hospital, he looked up to find General Patton standing beside his bed. Jumping up, he'd come to rigid attention. "What's the matter with you, Lieutenant," he asked. "Psychoneurosis, sir," he replied. Patton ordered, "Get up and go back to the front," and turned to leave. But abruptly he turned back and asked, "How long have you been a second lieutenant?" Then, upon hearing the answer, he departed. But when the patient had reached his outfit he found a letter promoting him to first lieutenant.

12 Mar 45. Misfortune. Severely sprained left ankle playing volleyball, officers against enlisted men. Stepped into a deep heavy truck rut, now obscured by new green grass. It was extremely painful, with marked swelling, but X-rays taken at 109th GH disclosed no fracture. (Years later I found that ankle ligaments had been torn, rendering the left ankle somewhat unstable to this day.)

I became febrile again, with the abdominal pains of a "stomach" ulcer, and with only a loaf of bread to assuage the pain—since the mess was served several hundred yards away.

Major Banks urged me to return to the 109th GH but I respectfully declined. The 81st was expected to move out any day to cross the channel to France and I was determined to stay with my unit. But as I was about to enter the gangplank to the good ship Sobieski on crutches at Southampton, the full colonel checking off each man said, "Lieutenant, it looks like you should be going in the opposite direction."

The *Sobieski*, apparently named after an ancient Polish king, was a splendid ship, far above the quality of HMS Vollendam, on which we'd crossed the Atlantic. Good food and a pleasant lounge. The only complaint was that E, above middle C, stuck on the piano.

We were fully dressed, had abandon ship drill, and wearing our life preservers, as we crossed the treacherous English Channel, infested with German submarines, under heavy destroyer escort.

As noted previously, the port of Le Harvre was in a shambles. We quickly boarded a train for Paris. There we had a few hours in the train station, where I saw a truck load of liberated French prisoners of war. They were dirty, listless and milled about in disorder. But just then a band appeared and began playing the Marseilles. And as by magic, the disheveled soldiers began slowly to straighten up, gather in formation, and marched off with steadily increasing pace and force.

A train took the 81st from Paris to Luneville. The long train ride across France carried us past many names immortalized by World War I. Chateau-Thierry, for instance. And as for the Marne River, one could have almost jumped across it. Shell holes pockmarked the terrain on all sides.

At Luneville near midnight we were directed to a girls school that had been taken over as a hospital. The toilet facilities were new to us, to say the least. One simply planted a foot on each side of the receptacle. We were told to go in, find an empty bed and get in it. I awoke to find an amputee on each side.

(By now the allies had repulsed the German onslaught through the Ardennes forest [The Battle of the Bulge].)

By truck convoy we left Luneville for "Mannheim," crossing the Rhine at Worms on a pontoon bridge, the previous bridge a wreckage about 50 yards downstream. Buildings were still smoking and dead horses littered the side of the road. Returning civilians were apt to be a woman pulling a miserable little wagon, with an old man pushing from behind, and a child leading a goat. Few able men were to be seen. When the trucks made a "rest" stop, there was no choice but to urinate from the road, while civilian women trudged behind. It would have been foolish to step off the road, for land mines had not yet been cleared.

As the 81st neared Mannheim, it became enmeshed in a tank column on its way to assist the attack to take the city.

Whereupon, it was decided that the orders had meant to read Marnheim. Thus, after much trial and error to find the route, we came abreast of the 59th Evac Hospital, at 0500, which put us up in empty ward tents for what there was left of the "night."

1 Apr 45. Easter Sunday. Only a few were out to attend the sunrise service. But with our family scattered afar, I knew each member was preserving our family tradition of singing "Jesus Christ is Risen Today" and "Angels Roll the Rock Away" on Easter before breakfast.

Dieburg. The 81st moved on to Dieburg and set up in an open field to receive patients.

4 Apr 45. Liberated Governmental wine cellar. With Adjutant Hurand's permission (Major Banks was away at

7th Army headquarters), several of us took an ambulance and drove a considerable distance to Neustadt. Here were green grass and blooming fruit trees in each direction of the long valley. Absolutely unscarred by the war. We selected two hundred sixty bottles of white and red wine and returned to the 81st at Dieburg. But we found there that Major Banks had returned, found us gallivanting after wine and planned to court-martial us.

All officers were instructed to gather at the headquarters tent. But instead of a court-martial, Major Bounds ordered me to come forward, offered a handshake and announced that I'd been promoted from 1st Lieutenant to Captain! Several others were promoted also.

Sadly, it must be recorded that our liberated 81st wine cellar was short lived. We had divided the 260 bottles of wine among the three units, and Major Corley had sharply limited our bottles to the men of our C-Unit. However, A and B Units had distributed their total allotments to their men, and some got drunk. When Major Banks returned from Headquarters and grasped the situation, he ordered Major Corley to take a detail of men and axes and smash every bottle in camp. What a loss.

6 Apr 45: Patients at last. Major Banks returned from headquarters this morning with instructions to combine all three units immediately and prepare to receive patients as a station hospital the next day, capacity 450 beds. Tentative lineup: CO – Major Banks; executive officer and Chief of Radiology, Major Corley; Chief of Surgery, Captain Bounds; Chief of Medicine, Captain Hardy; Ch. Nurse, Captain Connelly; Ch. laboratory and pharmacy –

The itinerary of the 81st Field Hospital in WWII,
Reproduced by permission of the University of Pennsylvania
Press. (Memoirs)

Captain Cummings; A&D (admissions and discharge),
Captain Martin.

7 Apr 45. Miraculously, we are ready today to receive
flocks of patients. The first was a Russian civilian freed by
the advancing Allies, his right forearm and hand being
markedly swollen from the infection of a hand wound.

8 Apr 45: Sunday. Today approximately 170 patients,
Displaced Persons all, were admitted. Chiefly Russians.
Diagnoses: Malnutrition, massive tuberculosis, hepatitis,

peptic ulcer, arthritis, cirrhosis, bronchitis, pyorrhea alveolaris, pleurisy, diphtheria, leprosy, Hodgkin's disease, dysentery, gastroenteritis secondary to overloading half-starved stomachs, malaria, edema of undetermined etiology, and idiocy.

9 Apr 45. Long day of screening patients for tuberculosis by means of chest X-rays. Many French and British colonial troops have come in. (Our enlisted men were amazed that the black members can speak French.)

A SHOWER. A shower company had set up their equipment nearby. I learned in the Army that it is not essential to take a bath every day—or indeed, every week.

10 Apr 45. Tuberculosis rampant. More patients in and many out. Several with tuberculosis have died.

11 Apr 45. Walt Martin busy as a hound dog with fleas. Admitted seventy-nine more tuberculosis patients today. Our nurse Ruth Udy was to contract tuberculosis herself in caring for these patients.

13 Apr 45. "Roosevelt ist tod" (is dead)—this from a Russian soldier.

14 Apr 45. "Bed check Charlie," the German pilot who's given us several scares with nightly strafings of the adjacent highway, killed one American soldier and wounded several others in a convoy last night. Today he is reported shot down and is said to be a patient in the 27th Evac Hospital.

24 Apr 45. C-Unit ordered to move to Heilbronn Reserve Lazaret, at Heilbronn. We went and monitored the evacuation of the German patients. Sadly, the war had drained the enlisted men transporting the patients to the rear of most of their humanity, and I was almost embarrassed to be an American.

And here I had to face a personal confrontation. There were a few werewolves (armed German civilians) about and I had directed a buck (3 stripes) sergeant to place sentries around the stone walled perimeter and at the front gate. I was busy all day with concerns such as the Chefarzt (chief physician) and the Oberschwester (head nurse). Both wanted to stay and continue to work in the hospital, but this was not an option.

But to return to the sergeant, he had done nothing about sentries. He had spent the entire day looking for and collecting souvenirs (looting, if you will). He had ignored completely my order, presenting me with a prickly problem. He was an amateur boxer and was very popular with the enlisted men. But to disregard this transgression risked the very core of military discipline. I was not sure that my action would be supported by my superiors, but I "busted" him from staff sergeant (3 stripes) down to buck private.

To his credit, he took it like a man, buckled down and became head of the plaster cast room. Three months later I recommended that his three stripes be restored.

Heilbronn itself was a huge pile of blasted masonry and other rubble. The "roads" and streets were simply cow trails through all the destruction. We learned that on 4 Dec 44 American bombers had appeared suddenly above the city of 60,000, and, after 25 minutes of saturation bombing, between fifteen and twenty thousand people lay dead.

Astonishingly, the large German hospital at the edge of town, bearing huge red crosses on its roof was unscathed, with the exception that all its windowpanes had been shattered by the blast effects.

Here again, I was Chief of Medicine and Laboratories. The water supply from the town was unpredictable. Electric current was provided by a small generator in the basement.

25 Apr 45. Spent the morning lining up German civilians to remain in order to operate the laundry, kitchen, cleaning, heating plant, and other hospital machinery. This relieved us from having to uncrate our own X-ray and other equipment. We could pay these workers no money, but they were free to help themselves to the food stores of the departing Germans. Potatoes were present in abundance.

Frau Elizabeth Wacker, blond, buxom and in her forties—ran the German X-ray equipment. Well educated, her husband, a minister, had been killed on the Russian front. Her brother was a medical student at the University of Tubingen. One day I said to her "Du bist wie eine Blume." (You are like a flower.) The next day she brought in the full text of Heine's poem in a slender volume of poetry. She and I communicated in German.

I accepted another woman to work in the laundry. She spoke English very well, having learned it in school, supplemented by travel in England and America. Now penniless, her husband had formerly been a leading industrialist in Heilbronn. When I asked her if she wished to continue to work in the laundry, she replied, "One must eat, Herr Hauptmann."

The range of illnesses of patients admitted at Heilbronn was very similar to that of the patients cared for at Dieburg.

30 Apr 45. German civilians say that Hitler was wounded yesterday by the Volkstrum.

2 May 45. Hitler is dead. Mussolini and daughter reported murdered by Italians and hanged by the heels.

7 May 45. V-E Day. The Germans have surrendered.

8 May 45. Churchill, King George, General Eisenhower, Bradly, Montgomery, Alexander and Tedder have all broadcast this evening.

28 May 45. What a pleasant surprise. Billy Harris (medical school classmate from Birmingham) turns up. He was with an artillery unit and had seen our 81st FH marker when his unit had passed through a few days before.

As we were passing the receiving office, a group of patients were sitting there awaiting discharge. Suddenly a pretty, flaxen-haired young Polish girl in her teens who had had pneumonia, stood up before me, extended her hand quickly, and blurted "Wiedersehen, Herr Doktor!" Then, overwhelmed with what seemed to her a rash behavior, she sat down again, averted her gaze, and blushed in confusion. As we passed on to relieve her embarrassment by our absence, Billy said, "Jim, it's worth all the effort when you see things like that, isn't it?"

1 June 45. Unit alerted for direct movement to the CBI! (China, Burma and India). It will be a long war for us. Had hoped to finish training by age 30 but not possible now.

6 June 45. A twin turns up. Having been at army headquarters, Julian had known all along where the 81st was. We'd not seen each other for two years.

9 June 45. Today we finished packing the equipment, said wiedersehen to Frau Wacker, and left the Heilbronn Reserve Lazaret to the mercies of the German military personnel that we'd imported.

9 June 45. We moved to Schwetzingen, on the Neckar River a short distance above Heidelberg. Major Reisman, commander of Unit B, had had the civilians moved from several adjacent houses. I instructed our enlisted men, very firmly, not to loot anything from the private home. The war was over. However, one of the nurses ran her index finger around in the Hausfrau's face powder, somewhat ingeniously I thought, and discovered the Hausfrau's wedding rings. And, I suspect, she kept them, an officer herself.

This pause in Schwetzingen was used to recheck the 81st's equipment prior to its being shipped through the Panama Canal for the invasion of Japan. Meanwhile I was sent to 7th Army Headquarters at Augsburg on official business. We traveled 400 miles in an open jeep. On the way down we crossed the "beautiful blue Danube." However, Der schone blaue Donau was not pure blue; it had a bluish-green color. We crossed on a temporary bridge, the original one being a tangled mass of iron a few yards downstream. The autobahn was a peerless concrete road, and was actually used for plane take-offs and landings.

11 June 45. Moved out from Schwetzingen and began the train trip to territory of Van Gogh fame, on very old, wooden-seated railroad coaches. I threw my bedroll on the floor, blew up my air mattress and slept.

Morale in the 81st is very low, as we begin staging for the long, long sea voyage to the Japanese empire.

14 June 45. St. Victorette Staging Area. We arrived here at 0400 hours. The huge camp was only about 0.25 miles from the railway station. Approximately 30,000 troops in this tent village. Two officers to each sidewall tent. Dust hovers over the area in great red clouds. Dust in clothing, food and lungs.

Appointed I&E (Information and Education) officer. Not particularly desirable assignment but suitable to my temperament and inclinations: (1) practice in public speaking, (2) precludes a less desirable assignment, (3) Adjutant Hurand works so hard that none of the rest of us can complain; he's the backbone of the outfit. I am to read up and lecture the enlisted men on Japanese army tactics.

19 Jun 45. Went to Marseilles today. Considerable bomb damage. Everything dirty and ill kept. The marché noir (black market) swarms about each entering GI truck, in the form of many nationalities—Frenchmen, Senegales, Moroccans, Syrians, and derelict Englishmen—and purchases anything for sale. (On a later visit, to see how the black market worked, I acknowledged an Arab, in full regalia, who had approached me. We entered a nearby bistro (bar), where he paid me $14.00 (in francs) for a carton of cigarettes that I had bought for 50cents in the PX.)

Talked with the enlisted men. Traced Japanese conquest from 1854 (Admiral Perry) to the present with McArthur back in the Philippines. (My speech delivery is creditably good and my manner self-assured. As Dr. Pepper always advised, the latter results from careful preparation.)

21 June 45. A bull session with the EM. (1) Postwar medicine, (2) peacetime conscription; most are for it; we are all afraid the U.S. will forget too soon. Perhaps the British won't and certainly the Russians won't.

27 June 45. Have just been censoring letters, the inevitable daily chore. The excuses for ending a letter at a point often tax credulity. For instance, one EM writes, "Well, haven't much to do today so will close." Another writes, "If the war will only last long enough I will get out on points."

26 July 45. Churchill's government has just fallen. I asked some British officers at the Marseilles Officers Club how that could have happened, with all that Churchill had done. "Easily, old chap, Churchill was a wartime leader. We now needed someone to rebuild the country."

9 July 45. Our hospital equipment is to be packed in three days, for shipment to the attack on Japan.

Lt. Colonel Banks, our 81st's commander, was wounded in the head and partially paralyzed. A soldier some tents away had been cleaning his souvenir German Luger pistol, and the accidental firing had struck Lt. Col. Banks as he sat on his cot in his tent. Within days Major John B. Moring, Regular Army, was sent down from Germany to command our 81st.

30 July 45. Held last orientation conference with the EM. The fall of Churchill's government, the portent of the enormous Red Army, universal military training in the U.S., tropical medicine and the Japanese soldier were some of the topics considered, in the rough and tumble discussion.

I reserved the closing moments of the hour for a few remarks about venereal disease. Before St. Victorette not one man had reported VD. In them I gave what I hoped was an alarming description of the ravages and heartbreaks that could result from such disease. Neither penicillin nor arsphenamine could cure all syphilis, and it was still a frequent cause of heart failure and insanity. Likewise, a single "dose" of gonorrhea might possibly prevent a man from being a father.

Men, for heavens sake use a pro!

7 Aug 45. "Atomic bomb" dropped on Japan. How in hell could such a small object do such damage? Even more incredible: How had the United States, of all nations, managed to keep the bomb a secret?

8 Aug 45. Wednesday. Russia declares war on Japan.

9 Aug 45. Rise and shine! This was it! Everyone was awakened at 0430 hours and told to get ready to move out. Still dark. Breakfast (cooked by German POWs) was eaten in fading darkness. Trucks arrived at 0630 hours. The 81st was checked out at the post entrance at exactly 0700 hours.

As we moved away from the gate, a chilling breeze was sending spasmodic flurries of red dust about the camp. The sky was cool and serene, with not a cloud to be seen, not even a little one, not even one the size of your hand.

The trucks moved to within fifty yards of our ship. She was the George O. Squier, a Navy transport ship. Unlike the Vollendam, the General Squier had individual lockers in the officers' staterooms, and thus the gear was not a problem. There were eighteen officers to each cabin. Having claimed our bunks, we went back on deck and watched as the troops were loaded, all day long, until there were almost 3000 aboard.

At 1700 hours, the anchor was weighed and the vessel put calmly to sea. As we stood on the decks watching Marseilles fall behind the horizon, we knew that an era had passed. Now—at last—we must wrench our minds away from the ETO and anticipate the orient.

The food on the Squier was excellent—fresh eggs, fresh meat, fresh vegetables, fresh fruit, good coffee. Everything the Army had not had in the ETO. Two meals a day but good snacks to be purchased at the canteen at midday.

11 Aug 45. Saturday. Passed the Rock (Gibraltar). Africa visible on the port side. As we passed through the narrowest part of the strait, a number of sleek porpoises raced playfully along beside the ship.

The next few days were ones of countless rumors about the future of the 81st.

14 Aug 45. Tuesday. The Japanese have surrendered! But, so what? So we were still bound for the CBI.

15 Aug 45. It was late in the afternoon. The moody vessel wallowed along through a glassy sea so smooth that not a ripple scarred the rolling ground swell. The enlisted men's long lines were feeding down into the mess halls and out the other side. The officers listened listlessly for the first dinner call, as they watched a taunting sun inch toward the West they longed to see.

And then it came!

Suddenly a voice came over the loud speaker system. *Now hear this. This is the Captain speaking. All passengers aboard will be interested to learn that this ship is altering its course and will dock at Newport News.*

Interested? God! We were wild. A spontaneous roar began in the very bowels of the ship and tore right to the heavens above. We had never before such joy! *It was the happiest day of my life.*

Let's have a drink. Liquor bottles ("prohibited aboard ship") were produced on all sides and some got drunk. I did not need a drink, for I was drunk on the realization that I'd just been given at least two years to my life.

And as we looked backward, we could see the northward curving of the wake of the ship, for miles behind.

We disembarked at Newport News and were given leave, to reassemble at Camp Sibert, about sixty miles north of Birmingham and near Gadsden. I don't remember much about our brief stay there, except for one embarrassing encounter. Hurand had suggested that we run down to a state store in Birmingham and replenish our store of alcoholic beverages. Down several steps, the liquor store was on the left and a dahlia flower show on the right. Well, just as Hurand and I exited the liquor store, my Aunt Cokie exited the dahlia show—and she was currently the president of the Alabama Christian Temperance Union! What could I do, being laden with the booze? I had to brave it out. I said, "Aunt Cokie, this is Captain Hurand," and we sped away.

I had returned to find Mother dying of metastatic cancer. Her noble spirit had been the major force in the development of my intellectual orientation.

1 Nov 45. The 81st was ordered to move to Crile General Hospital near Cleveland, Ohio. There our 81st mascot, Heartless Herman, was laid to rest, and the 81st medical officers worked in the Crile GH. I don't remember many particulars of my service there, but I once again was reminded that anything one learns may be useful in the indeterminate future. Upon arrival, I was assigned to one of the medical wards. The captain currently managing the ward was delighted with my arrival. He said he'd long awaited the arrival of the 81st so that he could go on leave. He suggested that we go to his ward and go over each patient, so that he could leave early the next morning. This we did.

Well, I was just settling in on the ward the next morning, meeting the nurses and so forth, when the phone rang in my office. Colonel D., Chief of Medicine, was bringing a general from Washington to make rounds with Captain J. I informed him that Captain J. had gone on leave and that I was currently in charge. He was clearly annoyed but he said, "Captain Hardy, I don't suppose you could take a general and me around the ward?"

"Sir, I'll do my best." Going down the long row of beds, Colonel D. selected a chart at the foot of the patient's bed and read out the diagnosis: Sarcoidosis. He then said, "Captain, could you tell us something about sarcoidosis?" (He clearly didn't expect much.)

Well, as a senior medical student I'd had a patient with sarcoidosis as a special project and had been gathering further information ever since. Needless to say, I "unloaded" on Colonel D. and the General.

JDH at the Pentagon – 1946. Reproduced by permission of the University of Pennsylvania Press. (Memoirs)

That evening at the officers' mess, I had sat apart from everyone else because I wanted to eat quickly and catch the bus into Cleveland. Colonel D. never ate with anyone. But when he came in this evening, he went through the line with his tray and walked all the way across the hall and sat down beside me. "Hardy," he asked, "Where did you go to medical school?" He then asked what my plans were for after my discharge from the Army and asked if I would like to come to the University of Kansas, where he would be Chief of Medicine. I thanked him but said that I hoped to return to Penn in surgery.

14 Dec 45. The 81st FH was deactivated and made its last move—into the pages of history.

11 Feb 46. The Pentagon. Ordered to assist in the General Dispensary caring for officers. It offered an opportunity to learn something about our capitol and to become addicted to the "Washington Post."

Several patients stand out in memory. One, General Dwight D. Eisenhower, sent down for nose drops.

Another, a young Army Air Force colonel. came in because of weight loss, despite a ravenous appetite. "Colonel," I said, "Your youth weighs against cancer and since you have no goiter, you must have diabetes." "I can't have diabetes," he exclaimed, "I'm a West Point man." But within minutes we had demonstrated sugar in his urine.

Still another was a major who'd been in the Pentagon throughout the war. He dragged in almost every week, complaining of his back. He was "bucking" for a "complete disability" discharge. Unfortunately for him, I'd happened to see him downtown Saturday night, walking briskly with a blonde. Thus, when he dragged himself in to see me the following week, I said, "Major, did you have a good weekend?" He replied, "No, Doc, I was in terrible pain the whole time."

"Major, I happened to be downtown Saturday night when you sped past with an attractive female on your arm."

At this, he became furious and said that he would have me court-martialed for lack of respect for a superior officer. But I replied that he would be unsuccessful because he had no witness.

The fourth patient was seen the day I had been named Chief of Otolaryngology. The colonel called me and said that the chief of ENT had just been discharged and that he was naming me Chief of Otolaryngology. I protested that I'd had little experience but the colonel said, again, "You are appointed, here is a book, and there is a general waiting in the chair."

So I went around to the ENT section, told the nurse to activate everything that shown or moved, that I would review the patient's chart and enter with a flourish.

When I opened the chart, I read that the general was a General Simmons. Could he be the General Simmons that Dr. T. Grier Miller at Penn had mentioned several times? He was. He was in this time to have his right antrum punctured again for purulent sinusitis.

"General," I said, "I've just been appointed as Chief of Otolaryngology. I've had little experience. I recommend that you go over to Walter Reed Hospital."

And he sped down the hall.

At this point I still had not had a definite commitment from Dr. Ravdin at Penn that he could take me on into his residency in general surgery. So I wrote him that I would come to Philadelphia in early July, to gain a decision either way, for I had to make a living, one way or another. When I arrived in the University Hospital, I encountered Dr. Ravdin and his entourage in the hall. Someone introduced me to Dr. Ravdin and he said, "I remember Hardy, he's gained weight." Which I had. He turned and gazed across Spruce Street toward the Wharton business school for an interminable time (it seemed to me) and then turned back and asked, "When do you want to start to work?"

"September the first."

The day before I was to be discharged from the Army, the colonel called me in and said, "Hardy, the army has a place for you."

"Colonel," I replied, "I respect the army very much and I value my experience, especially in command. But, going on three years, I really have not found my place in the army."

"Good luck, then," he replied, "But regulations say that I had to ask you."

July 8, 1946. Discharged from the Army. I had shared in the Sturm und Drang (storm and stress) of my generation.

CHAPTER 5

~⁓

The Residency In General Surgery

September 1, 1946. I arrived in Philadelphia with keen anticipation of doing surgery. I had already contacted the American Board of Surgery regarding what I would need to do to become eligible to take the Board examinations. The Board had been set up in 1937 with the purpose of standardizing surgical training and certifying only those who had had the requisite years of formal surgical training and could then pass a two-step examination, the first a written and, if successfully passed, an oral examination. Some board member would propose, from time to time, that the oral second part be dispensed with. But most agreed with Jonathan Rhoads' comment that the oral exam did at least permit the examiner to see whether or not the candidate had two hands.

The Board informed me that the five-year program could, for me, be as follows: one year's credit for my internship-medical residency, and one year for my going on two plus years in the Army. Then, I would need three solid years of clinical surgery.

I reported in to Dr. Isidor Ravdin, Chairman of the Department of Surgery, in his office. Instead of there being two professors of surgery with two almost equal departments before the war, there was now to be only one department but with the two separate clinical services maintained.

But instead of telling me when I would get to do an herniorrhaphy, he looked at me squarely and asked, "Doctor, what do you plan to investigate?"

"Cachexia, Sir," I replied just as firmly. He then said, "That is a stone wall. What would you actually do?"

I then told him that before the war when I was a resident in internal medicine, I was fascinated that cancer patients often lost appetite, lost weight, wasted away and died, without major organ dysfunction; that I planned to tube these patients and force feed them, to determine if they could fabricate tissue; that to know whether or not a weight gain was due simply to water retention or to the fabrication of new tissue it would be necessary to measure body composition. We already had a reasonably reliable method for measuring blood volume and the thiocyanate method for measuring extracellular fluid. But that the methodology for measuring total body water was in its infancy. Two Germans, von Hevesy and Hofer, had studied a single man and Moore at Harvard had studied a single patient using the gradient tube method. But the methodology for measuring total body water with heavy water (D_2O), using the dilution method, was in its infancy.

Dr. Ravdin was skeptical but he did provide money for purchasing two ampules of heavy water from Norway.

But my first "clinical" assignment was to be to Surgical Pathology. I liked pathology and enjoyed reviewing the

106

ISIDOR SCHWANER RAVDIN

Reproduced by permission of the University of Pennsylvania Press. (Memoirs)

daily load of slides with the pathologist. And it is essential that the surgeon know at operation what tissue is normal and what is not normal.

But without clinical duties I did have considerable free time to begin assembling the apparatus necessary for measuring D_2O at three parts per million. For this I bought a 100 liter aquarium from a tropical fish dealer in South Philadelphia. A very delicate thermoregulator was blown by the university's master glass blower, James Graham. And the dropping cylinder which permitted the dropping of absolutely uniform sized droplets was constructed by the university's master machinist, a duplicate of such a cylinder loaned by David Rittenberg of Columbia University in New York. The thermoregulator had to regulate the temperature in the water bath to within 0.001 degree centigrade. We eventually used infrared bulbs which stuttered continuously when all was working in unison. However, this was to be achieved several years later. In the beginning, I'd had little idea how demanding the achievement of the heavy water measurements would prove to be.

Meanwhile, with no patient responsibilities, I was free to leave the hospital on short notice. Thus Dr. Ravdin called me one day and asked if I would like to drive up to Bethlehem, Pennsylvania, for a consultation. And during the drive he asked me many questions about Dr. Isaac Starr, with whom I'd done research before the war, and about Dr. Francis C. Wood, who had been the faculty sponsor of Alpha Omega Alpha and whose 5-student elective at the Children's Heart Hospital I had taken my senior year. Dr. Ravdin knew, of course, that I'd been a resident in medicine before the war. He asked which one I would choose as the new Chairman of Medicine. I was reluctant to choose either one against the other, but they were very different and I pointed out the special qualities that each had. (I did not know at the time that Dr. Ravdin was on the search committee for a new Chairman of Medicine, but Dr. Wood was eventually appointed.)

When we reached Bethlehem, the surgeon requesting Dr. Ravdin's consultation met us and led us to a sun parlor where the patient's relatives waited. After introductions, we were led to the patient's private room. He was a late teenage scion of a wealthy and very prominent Bethlehem family. He had had an appendectomy but had developed postoperative complications and was running a high fever with anorexia and weight loss. After examining his abdomen, Dr. Ravdin asked for a glove and lubricant. The patient's surgeon assured Dr. Ravdin that a rectal had been done by his assistant and that no evidence of an abscess had been felt. However, there was no note to that effect on the patient's chart, and it soon developed that no rectal examination had been done. Dr. Ravdin immediately felt a bulging against the rectum, and diagnosed a large intraperitoneal abscess. He then led the surgeon to a private room, and laid out what he'd found and what he thought should be done about it. Dr. Ravdin went back to the relatives and told them his findings and repeated his recommendations.

In brief, a limited laparotomy permitted the drainage of the abscess and the patient recovered promptly.

I learned from this Dr. Ravdin's tact and preservation of professional courtesies. But he also made sure that the family knew what he'd found and what he had recommended be done.

I have no idea what Dr. Ravdin charged for this trip, which had taken almost the entire day. But he always charged reasonable fees.

(N.B. It used do be said that the consultant's main job was to do the rectal examination.)

Two missions. The Professor sent me down to Baltimore to Fort Howard Veterans Hospital and on an another occasion all the way across Philadelphia one rainy night to learn about a man who proposed to store blood in plastic bags instead of the standard glass bottles.

At Fort Howard I met with Dr. Everett Evans, burn expert at the Medical College of Virginia in Richmond, and with Dr. Margaret Sloan, Executive Secretary of the National Research Council. Our committee was to inspect some clinical studies involving two new enzymes, streptokinase and streptodornase. We were then to recommend whether or not the National Research Council should extend substantial support for large-scale commercial production. We were impressed with how these enzymes had cleared up infected wounds. However, we decided to recommend only that the investigator be invited to report his results to a meeting of the full National Research Council in Washington.

As Dr. Evans, Dr. Sloan and I were being driven back to the Baltimore train station, I overheard Drs. Evans and Sloan discussing what funds remained to the Council to distribute before the end of the fiscal year. When Dr. Sloan mentioned a large amount, Dr. Evans said, "You call Mike DeBakey tomorrow and tell him he must accept seventy-five thousand dollars." Grant policy at the top!

The other mission I was sent on was the one across Philadelphia on a rainy night. The inventor had tough plastic bags which he had filled with fluid and then dropped over a distance of from ten to twelve feet, and they did not burst! I duly reported back to Dr. Ravdin, but it was to be some years before blood was stored in plastic bags and not in glass bottles.

In January, 1947, I rotated off Pathology and began on Dr. Ravdin's private service. The other resident was Archibald Fletcher, who had had one year of surgical training before going to the army. We operated on a large volume of patients most days—thyroidectomy, breast surgery, cholecystectomy, colectomy, hernias and varicose veins. The Professor had few surgical complications and almost no deaths except when the patient had far advanced cancer.

Dr. Ravdin relinquished the chairmanship of surgery to Jonathan E. Rhoads at age 65 and became vice-president for medical affairs.

But to return to my surgery residency. I began clinical surgery on Dr. Ravdin's (private) service on January 1,
110

1947. He had an astonishingly good memory for patients' names and those of their relatives. He demanded that residents not come to the operating room without breakfast. He insisted that tubes of paste be squeezed from the end instead of the middle. Like most good surgeons, he reduced the details to a meticulous routine, addressing thereafter the major decisions inherent in the infinite variations of the individual patient's pathologic condition.

He had a superb suture (scrub) nurse who slapped the next instrument into his hand without his having to turn or call for it, in many or most instances. One day Dr. Blalock of Johns Hopkins was looking down from the observation gallery and said, "Rav, that young lady should be a member of the American Surgical Association!"

Later, when I was operating independently and Dr. Ravdin was out of town, she was scrubbing for me. One day I said to her, "Miss (Phyllis) Roseman, I bet you could do this gallbladder operation as well as I can." To which she replied, "Better!"

One evening Dr. Ravdin called me from his home to say that Dr. F. was sending a private patient with possible acute cholecystitis and that I should call him once I had examined the patient. Well, I kept calling the Emergency Room, time after time but the patient did not come in. Finally, at about ten o'clock I called the Professor at home to tell him that the patient had not come in. He told me to get some sleep.

Shortly thereafter I encountered Dr. Ravdin's assistant and told him about the "no-show" patient from Dr. F. He looked startled and said that the patient had come to the Emergency Room hours previously, had no note from her doctor; that it had been assumed that she was a "service" patient and not a private patient; and that there being no "ward" bed available, she had been sent to the Graduate Hospital about twenty blocks away.

I said that I must call Dr. Ravdin at once and tell him what had happened. Clearly, Dr. Ravdin had long delayed his call to me.

The Professor was considerably exercised and his assistant was absolutely stricken.

I went on up to my room, but as I sat there it occurred to me that if we could admit 174 patients to our 81st Field Hospital in a single day, it ought to be possible to retrieve a single patient from the Graduate Hospital. Thus I called the surgery resident at "Graduate" and told him the situation; that Dr. Ravdin was very upset. He was very doubtful. He said that the patient was already in bed, had an intravenous drip, and that her husband had taken her clothes home. Whereupon I countered with the assurance that I would bring University Hospital bed clothing. He finally agreed but then I couldn't get a taxi. It was pouring rain. But Quinnie, the night operator, took over. Leaving the switch key open so I could listen in she said, "Hello Yellow Cab. We have a case of life and death out here at the University Hospital. A patient must be moved immediately from the Graduate Hospital. Pick up Dr. Hardy at the University emergency room and he will support the patient during the trip." Yellow Cab responded at once. Taking along University bedding, I brought the somewhat startled lady back.

Storming in the next morning, I.S.R. was astonished to find his patient resting comfortably in a borrowed bed on the tonsil ward.

BREAST MAMMOGRAPHY. One day he told Dr. Fletcher and me that he did not want anyone to accuse him of doing unnecessary surgery, but that he was admitting a large lady with voluminous breasts for a breast biopsy. He went on to say that he could feel no lump in her large breast, but that Dr. Jacob Gershon-Cohen at Graduate Hospital had been following a group of about seventy-five women with periodic mammograms, and that he had "diagnosed" cancer at a specific site in the involved breast. At operation we found a cancer at the exact site that Dr. Gershon-Cohen had predicted. Even so, it was to take years before many or most radiologists accepted the value of mammography.

Dr. Fletcher rotated off and J.W. replaced him, this time I being the chief of the two of us. One day we were operating when a call from the emergency room announced the arrival of a private patient for Dr. Ravdin, appendicitis suspected. He instructed me to drop out of the operation we were doing and go down to the emergency room and size up the situation.

Meanwhile the next patient for operation was a boy with a groin hernia.

That afternoon, as we were making "work" rounds (as opposed to Dr. Ravdin's rounds) the boy's mother said, "Doctor Hardy, my son's hernia was on the left side but the bandage is on the right side." Startled, I took the junior resident aside.

"Which side did you operate on? The mother is right. How did this happen?"

"Well, Dr. Ravdin asked which side and I said the right." (He was a very bright man, usually right, but never able to say that he did not know.)

113

"I must tell Dr. Ravdin at once," I said, but he begged me to let him tell the chief, saying that otherwise he would never be named a chief resident.

Against my better judgment, I agreed, but Dr. Ravdin later called me up to his office and gave me a severe dressing down. "You are senior resident. You should not have let me operate on the wrong side. It's your fault. You were in charge!" Finally he subsided. (He was right, of course.)

"Well, Professor, I accept the principle that the senior resident bears full responsibility. But I did know which side the hernia was on, and I would have been there had you not sent me down to the Emergency Room." Actually, as is true in about one-half the cases, the boy had bilateral hernias; hence the mistake had not been suspected during the operation. The other hernia, on the opposite side, was repaired without event.

I would not want to leave the impression that working for I.S.R. was a grim activity. It wasn't—it was fun. He was just volatile. His explosions, usually in the operating room (again, understood by every surgeon) were like a summer thunderstorm, impressive momentarily but soon gone.

Dr. Ravdin had a good sense of humor. One day when the American Medical Association was meeting at Atlantic City and Dr. Frank Lahey of Boston was presiding at a program on colon cancer, he asked the audience if there were any questions or comments. At this, a man stood up amidst the thousand or so audience and said loudly that Dr. Ravdin, on stage as a member of the colon panel, had made a bad mistake in his case. (He'd had an abdominoperineal resection of his colon and rectum for cancer, and had not yet regained his ability to void, some weeks after the operation—a fairly common temporary complication of this operation.) We had discharged him the day before, wearing a catheter.

Dr. Lahey turned to our Professor and asked, "Rav, do you wish to comment?"

Dr. Ravdin strode across the stage to the lectern and said, "Yes, we did make a mistake in the Doctor's case: we discharged him a day too soon!"

When Rav had to go out of town he signed out his service to me. He knew I would call Dr. Rhoads or Dr. Johnson if any patient had a serious problem. One day he said he had to go to Washington immediately. (It was later known that he had been summoned to assist General Heaton at the operation on President Eisenhower for a small bowel obstruction.)

The two times of the week when Dr. Ravdin was most visible to all the members of the Department were Grand Rounds and the monthly mortality conference. The grand rounds consisted mostly of showing patients and discussing their problems, but a brief talk by someone was at times solicited. At one session Dr. Ravdin said, "Dr. Hardy, discuss tetanus briefly."

I replied that I'd never seen a patient with tetanus but that I would offer what I knew. Dr. Ravdin was much surprised, for his 20th General Hospital in Assam had cared for numerous cases in Chinese soldiers. But the fact that I'd seen no tetanus was that, in Europe where I'd been a captain in the 81st Field Hospital, both the German and American soldiers had been inoculated against tetanus; whereas, in the Orient, none of the Chinese soldiers had been inoculated against tetanus.

Mortality and Morbidity Conference. The monthly mortality conference was conducted with fairness and firmness. I can still hear the Professor asking the surgeon who had to present a death or a serious complication: "Doctor, would you have had this operation or had it on your wife?"

He urged the residents to develop a "surgical conscience."

The deaths were classified as follows:
> ET (error in technique)
> EJ (error in judgment)
> EM (error in management)
> ED (error in diagnosis)
> UC (unavoidable complication)
> EAM (error in anesthesia management)
> PD (patient's disease)
> (and, irreverently, TBG—trying to be God—
> attempting surgery that could not possibly
> have been successful.)

This session was sometimes embarrassing and painful to the surgeon involved, but it ensured that every possible therapeutic measure would have been taken to prevent the patient's death. (I adopted this classification years later when I became Professor and Chairman of the Department of Surgery at the University of Mississippi Medical Center in Jackson, but we stopped giving the patient's name when on legal advice it was found that trial lawyers were paying hospital personnel for tips that could prompt a lawsuit. We substituted numbers for the patients names.)

Rav set great store by loyalty. Once I had suggested that he fire a person who exhibited truly extraordinary ineptitude.

But, waggling his index finger at me he said, "Now, Jim, have you ever found her unpleasant?"

"No, sir, I haven't."

"Or have you ever known her to call in sick?"

"No, Sir," again.

"Have you ever had her fail to come in, somehow, no matter how deep the snow?"

No once again.

"Jim, she's loyal!"

As of July 1, 1948, I rotated off the Ravdin private service and on to the Rhoads ward (charity) service. Jonathan E. Rhoads, a Philadelphia Quaker, had a Lincolnesque appearance and I never heard him raise his voice to anyone, on any occasion. We made detailed teaching rounds for about two hours on Monday, Wednesday and Friday, and operated on Tuesday, Thursday and Saturday. Now, for the first time, I was allowed to perform simple hernia operations and leg

JONATHAN EVANS RHOADS

Reproduced by permission of the University of Pennsylvania Press. (Memoirs)

117

amputations, under supervision. One day the chief resident played a practical (but instructive) joke on me. We were to amputate a leg above the knee. I entered the operating room, to find that the scrub nurse (who I was dating) had already wrapped both prepped legs with sterile gauze and had the scalpel in her hand for me. I was allowed to start the operation and go as far as I could before the chief resident came in.

Well, I made the standard curving incision down to the *right* femur with a flourish. Just at that moment the chief resident, who now having finished his ten-minute scrub, came backing against the swinging door and, ostensibly talking to an invisible medical student behind him, said loudly, "With amputations, it is obviously important to amputate the correct leg. It is this patient's left foot that is gangrenous."

My heart skipped a beat. I *knew* it was the right foot that was gangrenous; but thereafter I never operated on any paired extremity without seeing it before the "prep" in the operating room. (A thoracic surgeon in Memphis with whom I worked several years later always insisted that the patient's chest X-rays be on the view box in the operating room. He rushed in one day, with the patient already anesthetized and draped. He sensed that something was not right. He looked up at the chest film, saw breasts, and said, "This patient is supposed to be a man." An inappropriate operation was thus avoided.)

In the spring of 1948 the chief resident on the Rhoads service told me privately that he had been instructed to pour the surgery to Hardy. He also noted that this meant I would be named one of the two chief residents my next (last) year. This was great news. The Ravdin-Rhoads-

Johnson triumvirate tried to get the other residents qualified by sending them to outside hospitals for part of their training, but the prestige and heavy operating went to the two chief residents.

I went on Dr. Johnson's service July 1, 1948. Dr. Johnson was a fierce disciplinarian where patients were concerned and the "tightness of his ship" was legendary. But here I was, his chief resident who, because of a quirk in the resident rotation schedule, had never yet been on the Johnson service. I asked his assistant how I should conduct myself on his service and he replied, "Say nothing unless called on and then you'd better be right!"

Dr. Johnson was the son of a Baptist minister and his wife the daughter of a Presbyterian minister. At marriage it had been agreed that they would go to the Baptist church for twenty-five years (where he became an elder), and then go to her Presbyterian church thereafter, which they did (where he became an elder in *that* church).

I got along with Dr. Johnson well enough. I did my work, answered when called upon, but volunteered nothing. One day after rounds he called me up to his office. "Jim," he said, "I've seen you on the other services talking like a magpie. What's the difference?"

"Well, Dr. Johnson, I asked several of my predecessors for advice." And I told him of the admonitions.

"Jim, I'm not a bad fellow when you get to know me." And it was his insistence for perfection, in every patient's care, his insistence that we fight continuously for the patient's life that gave me the training to be a success in the new and rapidly developing field of thoracic surgery.

He still did a lot of general surgery with the same infinite attention to detail, for there wasn't enough "thoracic" surgery to keep him busy.

119

One day we admitted a jaundiced patient. She'd had a cholecystectomy at another hospital, and had postoperatively drained lots of bile from her drain site. But as the drainage slowed down she became jaundiced. We sent for her chart at the other hospital. The operative note read "common duct exposed and divided."

Dr. Johnson said, "Jim, have you ever done an operation with the Professor?" I replied that I had not, since all his patients were private patients.

"Well, I think he would be tickled pink if you were to ask him. He specializes in common duct injuries."

I did ask him. He was obviously pleased and was a perfect assistant, somewhat to my surprise, for it is one thing to be the surgeon and tell the assistants what to do, but it is quite another thing to be the assistant and refrain from endless suggestions. We found the bile duct promptly, in all the old scar tissue, and we made an excellent repair. Well-placed sutures afford esthetic satisfaction.

With the end of my general surgery residency in sight, I had to make arrangements to support my forthcoming marriage July 1. I knew that thoracic surgery was the coming new field and I wanted to get more experience in it. But Dr. Ravdin had William Fitts as his assistant, Jonathan Rhoads had Cletus Schwegman as his assistant, and Dr. Johnson had Charles Kirby as his assistant.

But forced to make a move, I applied for a thoracic residency with Dr. Johnson. After much consideration it was decided that I would work with Dr. Johnson on Monday, Wednesday, and Friday; and with Dr. Rhoads on Tuesday, Thursday, and Saturday—this with considerable overlapping.

I was also to apply for a Clinical Research Fellowship of the Damon Runyon (cancer) Fund, based in New York.

This I did successfully.

BOARDS. In the late spring Archibald Fletcher and I took and passed the written and oral examinations. As for the written, we had selected ten questions for special study and four of those appeared on this written (discussion) examination.

As for the oral examination, I had drawn a nine o'clock first pair of examiners, and so I had gone back to the University Hospital (just over the fence from the Philadelphia General Hospital). I saw Bill Fitts and asked him what my two first examiners were known for. The one, from Jefferson Medical College was a retired Navy officer. He asked me how I would handle the situation if an atomic bomb fell on San Francisco. His partner, from Yale, asked me how I would treat the burns. Fitts had told me that Dr. Harvey was a burn expert and had proposed a special treatment. You can guess my response.

About this time I went downtown to buy favors for my groomsmen at my forthcoming wedding. They were all smokers and so I selected handsome silver cigarette lighters which had the shape of a swan. As I waited in line behind a gorgeous blonde, just for an instant I wondered if I might not be being a bit hasty with my marriage. But when the lady spoke to the cashier, with a loud raucous voice that murdered the king's English, I shuttered and was reminded once again that facial beauty is only skin deep, and that Weezie's beauty was not only facial but infinitely deeper.

In late June I departed for Decatur, Georgia, and my forthcoming wedding.

Shortly before I left Philadelphia Dr. Ravdin had commented, "Jim, you've done little research."

"Yes, Professor," I replied, "but I *am* Chief Resident." (It was expected that all residents have a research project—few did—but I well knew that the Chief Residency would go to him who did good surgery, and had sound clinical judgment, and took superior care of patients.) Actually, I had spent all the time I could squeeze out in setting up the D_2O apparatus. But privately, I determined, when I returned to Philadelphia a married man, I would redouble efforts to move my research activity into high gear.

CHAPTER 6

Courtship and Marriage

It will be recalled from the Army chapter (No. 4) that I first met Louise Scott Sams (Weezie) at my first "permanent" post, Stark General Hospital outside Charleston, South Carolina. And, as documented in my letter to my mother the next day, it was "love" at first sight. But it was to be five long years before she became a Hardy. Even so, the very next morning I sent Weezie a dozen long stem red roses with a card bearing the message "To the loveliest girl I know."

But we'd hardly met than I was ordered to report to McGuire General Hospital at Richmond. Our "romance" scarcely moved forward, and to make matters worse, a man on the Charleston beach had walked over to me from his party and asked, "Are you courting Weezie Sams?" I replied that I was. Whereupon he said, "You've got a lot of competition."

Nevertheless, once in Richmond I flew down to Charleston when I could get military leave, which was not often. Consequently, when I could get to Charleston it was as if Weezie and I were meeting for the first time. Suffice it to say that our friendship had not truly blossomed by the time I was sent overseas. Weezie was a poor correspondent and we exchanged very few letters when I was in England, France and Germany. Meanwhile, I did correspond frequently with a girl back in Alabama who was a splendid correspondent and who played the piano beautifully. (Weezie played nothing but loved music.)

When I returned to the States, I found Mother in the Baptist Hospital in Memphis with brain metastases. As I sat in the hospital's sun parlor, I reflected upon as to just where I stood in my life. I had two immediate goals: find my life partner and somehow get a residency in surgery. The Department of Medicine at Pennsylvania had kept a spot for me all through the war, but the war experience in Europe had changed my choice from Internal Medicine to Surgery. I had written the chiefs in Medicine that they should not hold a place for me any longer. I would try for surgery.

As for the life partner, I still admired the girl in Alabama, but I had not found my search in her. Meanwhile, I decided to call Weezie in Charleston: Correspondence and piano aside, Weezie had qualities that were special for me.

Thus, we began our meetings again. Hopeless that the distance between Philadelphia and Charleston would prove to be an insurmountable obstacle, I nonetheless determined to marry her if possible.

A few months later I did get the residency in surgery at Penn, but Philadelphia was no closer to Charleston than before.

When I could get permission from the Chief, I would take the coach train down at 30th Street Station late on

Friday afternoon and arrive in Charleston early Saturday morning. If Weezie was working that Saturday at her job in the post office, I would not see her until noon. Then I would have to get the train back to Philadelphia late Sunday afternoon, arriving there early Monday morning.

The ticket agent at 30th Street Station got to know me so well that, when he saw me coming, he would get out a ticket to Charleston. And, from time to time he would advise me "to marry that girl." (If I only could.)

At the University Hospital my telephone bill was impressive. Once, as I paid my bill to the hospital cashier, she said, "Dr. Hardy, if you don't go on and marry that girl soon you will be bankrupt."

Frustrated as I was, competing for a spot as Chief Resident and at the same time competing in Charleston, I was in a "short fuse" state. And this brought on a major error in tactics. I had learned that she had been to the beach with another (the competition). With jealousy at its zenith, I immediately sat down and wrote her a letter just dripping with vicious sarcasm. But no sooner had I mailed the letter than I cooled off and realized I'd made a serious mistake—that if she read that letter she certainly would never marry me. So, I went down to the West Philadelphia post office and told them my problem. They were sympathetic and, would you believe it, they found my letter and returned it to me! The Result: She ultimately did marry me and the Postal Service had made a friend for life.

Weezie and I became engaged in the summer of 1948 and we were married July 1, 1949. I had indeed been named one of the two Chief Residents in Surgery for the 1948-49 year. We would have preferred a June wedding but Dr. Lilly, who Weezie wanted to marry us, had commitments in Charleston and could not marry us until July 1.

Our marriage was held in the Decatur, Georgia, Presbyterian Church. The groomsmen included my four brothers and Julian, my twin, was my best man.

We spent our first wedding night at the Atlanta Athletic Club and the next at the Eola Hotel in Natchez, Mississippi—where Weezie's parents had spent one night of their wedding trip.

And then it was on in my new black Oldsmobile to Mexico, where Weezie had chosen for our honeymoon. As soon as we had crossed the Rio Grande River and entered Mexico, we began to get the throbbing Latin music on the car radio, and one evening at a roadside hotel the teenage daughter of a traveling Mexican family sat down at the piano and played flawlessly the haunting piece "Malaguena."

Arriving in Mexico City, I had developed a "brain tumor." I had the worst headache I could remember, but in about 24 hours it was gone: It had been a part of the altitude sickness.

After several days exploring the attractions of Mexico City, we left to drive on toward Acapulco but, in passing through Taxco, we liked it so much that we decided to remain there before returning to Philadelphia.

Several months earlier, Miss Berang, the deputy University Hospital director, had called me to her office. As usual, she was wearing her starched and spotless nurses' white uniform. But before she could say more than good morning, I said, "Miss Berang, I know what you were going to say. And I can tell you that I am moving

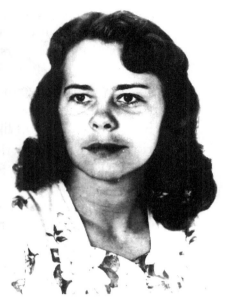

*Louise ("Weezie") Scott Sams at her 100 year ancestral home in
Decatur, Georgia at the time of her marriage.
Reproduced by permission of the University
of Pennsylvania Press. (Memoirs)*

out. I am engaged to be married and already have an apartment." (This after my having lived in the University Hospital for a total of five years.)

Whereupon she asked, "Do you have a refrigerator yet? If not, why don't you go over to the nurses' hotel that we rented for our greatly increased training during the war. Find a refrigerator you like and I will make you a good price."

I did and she did, and we used that refrigerator for ten years.

We returned to Philadelphia, set up housekeeping, and I began my residency in Thoracic Surgery.

CHAPTER 7

Resident in Cardiothoracic Surgery and Damon Runyon Fellow in Cancer Research

The appellation "residency in thoracic surgery" was in fact a misnomer in 1949. It was not a formal residency, it was an apprenticeship. Thoracic surgery was just beyond its infancy. Evarts Graham of St. Louis had performed a total pneumonectomy by simply tying ligatures (a tourniquet) around the pulmonary hilum, with no specific ligation of the bronchus and vascular structures. But by the late 1940s, pulmonary lobectomy with individual ligation of the bronchus and the vascular structures had come into fairly general use. As for "cardiac" surgery, the patent ductus arteriosus had been ligated by Gross of Boston, the coarctation of the aorta resected by Clarence Craaford of Sweden, and mitral valve stenosis was first corrected successfully by Charles Bailey of Philadelphia, though many other surgeons had contributed to the conquering of this malady.

As noted in a previous space, my assignment was to be attached to Dr. Julian Johnson (J.J.) on his operating days, but to assist Dr. Rhoads with his private patients in the office on Tuesday, Thursday, and Saturday mornings.

129

Moreover, I was given staff status and was free to have private patients of my own, if one should appear.

I found Dr. Rhoads considerably different in my new status. One day a stunning brunette came in and I examined her before going out of the cubicle to lead Dr. Rhoads in.

"Dr. Rhoads," I said, "that patient in the first cubicle is a knockout!"

"I take it to mean that you find her attractive. Well, let me tell you something about her. Women like that require a great deal of attention and I happen to know that her husband is a most frustrated and unhappy man. The most important requirement in a wife is she be loyal to the common enterprise."

I was startled that he placed beauty well down the list. But then I remembered my senior brother-in-law's comment about my sister, "Agnes is a wonderful woman. Why, I've seen her get out of bed with fever 104° F., dress and feed the chillun, and get them off to school."

Dr. Johnson had one of the three thoracic surgery services at Philadelphia General Hospital (PGH) and he also covered Valley Forge Veterans Hospital and a hospital in Wilmington, Delaware.

Charlie Kirby and I would go over to PGH late each afternoon or so, to answer requested consultations. All too often face masks were not to be found on the patient's wing, but I always found one somewhere. I had a profound respect for tuberculosis. Charlie would not wait, saying that if one had good immunological resistance he would not contract the disease.

One day Dr. Johnson called me at home. Caught! It was an unwritten law that no resident went out of the

JULIAN JOHNSON

*Reproduced by
permission of the
University
of Pennsylvania Press.
(Memoirs)*

hospital in the daytime, but Weezie had wanted me to see and help her decide about a piece of furniture that we needed to buy.

Dr. Johnson on the phone said sarcastically, "Jim, I wonder if you could favor us by coming down to my office?"

As I walked in he placed a chest film into his X-ray view box. "What do you think?"

I replied, "Somebody has a whopping cavity in the right upper lobe."

He said, "It's Charlie," who was sitting beside him.

He went on to say that Charlie would be put at bed rest in the University Hospital and after several weeks on the new wonder drug streptomycin, discovered by Waksman in 1948 (Nobel prize, 1952), and other drugs Charlie would undergo a right upper lobectomy. For long-term convalescence, he would be sent to a sanatorium at Lake Placid, New York.

But meanwhile, I must go to PGH that evening to attend the monthly staff conference on tuberculosis. I was to be certain that we (the Johnson service) got our share of patients needing an operation. The other two services were the Bailey (of mitral valve fame) and the Mendelson.

I arrived at the large conference room and took a seat well back. About 50 doctors, nurses and other personnel drifted in before the 7:30 meeting began. This June meeting was the last one before fall.

I was looking about, trying to see if I knew anyone (I didn't) but in doing so I had paid scant attention as the first patient's record had been read by her ward physician.

But suddenly I heard the moderator say, "Dr. Hardy, will you discuss the surgical management of this case?"

"Who, me?" and sat there with my mouth opening and closing like a fish on a wharf.

Everybody laughed and I was mortified, for I knew little about tuberculosis surgery in general and I certainly had no suggestions in this particular case.

Just then Dr. Bailey, seated on the first row, saw my predicament, and said, "I would continue to cover the patient with antibiotics, then do an upper lobectomy, and tailor a four rib thoracoplasty. Isn't that what you would do Dr. Hardy?"

Taking this broad cue, I said "Yes." (After the meeting I learned that this practical joke was played on every newcomer.)

The general surgery resident on thoracic surgery at PGH would pick up the consultation requests and then assign them in "rotation" to one of the three thoracic surgery services. But as time passed, I found that almost no major chest cases were assigned to the Johnson service.

Clearly, some type of favoritism was involved. And I suspected the reason. When only occasionally a major case was assigned to the Johnson service, Dr. Johnson would come over from the University Hospital (just over the high stone wall) and do the operation himself. Whereas, patients assigned to the other two services were operated upon by the resident, with only limited supervision.

I went to the operating suite and asked to see the list of thoracic operations performed in the last three months. It was just as I had suspected.

I confronted the PGH resident with these data. I did not expect or receive a confession. Instead, I said, "Jack, I understand your position very well. Let me make you a proposition. Let's collaborate: I'll do one case and you the next, in rotation." He agreed and we became good partners and friends. And would you know, it often appeared that the Johnson service got more major cases than did the other services (could favoritism have been involved here?)

It must be recorded that my research program was going full blast. I could get to the laboratory many afternoons and most evenings. In fact, one evening Weezie was with me and as the time wore on Weezie, now visibly pregnant, had curled up on a broad lab table and gone to sleep. Around midnight Dr. David Drabkin, the Chairman of Biochemistry, came by in a tuxedo to check on one of his experiments on his way home from a party. Seeing Weezie asleep, he declared that from now on that table would be labeled "Weezie Hardy slept here!"

My most memorable patient at PGH was a late teenage girl who had an abscess in the upper lobe of the

DAVID L. DRABKIN

Reproduced by permission of the University of Pennsylvania Press. (Memoirs)

right lung. Dr. Johnson required that such patients be placed on the operating table face down. Well, we had no sooner made the chest incision than the nurse anesthetist said that the balloon on the endotracheal tube had burst and that the patient had to be turned over on her back so that the endotracheal tube could be replaced. Somehow, we got the patient turned and without contaminating the open chest incision.

Next, well along in the operation, the anesthetist announced that the oxygen tank was almost empty and that a replacement had not arrived. It soon did arrive but by this time my nerves had become a bit frayed.

The presence of infection had made the lobectomy more difficult and bloody than usual, and I asked the anesthetist to start one of the six bottles of blood which I had been assured were on hand for this patient. But her blood had been used for an emergency during the night and there was none of her type remaining in the hospital!

What a calamitous situation: no blood, the bloody operation past the point of turning back, and Dr. Johnson out of town.

Just then I spied a telephone on the wall. I told the circulating nurse to get Doctor Brooke Roberts on the phone over at the University Hospital. He answered immediately. And with the nurse to hold the receiver to preserve my sterility I said, "Brooke, I'm in a desperate situation over here at PGH. No time for details, but bring me six bottles of O-negative blood from the University Hospital's blood bank."

I had immaculate confidence in him and within ten minutes or so he panted up the stairs with the six bottles of blood. The patient survived.

The University blood bank authorities were considerably exercised by this transgression, but just imagine J.J.'s reaction if I had lost that patient in his absence.

Louise Is Born. (29 July 1950). This event changed our lives more than we had imagined. Weezie's obstetrician had asked me if I would like to come into the delivery room to witness the birth. I did and it was one of the most moving experiences of my life. We had not known the sex previously but we promptly named her Louise Scott, after her mother and her grandmother. Her blue eyes and curly hair were those of her father.

When we got the baby home, I didn't know what to say to her. I had of course cared for many babies, but not my baby. Weezie said, "Say just anything, so that she will learn to recognize your voice." After this event, Weezie was no longer able to go to the lab with me in the evenings to run heavy water measurements.

For my thoracic research project, Dr. Johnson had directed that I operate on 25-pound pigs, take a segment of the infrarenal vena cava through a right flank wound, and then to make a left upper thoracotomy and place the vena caval segment into the aorta just below the left subclavian artery. I'd had almost no experience sewing blood vessels and my diener laboratory assistant had had almost no surgical experience at all. It was hard on the pigs, but we persevered, gained experience and did achieve survivors.

The pigs were allowed to grow to perhaps 200 pounds and then sacrificed. In brief, the incidence of aneurysm formation in the vena caval grafts was such it was clearly inappropriate to use such venous grafts in human beings to replace segments of the coarctation of the aorta that were too long to permit resection and then primary anastomosis.

Meanwhile, my research program was flourishing. And I was writing my first book, *Surgery and the Endocrine System*.

THE DECISION FOR MEMPHIS. As I began the last six months of my thoracic residency I had to make a basic career decision: Remain at Pennsylvania (a probable option), or go to some other lesser medical school that needed what I might have to offer, or enter private practice. Near the end of my general surgery residency I had been invited to Dallas to consider entering a private clinical group, of which Dr. Murphy Bounds (with whom I'd served in the 81st FH) was the leading surgeon. The guaranteed salary was certainly attractive, but the lack of a library or any other academic activity prompted me to decline. It was now clear to me that an academic institution would be needed for me to feel fulfilled professionally. Jonathan Rhoads had advised that I go down and look at the private practice job in Dallas, but he had followed it up with his estimate of my future. "Jim, I've followed you since you were a medical student. You are at home in the laboratory, a rarity in a surgeon. Let's say you put $50,000 in the bank the first ten years, what are you going to do then, make $50,000 more? If you can get your heavy water measurements working I think you would be useful to many departments of surgery."

I returned to Philadelphia and said, "Dr. Rhoads, I'm going to make that heavy water work."

As for staying at Penn, the prospects of progressing as an operating surgeon were limited: Dr. Ravdin had William T. Fitts as his deputy, Dr. Rhoads had Cletus Schwegman, and Dr. Johnson had Charles Kirby. With the chief resident on each of the two ward (charity) services rightly claiming the major portion of that surgery, there would be little left for me. And certainly any private patients I got would be few.

On the other hand, my research program had finally blossomed, with the heavy water now successful, and a series of metabolic papers in press or on the way. To move to some lesser school would certainly slow considerably my professional advance in this direction.

Finally, reluctantly, I made an appointment with Dr. Ravdin and told him that I felt I had to move to a lesser school that would welcome my research program and where I would be able to operate more. He was cool but did suggest that I contact Drs. Michael DeBakey in Houston and Carl Moyer in Dallas. Both were recruiting staff for new schools.

Actually, I had already met Dr. DeBakey, when he had come through Philadelphia two years before on a recruiting trip, but at that time I was just beginning the thoracic residency.

I took Dr. Ravdin's suggestion that I check with DeBakey in Houston and Moyer in Dallas. But as I was preparing for the trip, Dr. Rhoads said, "Jim, a friend of mine has just last year taken the Chair of Surgery at the University of Tennessee Medical College at Memphis. I think he could use a man like you. Why don't you stop by Memphis on your way back from Texas? I'll call him."

Both Drs. DeBakey and Moyer offered me a job but both departments posed special problems. Dr. DeBakey was frank that he could not promise me a ward service, though said he expected to gain further control at the city hospital. Dr. Moyer's department in Dallas was housed in WWII galvanized iron Quonset huts. He did offer me a job, but somehow it did not fit my needs. And, to boot, he seemed to be looking above my head half the time. (Upon returning to Philadelphia, I told Dr. Ravdin that I had got the feeling that Dr. Moyer was not long for Dallas—and he accepted the Chair at Washington University in St. Louis within months.)

But I did stop over in Memphis. I met with Dr. Harwell Wilson, Chairman of the Department of Surgery, and the next day for lunch with Dr. Orin W. Hyman, Vice-Chancellor of the University of Tennessee Medical Units in Memphis. (The University of Tennessee itself was in Knoxville.) Dr. Wilson had already shown me the several empty offices and laboratories assigned to Surgery in the new Pathology building. And in the connecting John Gaston (charity) Hospital I saw surgical problems of such

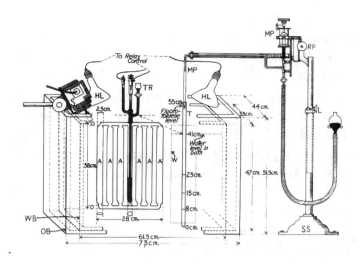

Apparatus used to control the temperature in the water bath within to .001 degrees Centigrade.

numbers, range, and severity as I had never seen in Philadelphia. Virtually no research was being done in the department of surgery. A possible salary of $9,000 per year was mentioned. Limited private practice would be permitted. It was the type of opportunity I'd been looking for.

I wrote my twin, Julian, who was practicing obstetrics and gynecology in Birmingham, for his estimate of the situation: Houston, Dallas, or Memphis? He replied with a most impressive analysis: that DeBakey would smother me. That since Moyer was a fluid therapy expert, anything I discovered there would be attributed to him. Julian recommended Memphis, without question.

I returned to Philadelphia and told Dr. Rhoads of my visit to Memphis. He then said, "The one requirement you must insist on is specific and regular rotations on the ward service. Without this you'll never be able to show yourself as a surgeon and they will label you as only a dog surgeon. Remember, if they really want you, they'll make room on the ward service. And you must get agreement to some private practice, even if very limited. Finally, if you do move to Memphis, try to see Harwell every day, if possible.

I talked with Dr. Wilson on the telephone, listing all the research projects I would pursue if I came to Memphis. Apparently he became alarmed and wrote me, "Now look, Hardy, don't come down and tell Dr. Hyman that you are coming to save it for him."

We scheduled a second visit and again met for lunch at the University's fine dining room.

With little preamble, Dr. Hyman turned to me and asked, "Doctor, what do you plan to do with your life?"

"I plan to work like the devil until I'm 45 and then, if I do not have a Chair of Surgery by that time, go into practice, at least largely."

"My," he said, "You are certainly opinionated for your age. How old are you?"

"Thirty-two, Sir." He then turned to Dr. Wilson and said, "Harwell, I think Hardy would be useful to us."

To me he said, "Are there any special considerations to be met?" (The $9,000 yearly salary had already been confirmed.) I replied that I would need nine months on the wards: six months on adult wards and three months on either thoracic or childrens surgery. (My pediatric experience here was to prove highly valuable several years later.)

Dr. Wilson said that he had met considerable resistance from the young surgeons now covering the wards, for they got a few private patients in this way.

Dr. Hyman then asked Dr. Wilson to try again to free up the rotations, that I did not leave for Philadelphia until the next day and that perhaps they could tell me something definite before I left.

Dr. Hyman then asked if we had covered everything. I then asked permission to earn a net of $3,000 per year from private practice. Any "overage" would go to the University. He agreed.

Dr. Wilson was able to get reluctant agreement from his junior staff members and the deal was sealed.

As the twin propeller plane taxied to the fence of the old airport in Philadelphia, I saw clinging to the wire an adorable little girl in a red jacket and with a sea of golden curls peeping from beneath her red hat. Smiling from behind her was her lovely mother. I told Weezie that we would go to Memphis in August.

The contract to move to the Medical College of Tennessee settled, I made an appointment with Dr. Ravdin to inform him before he heard it from anyone else. Up to then, I don't believe he thought that I really did mean to go.

I asked that I be relieved from all duties as of June 1, without pay. I wanted to finish up research I had been doing, finish my book *Surgery and the Endocrine System*, and formulate plans for the move to Memphis in August.

Meanwhile, however, many things had happened. First, the heavy water measurements were finally successful.

Dr. David Drabkin, my chemistry mentor, was as delighted as I was. He said that the Graduate Committee was impressed with my work, and that if I would write a thesis and pay a fee that he thought I could be awarded a Masters' Degree in Chemistry. I did and they did.

I first had the D_2O injected into *my* vein, for there was some lingering concern regarding its possible toxicity. The known amount of heavy water then equilibrated with all the other normal molecules of water in the body. After two hours a blood sample was obtained, treated appropriately and the highly purified water tested for the D_2O level: The dilution principle. My body weight was 61 percent (see figure) water. The leanest male (physician) was 73 percent water. The fattest male (physician) was 40 percent. Approximately one-half the D_2O injected into me had been excreted in the urine in 9 days, and "all" by 29 days. But presumably a few molecules escaped excretion indefinitely.

I soon presented some of this D_2O work before the Philadelphia Physiological Society and the Philadelphia Academy of Surgery. Walking out at the end of the Academy meeting, Dr. Johnson said, "Jim, that was pretty heavy stuff. I think I'll keep looking at the tongue to determine how well hydrated my patients are."

The first truly national presentation was to the American Physiological Society down at Atlantic City. My paper had gone well, but the next paper, from Dallas and also on the percentage of water content of mammals (dogs), had some animals recorded as 90 percent water. Preposterous. Such an animal would be flowing around like the amoeba seen under the microscope. Either his results were wrong or my results were wrong. And I wanted the large audience to know that I doubted the dog work. So, during the question-answer period, I arose and said, "Mr. Moderator, I would like to ask the essayist as to the character of his dogs?"

TOTAL BODY WATER (D_2O DILUTION SPACE)
AND BODY SIZE RELATIONSHIP

Subject	Mass, M	Stem length, L	Nutritive Index, N_o	N_o-N_m †	Percentage overnutrition above minimum value, $\left[\left(\frac{N_o-N_m}{N_m}\right) \times 100\right]$	Total body water		
						Amount	Per cent of body weight	Per cent deviation from maximum value
	kg.	cm.			Per cent	l.	Per cent	Per cent
Leanest (theory)	(56.4)	(91.0)	(0.42)†	(0.00)	(0.0)		(75)	(0.0)
J.M. ♂	60.9	91.0	0.43	0.01	2.4	44.5	73	2.4
H.G.B.♂	60.0	81.3	0.48	0.06	14.3	41.1	69	8.0
J.D.H.♂	77.3	83.8	0.51	0.09	21.4	46.6	61	18.7
J.R. ♂	66.4	76.0	0.53	0.11	26.2	37.6	57	24.0
W.B. ♂	121.0	90.2	0.55	0.13	31.0	60.6	50	33.4
S.G. ♂	116.0	81.5	0.60	0.18	42.9	48.3	42	44.0
M.McG. ♀	53.7	90.2	0.42	0.00	0.0	36.4	68	9.3
A.D. ♀	59.1	82.6	0.47	0.05	11.9	35.3	60	20.0
J.R. ♀	54.6	75.0	0.51	0.09	21.4	31.7	58	22.7
W.T. ♀	86.4	76.2	0.58	0.16	38.1	45.1	52	30.6
Fattest (theory)	(111.0)	(76.2)	(0.63)	(0.21)	(50.0)		(40)	(46.7)

* N_o = observed nutritive index = $M^{1/3}/L$ cm. (Cowgill and Drabkin, 1927)

† N_m = minimum nutritive index, or minimum value of N_o = 0.42

Data derived from the dilution of intravenously injected heavy water (D_2O) in the total body water.
Note on the right that the highest percentage of body weight represented by water was that of JM (73%), a surgery resident. The lowest percentage was that of SG (42%), a practicing physician. The fattest female was 52 percent water. JDH, of average "obesity" was 61 percent.

At this, the essayist drew himself up and said, "I'll have you know, sir, the character of my dogs was unimpeachable!"

STATUS OF MY DAMON RUNYON FELLOWSHIP. One requirement of one's having been awarded this fellowship was that the awardee come to the New York Memorial Hospital for Cancer and Allied Diseases. There would be a scientific program, put on by the fellows. I gave my heavy water studies.

Walter Winchell, Leonard Lyons and Sherman Billingsley would host a luncheon at the Stork Club while the ladies were entertained elsewhere. There Winchell stood up at the microphone and, in his characteristic staccato delivery, extolled the fight against cancer and the Damon Runyon Fund's participation in this fight. Leonard Lyons, the syndicated columnist and seated beside me, leaned over and said, "If Winchell's done nothing else, he's sure scared the hell out of the American people about cancer."

At lunch the second day, in the enclosed roof garden of the hospital, I was seated beside Mr. John Teeter, Executive Director of the Damon Runyon Fund. Making conversation, I asked how the Fund raised its money (from donations by the famous in the entertainment field). And then I asked him how research grants were decided? He replied that they had a scientific committee which appraised the scientific value and the promise of grant requests. However, he continued, he held back a small percentage of the total available funds to assign himself as "seed money" to young investigators just getting started—venture capital, he said he liked to call it.

That evening we all went to a costume ball for TV celebrities at the Waldorf Astoria Hotel. Weezie, now very pregnant, had rented an academic cap and gown, at the suggestion of her mother. During the evening one doctor at our table remarked to Weezie, "You know, your costume would be a fine idea if one were pregnant." Weezie just smiled.

During the evening Mary Martin rushed over from "South Pacific," in her sailor costume, and sang several songs from the musical.

We had had a memorable experience and, as I recall, took the train back to Philadelphia late that night, a 90-minute ride.

COLLATERAL RESEARCH. Along with the D_2O studies, I was heavily involved in studies of the patient's metabolic response to major operations. A principal need was to have dependable analyses of the urinary excretion of adrenocortical hormones for correlation with the water and electrolyte changes. And to this end, Dr. Ravdin had called the director of medical research at Merck's laboratories, I believe at Rahway, New Jersey, and he and I drove over there for a conference.

It was agreed that Dr. T. would do these chemical analyses on the urine that we shipped over. While we were there a Dr. Shope, a hog influenza specialist as I recall, asked me to examine some lymph nodes in the back of his technician's neck. I said, even before she came in, "Dr. Shope, the three most common causes of enlarged lymph nodes in the posterior cervical triangle are German measles, or a general node involvement such as in certain types of blood disorders, or head lice."

I took the technician into an office, closed the door, and said I wanted to examine her hair closely and there they were: innumerable nits (head lice, pediculosis). When I reported back to Dr. Shope he said that this technician cared for the ducks, which all had lice. I recommended DDT powder, this before Rachel Carson's *Silent Spring* had preceded the ban on the wide use of this chemical agent.

As time passed and we had sent over several hundred liters of urine from the patients studied in our University Hospital, I tried to contact Dr. T. but to no avail. Then one hot summer morning as I was helping the Merck driver load a large batch of urine specimens, I said to him, "You will of course store this urine under refrigeration just as soon as you get back to Merck."

"Doc, ain't no urine been stored under refrigeration over there. It's all sitting out in a hot warehouse, aint's never been touched."

All the urine that had been so laboriously collected was now useless for analyses. All that time and expense down the drain.

Fortunately, I was able to get enough steroid analyses from another source to correlate with the other metabolic data.

THE ATOMIC BOMB PROJECT. One day Dr. Ravdin called me to his office and said that, in 72 hours, I should place on his desk a proposal for the management of mass casualties of an atomic bomb on a major American city.

I immediately dropped everything else, read madly for a day, let my imagination run wild, transported whole populations across the country (recall that civilian air travel in 1951 was only a fraction of what it is now), and much else. I included thermal burns and radiation injury, the hazards for pregnant women, etc.

He must have liked what I wrote, for he called a meeting of several University Hospital leaders down at his home one evening and invited me to attend and enlarge on certain aspects of the proposal.

After that night I had given little thought to the matter until some days later the research laboratories secretary, Miss B.H., said to me, "Dr. Hardy, do you remember that proposal I typed for you about a week ago?"

"Yes, Betsy, what about it?"

"Well, I have just typed a large research grant proposal to go to Washington, for Dr. W. It consists substantially of what you wrote, some of it word for word, but your name does not appear anywhere."

This time I decided to take the matter directly to Dr. Ravdin, for I did not believe he knew that this corporate plagiarism had been so blatant. Belatedly, some minor adjustments were made in the text, but thereafter I was even more confident that the decision to leave Philadelphia was the correct one. I really didn't care about the use of the original ideas I'd put forward, for I had no immediate plans for such research. But I was deeply annoyed and indeed hurt that my material had been so preemptively appropriated (behind my back) without even permission or thanks.

It told me a lot.

SURGERY AND THE ENDOCRINE SYSTEM. In early July I placed this manuscript on Dr. Ravdin's desk. The next morning he called me to his office and said, "Jim, I had no idea. I have called Mr. Potter, President of the W.B. Saunders (Medical) Publishers, and he thinks they might want to publish it." After farming the manuscript out to knowledgeable critics, Saunders accepted it for publication.

MY LAST DAY IN PHILADELPHIA. How well I remember my last day in Philadelphia, home for thirteen years. It was a somber time. Reluctance at leaving, yes. Doubts about the future, yes. Aware of falling from grace in the eyes of friends and acquaintances, yes.

I went up to say goodbye to Dr. Ravdin last. It was after five o'clock and the secretaries had gone. The door to his office was partly ajar, and I could see that a barber was cutting his hair. Not venturing to go in and intrude, I simply said, "Goodbye, Professor."

He cut his eyes to the right toward me as the barber snipped here and there and said, "You'd better stay!"

"No, Sir, but thanks."

The car was packed and I was out of the apartment. Weezie and Louise had gone ahead. There remained only to take the final, corrected manuscript down to the W.B. Saunders Company in the city. I drove across to the Schuylkill River (here my Rubicon) and got inside the publishers building. Once there I continued correcting the manuscript. When the final occupant left, she put on the night lock and told me to pull the door closed firmly when I left.

I had finished the manuscript. I tilted back in the swivel chair for a moment, looked out at the lights and skyline of Philadelphia, thought of all I had learned and experienced there over the past thirteen years—my whole adult life thus far—and asked myself: Why am I really leaving?

The answer, I knew, was that I did not really fit the mold. I did not think my personality would be spiritually successful in the system, which was too regimented, too pyramidal. I needed more room to grow as an operating surgeon over the next ten years. I wanted to be employed to the fullest.

I walked out, closed the front door, got into the black Oldsmobile, and drove south through the rain toward an uncertain destiny.

CHAPTER 8

Research—The Early Years

As with Alice, research has been the golden key which opened the little door to the tiny garden where I mounted my magic carpet to the world.

THE ANATOMY OF DISCOVERY

Investigation takes many forms but the two commonly accepted classifications are basic and applied. The term "basic" in its strictest sense implies a search for information never known before. The Nobel prize is awarded for such basic information (usually). On the other hand, applied "research" usually implies the use of known information to achieve some specific goal. For example Watson and Crick's discovery of the molecular (double helix) structure of DNA (desoxyribonucleic acid) required basic research (Nobel prize, 1962). In contrast, John H. Gibbon's development of the heart-lung machine, while a monumental contribution, was apparently denied the Nobel prize because he had applied previously known information.

My own basic research had to do with the use of heavy water (D_2O) in studying body composition. And yet, there can be an in-between category in which known methods are used to search for answers to bodily function and dysfunction, as that associated with recovery from trauma or surgical operations. This has been the category into which much of our research would fall.

The great Scottish anatomist and surgeon, John Hunter, wrote in 1740 that "There is a circumstance attending accidental injury that does not belong to disease, namely, that the injury done has in all cases a tendency to produce the disposition and the means of cure."

Enter endocrinology.

Our most extensive applied research has been in the transplantation of organs.

PILGRIM'S (JDH) PROGRESS: WHEN DID IT ALL START? (You've Got To Be Carefully Taught, Before It Becomes Too Late.) As noted in Chapter 3, my first research came as a freshman in medical school when I joined three fellow students in an elective research project which involved the effect of olive oil introduced into the duodenum on gastric secretion. We ourselves were the "guinea pigs." Our supervisor was Dr. Joseph Doupe, down from Canada. I had then presented our material to the entire class and faculty. I was afterward called in by Dr. Henry C. Bassett, Chairman of the Department of Physiology, and asked what my plans were (regarding research). I replied that my objective was to finish medical school.

During the sophomore year I did no "bench" research but I wrote a paper (required?) entitled "The Relationship Between Nutrition and Hookworm Disease."

The junior year was too heavy to do anything other than the prescribed studies in all the many branches of medicine, surgery (general, urology, ENT, ophthalmology, orthopedics), obstetrics and gynecology, pediatrics, public health and psychiatry.

One happy event the junior year, however, was that I was elected to Alpha Omega Alpha, the "Phi Beta Kappa" of medical school. This meant that I ranked among the top five students in my class.

Meanwhile, I had my own projects. As noted in Chapter 2, I competed for the Medical History Prize and I was told by the Dean's secretary, most confidentially, that my thesis "The History and Importance of Military Field Hygiene" would win the prize. I most confidentially told only Julian. But at graduation another name appeared in the History Prize slot in the program. He had turned in his paper at the last minute.

But not all was lost. Two weeks later Julian and I took the Alabama State Medical Licensure examination in Montgomery and four of the ten discussion questions dealt with major portions of my medical history paper. I was later informed, unofficially, that I had made the highest mark of those taking the examination.

See the Army chapter where I did so well when asked about sarcoidosis that I was offered a medical residency at the University of Kansas after the war!

The internship has been described earlier. I did not have time to do research but I *was* able to begin piano lessons.

It would be tedious to itemize all my subsequent research projects. The bulk of them had to do with the metabolic effects of surgical trauma and the transplantation of organs.

In sum, the resulting publications approached five hundred.

PLANNING RESEARCH. In my terms on N.I.H. study sections, the applicant was at times more likely to be successful if he requested support for two or even three years, than if he asked for support for only one year. Why was this? It was because the voting members of the study section were all experienced investigators themselves, and they knew that it would probably take at least a year even to get the experiments set up.

Reading. In most instances the first requirement is to determine whether the prospective research has already been done and published. If it has, the investigator may decide to select some other target; or, he, after reading the previous report carefully, may see the opportunity to advance some facet to gain useful information. And here mathematics may come into play. An experienced mathematician may see special significance in others' data that was not perceived by the original investigator. In fact, Dr. David Drabkin, in whose chemistry laboratory I worked for several years, made a (successful) habit, almost a hobby, of recalculating others' published data and publishing additional conclusions.

Methods. The methods selected for use must be the best currently available.

Protocol. Take time to develop a comprehensive protocol. Try to gather, from the outset, with the first experiment, all the different types of data that will ultimately be needed or at least useful.

Consult others in the field and promote brainstorming, cross-fertilization opportunities as the experimental protocol is being developed.

Costs. Can the project be conducted successfully with the funding available?

The Data Book. It goes without saying that data should be entered into the data book immediately, dated, and the book kept in a safe place.

Personnel. Are the technical personnel available capable of running the experiments without major supervision?

PUBLICATION. One hears it said occasionally that it does not matter who gets the credit. This is of course naïve. It does matter, for it represents the fruition of the research performed. For the scientist in full-time research, it is a matter of vital importance: It may decide his funding, his salary, his academic promotion, local and national reputation, and the welfare of his family. And these considerations take on special force and delicacy when a pure scientist is collaborating with a clinician, whose promotions may be gained primarily from the clinical sphere of his or her activity. Into such collaboration can creep invidious terms such as Greek slave or "truffle swine" (one who exposes a truffle but the farmer [substitute departmental chairman] scoops it up and bags [publishes] it).

The Order of Names. Again, at the very outset of a collaborative venture, a listing of the names of the investigators should be drawn up: first author, second author, last author, etc. Of course, this order or even the composition of the listing can be altered over time through specific contributions, departure of one of the members, and so forth. But the authorship can always be modified with a codicil.

This early attention to authorship ensures that credit will be given where credit is due, and it preserves harmonious relationships. "Good fences make good neighbors."

Priority. Knowledge of who did it first is obviously important. But it can take up to a year before a submitted manuscript appears in the published journal. Thus, if a truly important discovery has been made, priority can be established by a "letter to the editor" or some short-time segment of the journal. It is also useful to call the editor to alert him or her and to ask for advice.

The Department Chairman and Publication. When may (should) the department chairman place his name on a manuscript submitted to him for approval and forwarding for publication? This consideration has plagued many medical schools throughout the world. Of course, if the chairman furnished the idea and the grant funds and corrected the manuscript, there is justification for tacking on his name. But many departmental chairmen put their name on virtually every paper that comes from their department. In my view this borders on dishonesty, and it can lead not only to personnel unhappiness but to reputation destruction of the chairman if he or she so became the victim of laboratory fraud. For example, the lowly research assistant at one of our major mid-west universities made an astonishing and monumental discovery: He had found that skin taken from a black and unrelated mouse, if stored appropriately, would be accepted on the back of the white mouse without rejection. The chairman embraced this assistant's discovery wholeheartedly and spoke of it nationally. But other laboratories could not duplicate these results. In brief, it was discovered that the assistant had simply painted a patch of hair on the back of the white recipient with black shoe polish.

In a major northeastern university, the previously obscure researcher began to make epochal heart discoveries, one after another using radioactive C-14. The chairman embraced these results and participated in their publication. But, unfortunately, the investigator's laboratory assistant became disgruntled and suggested that the administration take a Geiger counter and check the stored hearts for radioactivity. There was none.

LABORATORY FRAUD. The two instances of laboratory fraud cited above were not peculiar to those two universities. We at the University of Mississippi had our own instances of fraud, incompetency and neglect. Parenthetically, I should note that I endeavored to have each surgical resident do a laboratory project of limited scope, analyze the data, write it up and hopefully give it at a regional or national meeting.

Fortunately, all four of our irregularities were detected before publication. The first, and the most egregious, had to do with a senior surgical resident. His assignment was to perform gastrectomy but with immediate reimplantation of the stomach in dogs, this to study the effects of this maneuver upon gastric secretion in the animals. In my periodic review of various projects with my chief laboratory technician, she said that "these results don't make sense." It was soon confessed that the related blood samples had simply been drawn at random from the dog colony, with no operation having been done on any of the "experimental" animals.

A second lapse had to do with another resident. His assignment had been to see to it that inbred purebred beagles, bought at considerable expense from a breeder in Tennessee, received the prescribed atherosclerosis producing high fat diet. But when I opened the abdomen of a first animal, at the prescribed time, I found the aorta completely free of the expected atherosclerotic plaques, as was the case with a second dog. And it was soon established that the beagles had never received the special diet.

The third research lapse was signally instructive. The new chemistry technician presented herself as having had her major in chemistry at the University of Wisconsin. Up to this time, we had depended on the Personnel Office to check on the credentials of job applicants. But when we realized that she really did not know what she was doing, we checked with the University of Wisconsin ourselves. We discovered that she had had one year of freshman chemistry but none thereafter.

The fourth circumstance had to do with a computer technician. I myself knew virtually nothing about computers but two staff members were well versed in this field. They had hired a technician from a local college who was purported to be well versed in computers.

Well, I received a request from the N.I.H. to send a status report on this work and I asked my chief chemistry technician, the computer technician and her two staff supervisors to meet me in the conference room: My chief chemistry technician, with me from Memphis some years ago, had told me that the data submitted to her "did not make sense."

Sadly, to be brief, the computer technician simply had not known what she was doing and the data recorded were totally unreliable.

The Nobel prize. This coveted accolade is the ultimate research achievement. I was asked to write in support of three worthy candidates, but only one of these was actually awarded the prize.

RESEARCH ACCESS DERIVED FROM MY OWN RESEARCH.

The Surgical Biology Club. In approximately 1952 Francis D. Moore of Harvard and the Peter Bent Brigham Hospital pulled together about ten surgical investigators to form a Surgical Biology Club. The group would meet on Sunday just ahead of the Clinical Congress of the American College of Surgeons. The motto was to be "exchange without piracy." Several papers would be presented and free discussion encouraged.

The group was enlarged to about twenty-five over the years. And, incidentally, at one session Drs. Zollinger and Ellison presented several patients with pancreatic tumors associated with a severe peptic ulcer syndrome. The birth of the Z-E syndrome.

The N.I.H. Surgical Study Committee. This assignment lasted three or possibly four years and its mission was to assess the merits of the many grant requests received in the surgical field. There were about twenty members and each grant request was assigned to three members, each of whom wrote a critique and presented it to the committee as a whole. A secret vote was then taken.

The Anesthesia Training Grant Committee. At the end of my service with the Surgery Study Committee, I was asked to serve as the lone surgeon with about nineteen academic anesthesiologists. Congress had declared Anesthesiology, Pathology and Radiology disaster areas because relatively few medical students elected to train in these specialties and the resulting shortages had become serious.

We gave out a lot of money in the effort to enlarge the anesthesiology pool, but it was to take some years before the entries in the training grant pipeline emerged to enlarge the national capability in this discipline.

The Advisory Committee on Technological Application. Dr. Clarence Dennis had joined the N.I.H. and been assigned to assess technological instrumentation and its promises. He urged me to join his committee and I finally did so. However, although we then had an ongoing ten-man team inserting an artificial heart in calves, I myself had limited my investigation to transplantation of the heart.

Unfortunately, this Committee of about fifteen specialists did not have a clearly defined mission, and after two or three years it was discontinued.

The Clinical Research Committee of the American Cancer Society. This committee of about twenty investigators met in New York City every three or four months to assess grant requests. It seemed to me that the Executive Secretary had a few applicants toward whom he was especially lenient. I decided that we must be fair and require a uniform detailed application from each applicant. Thus, when Dr. Charles Huggins of the University of Chicago sent in his annual request conveyed by little more than a letter, I insisted that he be required to send a formal application, just like everyone else. This caused obvious distress on the part of the Executive Secretary but I carried the day. After all, Dr. Huggins had time to send in his formal request before running out of his existing funding.

However, in the interim he won the Nobel prize. He then sent in his previous letter and I remained as silent as a mouse.

CHAPTER 9

The University of Tennessee College of Medicine, Memphis

By driving most of the night I arrived at Bristol, Tennessee, the next morning. I assumed that I was almost there but Tennessee extends approximately 500 miles from east to west. I arrived at the Peabody Hotel in Memphis late in the afternoon. There, waiting in her room, was a round-faced, brown-eyed, brown-haired lovely and very pregnant person in a pink slip. A joyous vision that I knew I would remember forever.

Our first house was one rented on the outskirts of Memphis—dusty roads, Johnson grass elephant-eye high, and floor furnaces that burned little Louise's hands when she fell on them. Harwell Wilson brought out a roast duck, but his new Cadillac slid into the ditch and by the time we got it out the high spirits of his visit had somehow been dissipated.

Next, I surveyed the prospects for doing research. I had brought the heavy water equipment from Philadelphia in my car. But all that the Tennessee College of Medicine furnished was two empty laboratories, one of which contained a chair and a desk.

I asked Dr. Wilson if he would allow me to spend a few hundred dollars of budget money to purchase even basic laboratory equipment. He said that there was not much of a departmental budget, but that he would take it up with Dr. Hyman, Dean and Vice-Chancellor. Nothing happened. Meanwhile I was flooding the mails with grant requests, but the granting agencies replied that it did not appear that the University provided even the basic laboratory equipment that a granting agency had a right to expect.

I asked Dr. Wilson if I might go over and see Dr. Hyman myself. He listened to me briefly and then held up his hand. "Hardy," he said, "We pay your salary but it is up to you to get money for research." (I later learned that he'd had many disappointments after putting up money for research. And, two years later he insisted that he would pay a fellow who wanted to work with me without pay: "Hardy, you don't get something for nothing.")

I went back to my office and wondered just what had I gotten myself into.

But suddenly an idea flashed into my mind: The Damon Runyon Fund: "Venture capital," "Seed money."

I picked up the phone and called John Teeter in New York, reintroduced myself as a former Damon Runyon Fellow, and told him my situation. He told me to write out a grant request form, such as required by the N.I.H.

Within a few months I received an award of $4,000. I immediately bought the basic laboratory equipment, included it in the previously unsuccessful grant requests, and mailed them off again.

After several months I had approval from the American Cancer Society, the N.I.H., and the Research

ORIN W. HYMAN

*Reproduced by permission of
the University of Pennsylvania
Press. (Memoirs)*

and Development Section of the Army Surgeon General's Office.

My getting the American Cancer Society grant was illustrative as to how chance encounters can affect one's future. One day Dr. Douglas Sprunt, Chairman of the Department of Pathology, came down to my office. "Hardy," he asked, "How do you know Owen Wangensteen (Chairman of Surgery at University of Minnesota)?"

"I wouldn't say I really know him. But he came with Dr. Ravdin to my laboratory at Penn. I had said that fat contained little water by body weight. That the fattest physician we'd studied had contained only about 40 percent water but that the leanest man had contained 70 percent. He then turned to our rotund chairman, Dr. Ravdin, and with a twinkle in his eyes asked me what percentage of body weight I thought he had." Then, after Dr. Ravdin had had to go on to other duties, Dr. Wangensteen had stayed with me for about an hour.

"Well," Dr. Sprunt said, "You sure made a convert out of him. Your grant request was about to be turned down there in New York yesterday, but he stood up, said he knew you personally, that you would learn how to write grant requests better, but that you certainly must be supported. And you got the grant."

Once a pauper, I now had more money that I could use effectively. I told Dr. Wilson that I was going to send back the money on one of the three grants; that now even with multiple technicians and two research fellows, I had more money than I could use. I wanted to establish a reputation for using grant money effectively.

Dr. Wilson was much concerned. He said that the University got a lot of overhead money from such grants, and I had better go talk with Dr. Hyman before I did something so rash as to send back money.

I did, and Dr. Hyman was clearly disturbed. He proposed that I pay my $9,000 University salary from the grants.

"Dr. Hyman," I said carefully, "If the University were paying me not one dime, I could hardly feel appreciated."

I sent back the money.

On the night of October 30, 1951, Julia Ann Hardy was born. But it was a rather untidy affair. Weezie had been examined by her obstetrician a bit earlier, and he and I were chatting in the hall. Meanwhile, Weezie called the nurse and told her that the baby was coming *now*. The nurse said, "No, dearie, the doctor has just recently examined you." At which, Weezie asked her, "Have you ever had a baby?" No she had not.

Weezie thereupon insisted most vehemently that the baby *was* coming.

Just at this point the baby's head appeared and she was rushed to the delivery room to finish the birthing of a little girl.

Weezie never forgave the obstetrician, who was a good friend of mine and she absolutely refused to have him again with her next (third) girl. She remained relentless and it became obvious that I must either get a new obstetrician or deliver the baby myself at home.

I went over to the Baptist Hospital to consult Dr. Wilson about this impasse. He broke out laughing and said, "Join the club." He said that his wife, Helen, had gone in for her postpartum examination. The obstetrician had examined her with one hand while he continued to hold his cigar in the other! She swore she would never go near him again, though he was the leading obstetrician in Memphis and a principal referring physician for her husband.

Dr. Wilson recommended another obstetrician for our next (third) daughter.

Meanwhile, our research program was beginning to take form. The various parameters of operative metabolism, begun at Penn, were to be pursued, particularly with the standard three-stage thoracoplasty operations done at the adjacent West Tennessee Tuberculosis Hospital. Too, I had reviewed 500 charts of burn patients admitted to the John Gaston Hospital, and this review had been the basis for the Army Grant entitled "The Cause of Death in Thermal Burns." In due course, by performing several blood cultures on every patient with major flame burns admitted to the John Gaston Hospital, we found (as did others) that the "toxemia of burns" was due to bacterial invasion of the blood stream.

TEACHING. As the first full-time member of the faculty, I was assigned to teach the entire course in general surgery to the medical students: and the entire course was repeated every three months—for the medical school was on the quarterly system, with a class graduating every three months.

Our research laboratory was the only laboratory in Memphis set up to measure corticoids, 17-ketosteroids and catechol amines, and since we were called upon to furnish such measurements to private practitioners, we got an occasional private patient from this source.

COLLATERAL MATTERS. The year 1952 brought progress in a variety of other directions.

First, the volume of Gaston surgery was large and I covered general surgery on one or the other adult wards six months a year and three months on the children's ward (an important experience for later in Jackson). But I had never got a rotation on thoracic surgery and I knew I needed to be *doing* thoracic surgery to feel comfortable in the upcoming thoracic board oral examinations in Chicago. I had already taken and passed the first stage, the written examination.

I went to Dr. Wilson and asked, once again, about the thoracic rotation. He said, "Jim, it's embarrassing but I just have not been able to get Dr. Carr (Chief of Thoracic Surgery) to put you on the thoracic rotation. It is one of the promises to you that I just can't keep. I'm very sorry."

The problem was, of course, that Dr. Carr had over the years managed to keep thoracic surgery for "pure" thoracic surgeons. And to let a general surgeon (me) demonstrate thoracic surgical capability would threaten the private practice of the purists.

THE JOHN GASTON HOSPITAL

HARWELL WILSON
Reproduced by
permission of the
University of
Pennsylvania Press.
(Memoirs)

I knew Harwell had tried. I said to him, "Dr. Wilson, I can suggest a solution if you and Dr. Hyman will approve. They need help over at the West Tennessee Tuberculosis Hospital. They would give me a contract to do one or two lung operations each Wednesday. Dr. Wilson was relieved and the Vice Chancellor also agreed, under the circumstances. Thus I began a very productive endeavor and the assistant Chief of Surgery, Francis Cole and I began heart surgery in Memphis.

The Chief of Surgery was Frank Alley and one day he said to me, "Jim, my secretary is not well but she's seen a variety of doctors. You are the only one of us over here who is both a thoracic surgeon and a general surgeon. Would you be willing to take a look at her?"

"I'll examine her just as soon as I finish the pulmonary lobectomy that I'm scheduled to do this morning," I replied.

167

I got E.B. and a nurse and went into an examining room. In taking the history, I noted that she had a sort of husky voice, did she have a cold? No. She did say that her menstrual periods had become irregular.

On physical examination I noted a sense of fullness in the right upper quadrant of the abdomen. The pubic hair extended upward toward the umbilicus, instead of the usual female transverse pattern. I found nothing else on the physical examination, and told E. that she could get dressed. I did not do a pelvic examination because she said that she had just recently been examined by her gynecologist.

But as I was walking up the hall into an office where I could write up my findings, I said to myself, "You did not do a complete physical examination, the first requirement of a good doctor." I whirled around and hastened back, summoning the nurse again and telling E.B. that I wanted to do a pelvic and rectal examination.

I had hardly sat down when I saw a markedly enlarged clitoris. Touching it gently with the gloved finger I asked her, "How long has your clitoris been enlarging?"

"Oh, I've been so embarrassed. Certainly for some months. And about my voice, I now remember that I had to drop out of the church choir. I used to sing soprano."

"E.," I said, "I think you may have a masculinizing tumor of the adrenal cortex, probably on the right side. We can establish or rule out this diagnosis by measuring the level of 17-ketosteroids in a 24-hour urine specimen."

This level was enormous, forty times normal for a female. It almost certainly pointed to a malignant tumor.

I removed the large adrenal tumor from beneath the right lobe of the liver.

The 17-ketosteroid level fell immediately to normal, but I warned that we would need to check her urinary 17-ketosteroids for years to come.

Sadly, when she returned six months later, the steroids had again risen markedly, indicating fatal metastases.

Her caring boss had bet her fifty cents that she was cured after the operation. This time he came in, looked at her silently, placed a 50-cent piece on the bedside table, and rushed out of the room.

It remained to me to tell her that she had a recurrence. But I sensed that she had already known.

"E.," I asked, "Just when did you first know your diagnosis?"

"It was the nurses whispering to each other. And what *you* did not say. But when my husband, a dental student, came in and said, "Honey, let's not go to Colorado to practice (dentistry), let's just stay here in Tennessee. Then I knew."

With a growing family, we bought a spacious, old, two-story house not far from the University and close to the zoo. In fact, Weezie's visiting sister swore she'd heard a *lion* roar during the night.

My most important achievement was the passing of the thoracic board orals in November. I had already passed the written part of the examinations. A thoracic colleague, G.R., had already passed the oral and chest segments, but he had failed the pathology part of the examination and had to take just the pathology part again. I had reviewed the chest X-rays from a wide variety of diseases. We went to the University of Chicago together. Usually the pathology section had been given last, following the clinical and X-ray examinations. But this year the pathology was given first, because the general election which made Eisenhower president was to be held the following day. This pathology examination consisted of showing the photograph of a gross specimen on the left screen and the microscopic picture of this tissue on the right screen. Well, I was pretty confident of my diagnoses as the number reached twelve, but thereafter some of the specimens seemed to be a repetition of the diagnoses of the first twelve.

I decided that I could not outguess the examiners and would have to put down my own diagnosis, even though the last eight had appeared to be duplicates of the first twelve. But I was far from confident that I had passed. (It was later learned that the last eight specimens were duplicates of eight of the first twelve!)

My first two examiners were Dr. Michael DeBakey and Dr. Edward Churchill, Chief of Surgery of the Massachusetts General Hospital of Boston. They asked a number of questions about thoracic surgery in general and then it was time to read chest X-rays. They put a film up in the lighted viewbox and asked me what I saw. I saw nothing abnormal, but then the discipline of my training saved me. My chief at Penn had always insisted that we get a lateral film in addition to the usual anterior-posterior film. I said, "I'd like to see a lateral film."

At this Dr. DeBakey put up a lateral film and there was a mass behind the heart!

They both smiled and wished me well with the other examiners.

Having signed out of the hotel, I went on to O'Hare Airport. But when I offered my return ticket to the young lady she looked at her list and then told me that I was not listed on the only Delta flight that would get me to Memphis that night. I was furious. I said, "That reservation was made weeks ago. I am outraged. What is your full name?" She said that she was not allowed to give it.

I then asked for the name of her superior in that office, preparing to write it down. She said that she could not release the name. I said I would call Delta Headquarters and that I would write them some letters.

At this she said, "Just a moment, Doctor," as she disappeared into the room behind the counter. I heard animated whispering and then she suddenly reappeared, saying brightly, "Doctor, we have found your reservation!"

Shortly thereafter I saw Dr. DeBakey coming down the hall. At the same moment he saw me and walked over. "Jim," he asked, "How do you think you did?"

"Well, Dr. DeBakey, that pathology was a puzzlement."

At this he took my right hand in a firm grip, looked me in the eyes and said, "Jim, don't worry. Do you understand, don't worry." I said, Dr. DeBakey, if you don't want me to worry, I won't worry!"

I arrived back in Memphis on time and decided that I would just drop by the office before going on home. But my secretary and the technicians were most surprised: "Why, Dr. Hardy, you weren't scheduled to come back until tomorrow!"

The year 1952 was notable for several additional events. My book *Surgery and the Endocrine System* appeared on the bookstands and was apparently the first such book ever published. I became a "consultant" to the Oak Ridge Institute of Nuclear Studies and learned much more about the uses of isotopes in metabolic studies.

In 1952 I was elected to membership in the Society of University Surgeons. And it was in 1952 that Jim Hendrix, a plastic surgeon also interested in burns, told me about a developing four-year medical school in Jackson, Mississippi. He said that he was going to move to Jackson so as to be in on the ground floor.

Meanwhile, we were publishing our research in a variety of surgical and other journals, and I commonly crossed the campus to attend the physiology and chemistry seminars. The scientists from the existing two-year medical school at Oxford, Mississippi, often came up to attend these seminars. And it was probably through this association that I was invited to give a lecture down at Oxford. My topic was "Normal and Abnormal Physiology of the Adrenal Cortex." It was well received and there was much discussion from the audience.

Our third daughter, Bettie Winn Hardy was born in the Baptist Hospital on June 26, 1953.

THE DOG LAB. Whereas the dog lab at Penn had had considerable support, even for metabolic studies on occasion, the dog lab at U.T. was poorly supported and in fact primitive. Moreover it was immediately adjacent to the student nurses' dormitory and thus the animals had to be "debarked" (vocal cords snipped under anesthesia) to reduce the noise. The lab was used, however, for short-term teaching. For example, by tradition the students rotating on surgery were afforded the opportunity "to operate." Four students at each operating table would anesthetize the dog and then perform an appendectomy. Moreover, the dog was expected to recover from the anesthesia and to live. It was during one such session, as we listened to a small radio, that Bobby Thompson hit his classic home run in the ninth inning that won the World Series. Leo Durocher, the Brooklyn Dodgers manager, was said to have swatted Bobby on the bottom and said, "Bobby, if you ever hit a home run, do it now!" Durocher was an aggressive competitor with the motto, "You show me a good loser and I'll show you a loser."

Another use of the lab was to instruct postgraduate physicians in cardiac resuscitation. After reviewing the general principles, I would suddenly stab the exposed cardiac left ventricle and, with blood spurting up in the air, the "students" were to quickly close the injury with sutures and then defibrillate the heart if it had developed ventricular fibrillation. Our defibrillator was primitive indeed, but Dr. Claude Beck of Western Reserve University in Cleveland had just recently spoken on cardiac resuscitation and the group at Hopkins had demonstrated that intermittent pressure on the closed chest could produce a cardiac output of approximately one-half the normal.

RADIOACTIVE THYROIDS IN CATTLE. Around 1953, one of the physiologists, with a special interest in the thyroid, found that bovine thyroids, harvested at the slaughter house, were radioactive. This brought on much excitement and federal agents descended upon Memphis almost immediately. This radioactivity could have come only from the atmosphere, and it was taken to indicate that the Soviet Union had exploded an atomic bomb.

FREEZE-DRIED AORTIC GRAFTS. During my second year in Memphis Dr. Wilson asked me to set up the technique for harvesting and preserving aortic segments as aortic grafts. This was soon after he and I had resected a large abdominal aortic aneurysm in the Baptist Hospital. He said that a specific young physician had volunteered to set up the aortic graft technique but that he had procrastinated and procrastinated until now it had to be done.

I knew that the procedure was in use at Vanderbilt and so I went over, learned the technique and duplicated the necessary equipment. (When I left Memphis for the new medical school in Jackson, Mississippi, a year or so later, I prudently took two of the freeze-dried aortic grafts with me.)

The Baptist Hospital in Memphis. By the end of my second year at U.T. I had begun to get a few private patients, and this introduced me to one of the best run such institutions in my experience. I do not remember the nurse's name who ran the operating suite, but she ran it in a firm but fair way. Two items: If the surgeon was late to scrub for his operation, he was promptly placed at the bottom of the day's operative schedule. But if the surgeon's case did not come until late in the day, he would have the option of doing the case no matter how late. For instance, I once performed a pulmonary lobectomy beginning at seven p.m. The family had come to town for the operation, but had no choice but to drive back home that night.

Another special experience. I had operated upon a very obese woman to repair a large abdominal hernia secondary to a previous operation. And I had ordered a bottle of blood transfused, for we had lost a fair amount of blood at the operation and blood transfusion was considered something of a tonic in those days. The next day several members of her family came to my office and asked if it was true that their mother had been given blood. Unsuspecting, I said that she had. Whereupon the family members became very angry and said that the patient was a Jehovah's Witness and that their religion prohibited transfusion.

Well, they did not sue me, but for several years thereafter I periodically received in the mail pamphlets demonstrating how the Bible prohibited transfusion.

Since I now had enough patients to justify my attendance, I began to go to the M&M Conference, held in the chapel of the Baptist Hospital. When a chronically ill patient had had no change since the last meeting, the resident presenting the case would say, simply: Hebrews 13:8. (The same yesterday, and today and forever.)

One afternoon two prominent internists came over to my office in the Pathology Building. "Hardy," they said, "We have a proposition for you. We have been following your chest work. If you will come over to the Baptist Hospital and rent an office, and sever connections with the University, we will send you all our chest work until you are well established. Furthermore, we speak for a number of other internists. We want the thoracic group in the Baptist Hospital to have some competition."

I thanked the two visitors, but said that I would have to think about it and discuss it with my wife.

There were several particular considerations which weighed against accepting the offer. First, it would mean my leaving academic surgery. Second, it would require my becoming a pure thoracic surgeon, whereas my research program involved most of the organs of the body. Third, it is easy to leave an academic post for private practice but it is hard to return and be truly successful.

Fourth, the University had been fair with me and I did not think I should move out in quite this way.

But the final deciding factor was Weezie. She said, "Jim, it's nice of the doctors to make the offer, but you would never be satisfied outside of academic surgery. We have worked too hard to change now. Let's stay with our objectives."

This was the last temptation I ever had to enter pure private practice.

I declined the offer.

THE SOUTHERN SURGICAL ASSOCIATION. I was asked to put on a program over at the beautiful new LeBonheur Children's Hospital. (I had just recently rotated onto the pediatric surgical ward at the John Gaston Hospital, where I'd found a boy who had been followed so long with long tube management of small bowel obstruction that that the metal tip of the tube had eroded through the small bowel wall and contaminated the peritoneal cavity.) And there was another similar case.

I said that I would be willing to put on a program but that I had to have a free hand.

The monthly staff meeting was held at five o'clock, after the physicians had been working since seven o'clock in the morning. The required attendance afforded something less than ecstasy, but the perennial moderator, the Chairman of the Department of Pediatrics, would always rise and proclaim that this extremely dull presentation was the best of his experience.

I arose and stated, "I am presenting two cases of small bowel obstruction in children because, in my opinion, they were grossly mishandled." I said that Dr. D. was not completely responsible, for he had not been on the service the entire time. I also implied that the radiologist had made an incomplete diagnosis.

By this time I had the riveted attention of the audience: I had actually named names!

I went on to state my review of the two patients' management.

When I closed and invited questions and comments, there was vigorous discussion. Dr. D. said that he had not been on the children's service the entire time, that he'd not been on the service for years. I replied dryly that that was what I'd said.

The radiologist got in a telling blow, to the delight and vigorous applause of the audience.

During the middle of my presentation Dr. R.L. Sanders, probably the most prominent surgeon in Memphis, had risen and stalked out. The next day at the Baptist Hospital he encountered D. and said my presentation had been the most disgraceful in his forty years of practice; that if D. wanted to sue me for slander, he would testify.

At this, D. laughed and said, "Dr. Sanders, you must have left early. At the end Dr. Hardy turned over the last sheet on the big easel which stated that "all participants were warned in advance."

The upshot of this was that Dr. R.L. called my boss (Dr. Wilson), said that I ought to be a member of the Southern Surgical Association and that he would like to be one of my supporters (which he did).

OAKVILLE TUBERCULOSIS SANATORIUM. Somewhere in 1953 Frank Alley, Chief of Surgery at the West Tennessee Tuberculosis Hospital where I operated on Wednesdays under contract, had a heart attack. As was the wisdom in those days, he was placed at bed rest for a time. He asked me if I could go out to the Oakville Sanatorium, at which he was also the chief, and do enough chest surgery to hold the city job, until he could recover. I said that I would go out there one morning a week if Dr. Hyman and Dr. Wilson would approve. The operating "room" there was simply a bedroom in the ancient dwelling and the place for scrubbing one's hands was the shallow clothes closet therein. Anesthesia was given by an experienced nurse anesthetist and there was a house physician who also served as my surgical assistant. Well, one morning I had closed the wound of a very obese black patient and turned away to sign the anesthesia record when the anesthetist yelled, "Quick, Dr. Hardy, she's falling off the table!" I whirled around and with the anesthetist and suture nurse we dived under her to break the fall.

The next day, on rounds, she said, "Doctor, you know what? I done dreamed I fell off the operating table!"

"Did you? Whoever heard of such a thing!"

THE "TURKEY THIEF" AND THE CAMPBELL CLINIC. Once when assigned to the men's colored ward (95% of the adult men in the Gaston were black), a man was brought in with a bad wound of the left lower leg. He said that the police had said he'd stole a turkey, but that the man who had stolen the turkey had run. The patient, being innocent, had not run but that the police had shot him anyway.

Orthopedics was consulted, this service being run by the famous Campbell Clinic, which served as the Division of Orthopedics in the University. The consultant recommended immediate amputation, to get the patient out of the hospital and begin fitting him with a prosthesis.

I disagreed and proposed that we debate the issue at the quarterly staff meeting and dinner the next evening. I well remembered Father's workman Jimmie Lee Johnson of my childhood. He'd had a similar gunshot wound of the lower leg, and had steadfastly refused amputation and eventually regained walking on his own leg. (In general, even an impaired leg that is serviceable is better more often than an artificial leg.)

But what a reaction I had precipitated! Dr. Wilson called me and said, "What are you trying to do to the Campbell Clinic?"

I explained.

He then said, "Hardy, you are new here. If you will not amputate, transfer the patient to the orthopedic service."

He was transferred.

SUPERVISION OF THE RESIDENTS AT THE GASTON. I had had culture shock upon arriving in Philadelphia to begin medical school in 1938. I had never heard black people addressed as Mr. or Mrs.

But back in the South, after thirteen years away, I experienced culture shock in the opposite direction. The residents would stand in the middle of the open (black) women's ward and tell unacceptable jokes relating to colored people.

I told the residents that such behavior must stop: That it was an insult to their patients and completely unacceptable as physicians. The residents were good men, they simply reflected the culture that they'd grown up with. They did not like my requirement but they did conform.

Next, I found a patient in shock on the ward, with all the residents operating on the sixth floor. When I asked the chief resident why he did not have someone taking care of the shock patient, he replied that Dr. Wilson wanted the residents to use the operating rooms to the fullest extent.

At this, I said to him, I cannot believe Dr. Wilson ever wanted you to be in the operating room when a patient already operated upon was in grave danger on the ward. Let us go right over to his office in the Baptist Hospital and learn what his instructions were.

At this, the chief resident said, "He didn't really spell out that an operation on a 'healthy' patient should take precedence over a critically sick patient on the ward."

I said, "Well, Jack, let's be sure we care well for those that we *have* operated on before we do more operating."

He was a good man. The service just needed the disciplined supervision that I'd had at Penn.

(And I had my reward. One day by chance I overheard him speaking to a junior resident who had failed to help with our clinical research program. The Chief's words were, "Dr. Hardy is going to increase the stature of our certificate. Help where you can.")

THE AMERICAN SURGICAL ASSOCIATION. A major event of 1952 was the giving of the first paper at the annual meeting of this august organization, which has at times been characterized as the priesthood of American surgery. The title was "Some Physiologic Aspects of Surgical Trauma."

Somewhere along the line, perhaps late in 1952, Dr. Wilson asked me if I would like to be recommended for chairman of surgery at the new four-year school being established in Jackson, Mississippi. I said I did. There followed an invitation by Dr. Pankratz, current dean of the two-year school on the University campus at Oxford, Mississippi. On another occasion I found myself seated at a luncheon in Oxford beside Dr. Billy Guyton, a former dean of the medical school, perhaps the leading ophthalmologist in Mississippi; and Arthur Guyton's father. He asked about my family and I told him we had three daughters and another child on the way. I told him that I did not want the girls to go to medical school: It took their youth and impaired marriage prospects. He said that I was wrong, that it would give them interesting work for life and that they would be surrounded by intelligent and eligible men to marry.

Doctor Pankratz continued to drop by my office for a chat when he was in Memphis.

On the afternoon of March 23, 1953, a tall gentlemen entered my office and introduced himself as Doctor Coggeshall. He sat down and asked what I was working on in the laboratory and what my future plans were.

I told him exactly what I had told Dr. Hyman two years earlier: that I was going to work like the devil until I was forty-five, and that if I did not have a chair of surgery by then I would go into private practice, at least to a major extent.

He then said, "Dr. Hardy, there are many young men at your level in the country but only a few of them will ever achieve a chairmanship of surgery. Perhaps you should modify your ambitions somewhat."

Just then it dawned on me that he was the famous Coggeshall, head of the medical units at the University of Chicago and at U.T. to give the commencement address to the senior class graduating that evening. He stood up and wished me luck.

Literally within the hour Dean Pankratz came into my office, up from Oxford for the commencement activities.

He had obtained his M.D. from the University of Chicago, but had not interned thereafter. He already had had a Ph.D. in anatomy.

"Jim," he said, "The faculty at Oxford has voted to offer you the chair as Chief of Surgery at the four-year school now being built in Jackson."

What timing!

I accepted at once.

When I got home that night, I embraced Weezie and said, "We've got a chair!"

From there on my thoughts were turning toward Jackson.

THE ALPHA OMEGA ALPHA LECTURE. The graduating class had asked Dean Roberts to invite me to give the AOA lecture that spring. I replied that I would be honored to accept but with one condition: that I could say what I thought needed to be done around here. He was dismayed and said he must take it to the boss (Vice-Chancellor Hyman). A few days later he called and said, "The boss says for you to go right ahead. But let me tell you something: You are strictly on your own!"

The AOA dinner was held at the Memphis Country Club. I was at the lectern, with Dr. Hyman on my right and the student president of AOA on my left.

I stood and began with: "I am deeply honored to have been invited to give the address this evening. However, that said, I want to state that the remarks I shall make are my own and do not necessarily represent the positions of the management!"

At this the audience roared, for everyone knew that Dr. Hyman ran the clinical affairs with a firm, if not an iron hand.

Basically my message was that more full-time people needed to be recruited. I pointed out that I was the only full-time faculty member that the Department of Surgery had ever had. That there were only three in the whole Department of Medicine.

My remarks were duly reported in the Memphis Commercial Appeal the following morning.

Whether my points had been influential or not, the medical school gradually developed full-time faculty in every department.

On several occasions Dr. Hyman made it clear that he wished me success. He'd once said, "Hardy, you'll do all right down in Jackson but they'll get at you through your family."

I wondered if he spoke from personal experience.

And he was most generous in allowing me to go back and forth to Jackson during the next almost two years.

CHAPTER 10

A New Four-Year Medical School and University Hospital in Mississippi

Beginning with Dean Pankratz's offer of the Chair of Surgery in Jackson and my immediate acceptance on March 23, 1953, my thoughts began to turn toward learning just what the "Chair" amounted to. There was still a good deal to do and to experience in Memphis at the University of Tennessee Medical College but, as the first clinician appointed for the medical school in Jackson, I had a vested interest in the selection of the others who would serve as clinical department chairmen. And I was soon to be more and more skeptical as to how it all would work out. One of the problems was that Dean Pankratz had not even served an internship and had long been cloistered at the two first years at Oxford. He had had little exposure to the many political problems which always beset a new medical school being developed in a small or modest sized community. And he was too prone to take the advice of less than expert friends.

For example, one day Vice Chancellor Hyman called me from his office over in the administration building and said he wished to congratulate me on our new chairman of Obstetrics and Gynecology down in Jackson. I replied, "Dr. Hyman, I don't believe anyone has even been considered as yet."

"Oh, yes, it's Dr. W. Better call Pankratz."

"You bet I will, Dr. Hyman, and thank you very much."

I called Oxford at once. "Dean Pankratz," I said, "Dr. Hyman has just called to congratulate me on our new Chairman of Obstetrics and Gynecology, Dr. W. How did this come about?"

"To tell the truth, Jim, he simply called me and said he wanted the job."

"Dean Pankratz, I would be depressed about our whole enterprise with this appointment. Dr. W. was finally eased out here after many absences and a serious chemical dependency problem. We will be the laughing stock of practically all the knowing physicians in Memphis."

"Don't worry, Jim. I'll just call him in Nashville and tell him that he can't have the job after all!"

I could just imagine the dismay at Vanderbilt, but I thought it better to have consternation there than to have him in the chair in Jackson.

Another example. Dean Pankratz called one day and said that he had just been talking with a young radiologist. He said that if I found him acceptable he would appoint him Chairman of Radiology in Jackson. I replied, "Dean Pankratz, I really am not qualified to recommend him and I should not have that much responsibility."

"Well, just see him and let me know."

The candidate came to Memphis and I discovered that

A New Medical School Is Established in Jackson

he had just finished a residency at Shreveport General Hospital, which at the time was not a University Hospital. After the usual pleasantries I asked him what he would do with the Department of Radiology. He replied that he would take X-rays. I acknowledged that I was confident of that but that a department of radiology in a medical school had far more requirements than just to take X-rays. I then asked if he'd ever written a paper that was published in a national journal. No, he hadn't. I then pointed out that he would have to train X-ray residents and technicians and teach medical students.

Abruptly, he said, "Dr. Hardy, I don't think I am qualified to head a department of radiology."

"Dr. Y.," I replied, "Why don't you join the staff of our institution or some other academic institution and learn all the responsibilities of a chairman. Then, I am satisfied that in due course you will have the opportunity to run a department of radiology."

I don't know what he did, but I was reminded of the reported exchange between Robert Hutchings and Abraham Flexner. Flexner, who guided major funding from the Rockefeller Foundation for educational efforts had recommended to Hutchings that he go abroad for several years and study at the great universities. But Hutchings did not go. Some time later, upon encountering Flexner, he said, "Dr. Flexner, if I'd gone to Europe like you wanted me to do I would not now be president of the University of Chicago."

Hole in ground, future University Medical Center, 1952

Reproduced by permission of the University of Pennsylvania Press. (Memoirs)

"Yes, Flexner replied, "But you'd be fit to be."

After this episode Dr. David Wilson, long since appointed director of the University Hospital (now under construction), and I called upon Dean Pankratz and asked him to appoint with Dr. Arthur Guyton a formal Search Committee which would scour the whole country to find eligible candidates for the remaining departmental chairs. We would then report to him. But Dean Pankratz did not agree. And to be fair, he eventually ended up with good people at every unfilled post. These were Robert Snavely (Medicine, Tulane), Robert D. Sloan (Radiology, Johns Hopkins), Blair E. Batson (Pediatrics, Vanderbilt and Johns Hopkins), Michael Newton (Obstetrics and Gynecology, Cambridge, Pennsylvania), Warren N. Bell, a Canadian who came to us from the University of

Pennsylvania (Department of Laboratories and Hematology) and Floy Jack Moore (Psychiatry) from the University of Pennsylvania.

Surgery Staff. It was now time for me to concentrate on the needs of the Divisions of Surgery. The original plans of the organizers had been that there would be a full-time paid Departmental Chairman but major support could be expected from specialty volunteers from out in the City of Jackson. For the medical school loomed as a far more expensive proposition than had been envisioned at the outset. However, I pointed out that teaching and research would be thin indeed with such a policy. And I was already under such a policy at the University of Tennessee. However, I was able to convince Dean Pankratz that at least three full-time faculty members would be needed to cover general, thoracic, and pediatric surgery, and one each to cover anesthesia and neurosurgery. Urology, orthopedics, otolaryngology, and ophthalmology were to be covered by volunteers in town. They were Dr. Temple Ainsworth in Urology. He was the dean of the urologists in Jackson and later president of the American Urological Association. Dr. Thomas Blake in Orthopedics, who was so well known that it was said that Mississippians could not distinguish between break and Blake. Dr. Walton Shannon, Oral Surgery and Dentistry, a fully established practitioner. Otolaryngology, Ophthalmology, and Plastic Surgery posed special considerations. As for ophthalmology, Dean Pankratz wanted me to appoint Dr. Samuel Johnson, who had recently finished his training at Tulane and had come to Jackson and set up a practice office. He had married the daughter of Dr. Henry Boswell, head of the Mississippi

Tuberculosis Sanatorium down at Magee, and a very influential person with the legislature. I was concerned that the long-term practitioners in Jackson would be affronted by this appointment, but I knew none of the ophthalmologists in Jackson, including Dr. Johnson. Dean Pankratz had asked for no other appointment and so I appointed Dr. Johnson. Sadly, none of the well-established ophthalmologists ever served the University. As for the Plastic Surgery appointment, more will come later. Otolaryngology was covered by Dr. Edley Jones in Vicksburg. These specialists in Jackson could not agree on one of their group, since presumably the prestige of the office would eventually unbalance the current private practice patterns. Dr. Jones was prominent in the national otolaryngology circles. He came regularly the 40 miles once or twice a week, and got a residency approved. The local specialists did give support to the residents. The affiliated Veterans Hospital would continue to function with its existing personnel but the services there would, over all, be responsible academically to the University Departmental Chairmen. Not long after I had been named Chairman publicly, I was invited to come down from Memphis to make rounds and accept an honorarium from the Veterans Hospital. There I met one John Busey. Looking at him carefully, I said, "I've seen you somewhere before." He responded with the usual banter of far away places. Then, seriously, I asked, "Were you ever in Philadelphia?"

"Only to pass through."

"Were you in military service?" Was he in the Army? Yes, he was. Was he in England? Yes again.

Then I said, "You were in the Army and you were

stationed at the 68th General Hospital."

With this he was stunned: "I was!" he said. "But how could you know that?"

I told him that while my outfit, the 81st Field Hospital, was checking equipment prior to crossing the Channel I had been sent on detached service to his 68th General. Arriving there in a jeep just after dark, I was told to rush over before the officers mess was closed. I was the lone diner in the hall when a Major came by and asked, "You are new here, aren't you, Lieutenant?"

"Yes, Major, I've just come in." He sat down and said, "Finish your meal and let's go over to the club and have a scotch."

"You were that major."

But to return to the prospective department down in Jackson. Dr. Watts R. Webb of Johns Hopkins Medical School had been well trained in thoracic surgery at Barnes Hospital of the Washington Medical School in St. Louis. Dr. Curtis P. Artz, a fellow member of the Surgical Biology Club, had had his residency at Ohio State University under Dr. Robert M. Zollinger. He then had served several years in the Army, especially at the Brooke Army Burn Institute at San Antonio. He was the best burn manager that I ever worked with. He would help cover general surgery but with a special expertise in burns and trauma. With my Thoracic Boards, I would collaborate with Dr. Webb on the lung and heart patients, assist with general surgery, and cover pediatric surgery on the strength of my considerable experience with children at the John Gaston Hospital in Memphis. Dr. M. Don Turner, Ph.D. in chemistry-physiology, would work with me in supervising the research activities.

There remained to appoint a neurosurgeon and to find an academic minded anesthesiologist. Dr. Orlando J. Andy was already known to me as a resident in neurosurgery there in Memphis, and I had played golf with him occasionally. I consulted his superiors and they said he was very bright, a good worker, but at times less than optimally focused on patient care details.

He had gone on to Johns Hopkins Hospital where he engaged in some clinical neurosurgery but was primarily interested in research, and in this he was a prodigious worker.

In Jackson, the leading (and perhaps only) neurosurgeon was Dr. Charles L. Neill, trained at Cornell. He was an excellent man, but I feared that his huge private practice would preclude his doing laboratory research. So, all things considered, I offered the chair to Dr. Andy and he accepted. But my lasting appreciation remains for Dr. Neill's loyal support of the University Medical Center through his vast clinical experience.

The full-time Chairman of Anesthesiology was yet to be found. This specialty attracted few medical students, and few of the ones trained were willing to accept the heavy administrative responsibilities and the financial strictures of an academic full-time position.

However, we were sent the name of Dr. G.E. Bittenbender, Chief of Anesthesia at the Veterans Hospital associated with Baylor University Medical School in Houston. I of course wanted to talk with "Bit," because friction between the anesthesiologist and the surgeon can create serious problems. I flew to Houston to interview the candidate in his own environment. After talking with Dr. Bittenbender, I next called upon Dr. Oscar Creech and

Dr. Michael DeBakey. It developed that they had performed a (right?) pneumonectomy on Dr. Bittenbender a year before, for a very small peripheral lung cancer, virtually on the surface of the lung. They said that if anyone was ever cured, he should be cured. They said that Dr. Bittenbender was a crusty person but not hard to get along with.

One significant problem was that "Bit," during his training at Charity Hospital in New Orleans, had had little experience with anesthesia for infants and of course had had none in his post as Chief of Anesthesiology in the Veterans Hospital in Houston. However, he could bring four nurse anesthetists with him. So, under our imminent needs, I offered him our position as Head of the Division of Anesthesiology and he accepted.

HOSPITAL BEDS. A total of 35 hospital beds would be assigned to the Department of Surgery. These had to be divided among the surgical specialties, and there was constant unhappiness on the part of one service or another that strived to develop an approved residency with such bed limitations. For adult surgery, however, we did have the affiliated Veterans Hospital patients.

THE CURRICULUM. Dr. Robert Snavely, being with me the chairmen of the two largest departments, were in agreement on most procedural matters. The medical student teaching at Tulane had been very similar to ours at Pennsylvania. We lobbied with our other faculty to push for only one class per year. Recall that I was under the quarter system at Tennessee, with a class graduating every three months. The two years of medicine taught at the University of Mississippi at Oxford "graduated" a class every six months.

By the time we all reached Jackson in the early

UNIVERSITY OF MISSISSIPPI MEDICAL CENTER
Department of Surgery
ORIGINAL FULL-TIME FACULTY
1955-1956

JAMES D HARDY, M D
PROFESSOR & CHAIRMAN

ORLANDO J. ANDY, M.D.
PROFESSOR (NEUROSURGERY)

G.E. BITTENBENDER, M.D.
PROFESSOR (ANESTHESIOLOGY)

M. DON TURNER, Ph.D.
ASSISTANT PROFESSOR

CURTIS P ARTZ, M.D.
ASSOCIATE PROFESSOR

WATTS R WEBB, M.D.
ASSISTANT PROFESSOR

WILLIAM F ENNEKING, M D
ASSISTANT PROFESSOR
(ORTHOPEDICS)

First full-time faculty, Department of Surgery. Reproduced by permission of the University of Pennsylvania Press. (Memoirs)

summer of 1955, the consensus had settled on only one class per year. In each department, teaching in specific specialties would be conducted by the appropriate expert. The departments of Pediatrics, Obstetrics and Gynecology, and Radiology would of course have their allotted time.

Space. The three major considerations for an academician are faculty rank, salary and space. While attending a meeting of the American Physiology Society in Chicago, I found myself seated with Dr. Arthur C. Guyton, Chairman of Physiology, and Dr. Louis Sulya, Chairman of Biochemistry, both at the two years of medical school at Oxford. They asked me where the space for the Department of Surgery was to be located in the building being built in Jackson. I replied that I did not know but that I was sure that had been taken care of by the architects. They then advised that I had better run down to Oxford and take a look at the plans.

I went, but to my astonishment I found that no special office or laboratory space had been assigned to Surgery. It had apparently been assumed that surgeons just stayed in the operating suite and did surgery there.

However, I approached Dr. Sulya, whose Department of Biochemistry was located on the third floor, and Dr. William Hare, whose Department of Pathology was on the second floor, as was the operating suite. They were generous and I eventually achieved adequate space.

LABORATORY PERSONNEL, RESEARCH SUPPORT
AND EQUIPMENT.

Personnel. Several of our laboratory personnel were free to move with me to Jackson: Mrs. Anne Cole (later Turner), Virginia Ward and Thelma Carter. Presently, though, it developed that Mrs. Cole was engaged to marry M. Don Turner, who was just gaining his Ph.D. in Physiology. I had learned in Philadelphia the great value of having basic scientists in a department of surgery, so I invited Dr. Turner to move to Jackson with us. Mrs. Cole had her masters degree in Physiology and was a superb assistant.

The medical school photographer, John H. Dickson, was most unhappy with his boss. He and I had made one or two movies together and he asked me if he could go to Jackson with me. I said that, first, I would have to talk with Dr. Hyman about it. That if he had no objection, I would ask Dean Pankratz if he could pay the salary. Dr. Hyman said he had no objection if Mr. Dickson wanted to go, and Dean Pankratz said he could pay the salary. (Mr. Dickson and I in Jackson made over 200 movies and countless photographs of surgical specimens at operation or otherwise. He was invaluable.)

Incidentally, this was not the only time Dr. Hyman assisted me in the move to Jackson. On one occasion, he said, "Hardy, you will do all right down in Jackson but they will get at you through your family." I wondered if he spoke from personal experience.

Equipment. Regarding laboratory equipment, I planned to continue the endocrine and metabolic research I had been doing at Tennessee. Thus, I asked Dr.

Top left: Hazel M. Mattox; top right: Virginia W. Keith; bottom left: Mary Ruth Ruffin; bottom right: Jane E. Peters. As every administrator of large enterprises knows, the degree of success achieved depends on the ability, the dedication and the loyalty of the secretarial-administrative infrastructure of those involved. We in the Department of Surgery were blessed over the years with exceptional women. Those above were very special representatives of the wealth of talent that served our Department of Surgery. Mrs. Mattox came aboard in 1955 and served until retirement. Mrs. Keith joined me in Memphis in 1953 and still remains "aboard" today, after these forty-seven years. Mrs. Ruffin began in 1956 and has typed-"produced" this book. Miss Jane E. Peters (now Mrs. Goudelock) moved into Mrs. Mattox's position when she retired and then served splendidly until I retired from the University, at which time she became Secretary to the Dean. Reproduced by permission of the University of Pennsylvania Press. (Memoirs)

Wilson what he wanted to retain at Memphis, and this I requested the granting agencies to permit me to duplicate. Therefore we were able to move to Jackson a virtually intact laboratory equipment for special chemistry procedures that we had been employing at U.T.

Research Support. The upshot of this was that we were set up and busily moving along later in Jackson when a ten-man project site visit committee visited us with respect to a large program grant in the cardiovascular area that we had applied to the N.I.H. for. Dr. Paul White of Boston, a world authority on heart disease (and later on a postage stamp), was the chairman of the committee. We had got all the way down to the hospital basement when he spied a men's rest room just across from the hospital's record room. He indicated that we, he and I, go into the "rest" facility alone. Inside, he looked around and then said, "Dr. Hardy, tell me how much money you need."

What an agonizing situation. If I suggested an excessive figure, I might get no money at all. But if I put it too low, I might have "left on the table" a substantial amount of support. Looking at him closely, to see if he flinched, I said $50,000 per year for the five years. At this he said, "If that's what you need, that's what you'll get." And that was exactly what we got.

Finding a House in Jackson. On every 213 mile trip to Jackson I would look for a suitable house to rent. This problem seemed insoluble until one day Dr. David Wilson, the Hospital Director, said, "Jim, I don't know why, but a two-story house has not been occupied and the place is now all grown up with weeds. But I was once there at a party and it is really a nice house."

I located the home and, believe it or not, a rabbit was sitting on the front porch. I went to the nearby filling station, the Shady Nook, and learned who owned the house and its large side-yard. The lady who owned it was mentally unbalanced, but I located her in Baton Rouge and found that the real estate firm Wortman and Mann of Jackson held the management contract. Through the lady's son, who came to Jackson, we rented the home— two stories, 3-1/2 baths, five bedrooms, and hardwood floors. The drawing room was perhaps 20 x 30 feet in dimensions, with a fireplace.

We were to live there almost five years. We would have bought it and lived there indefinitely, for it was located only about five minutes from the hospital. However, the lady who owned it said she had had her children there and that she would not sell it.

THE TOWN-GOWN PROBLEM. By this time the political clouds, once no larger than the proverbial cloud the size of one's hand, had begun to enlarge. Basically, the change had to do with money. Each time organized medicine in Jackson fired another salvo, Dean Pankratz would come to Memphis and propose a different contract. As this continued I became increasingly concerned over the whole enterprise. Meanwhile, they liked me in Memphis and Dean Roberts (Dr. Hyman was Vice-Chancellor) had told me to come back to University of Tennessee any time if I were forced to retreat northward from Jackson.

Then, one day, a Doctor Curtis Caine appeared at my office, sat down and said, "Dr. Hardy, we're not going to have you in Jackson if you insist in seeing private patients in the University Hospital."

"Dr. Caine," I said, "You will realize I mean no offence, for we have just met. But let me say this: We could put that medical school on a Pacific atoll if somebody wanted to pay for it and the Mississippi legislature has already voted the money."

With this, he departed and remained a rival thereafter.

When he reported back to his colleagues in Jackson, they asked Dean Pankratz to come to a dinner meeting of all the surgeons in Jackson. I and David Wilson were invited by the Dean to be present.

Unfortunately, my plane at Memphis was delayed by a mechanical problem, so three of us rented a small plane to take us to Jackson. When we got there, we had to circle the field until our Delta plane had landed!

At the meeting virtually all the surgeons I knew were seated around a long oval table, perhaps 40 or 50 more. Seated at the head of the table Dr. J. Harvey Johnston was chairing the meeting. I sat down in the empty seat at the other end of the table and ate hurriedly.

No time was lost. "Dr. Hardy," Dr. Johnston began, "I have in my hand a list of all the surgeons in Jackson. None will assist the medical school in any way if you insist on seeing private patients in the University Hospital." He passed the sheet down the line to me. I looked it over carefully and then said, "Dr. Johnston, the list is incomplete."

He then produced a second sheet which bore a single name, the one that had been omitted on the big list. "Now, Dr. Hardy, what do you say?"

"The list is complete, but my position has not changed in the slightest." I was deeply disappointed that the single name appeared on the second sheet. He was the only plastic surgeon in Jackson and perhaps the entire state. Moreover, he had been partially responsible for my coming to Jackson.

Dean Pankratz had sat there immobilized by this exchange.

At some point Dr. Johnston had asked if I thought I could influence him with $6,000. (I had insisted to Dean Pankratz that I must have dependable assistance in the clinic and elsewhere.)

"No, Dr. Johnston, I don't think I could influence you with six thousand dollars. I understand that you have the largest practice in Jackson and perhaps in the whole state of Mississippi. However, there would be a young well-trained surgeon who'd just come to town and badly needed $6,000. He would start in that position the following morning."

I returned to Memphis full of doubts. It was a Mexican standoff, it seemed to me, and I began to voice my misgivings.

Then one day I received a call from Dr. Billy Guyton, probably the leading ophthalmologist in the state, practicing in Oxford and Arthur Guyton's father: "Jim, what's all this that you are thinking of pulling out. I am surprised that you've not met Chancellor Williams. Could you see me tomorrow afternoon?"

"Certainly, Dr. Billy."

He drove up and then told his chauffeur to go get coffee and come back in an hour. He then turned to me and said, "Jim, tell me how you see things down in Jackson."

I did.

John D. Williams, Chancellor, University of Mississippi

David S. Pankratz, Dean, University of Mississippi School of Medicine

Reproduced by permission of the University of Pennsylvania Press. (Memoirs)

Before leaving he asked me to do nothing radical before I had talked with Chancellor Williams. "You will hear from him very soon."

Chancellor Williams called the next day and asked if I could meet with him the next day at the Peabody Hotel, often referred to humorously as the capitol of the state of Mississippi.

We chose two overstuffed armchairs near the duck pond. Small chat over, he too asked me to tell him how I saw the situation down in Jackson. I explained the town-gown problem. Dr. Pankratz, well meaning but unfamiliar with the nitty-gritty of medical politics, was too anxious to please and placate the medical establishment there. Thus he had several times asked me to accept some different contract. That clear policies had to be established and then steadfastly maintained. I noted that some of the most vociferous "surgeons" in Jackson had had little formal surgical training, but they expected to have operating privileges in the University Hospital. I wished to establish, from the outset, the American Board of Surgery qualification for members of the Department of Surgery.

I told the expense of a modern medical school and that some type of private patient plan would be needed to attract and then retain first-class surgeons, who would enhance the overall finances of the institution and would permit the full-time faculty to interface with important political and other prominent citizens.

He then prepared to leave. "Dr. Hardy, I am satisfied you are the man we want for our Chairman of Surgery. But before I leave, I want to tell you a story. A drummer was standing with the farmer on the outside of the barbed wire fence, and a bull was seen to plant himself in the middle of the track and prepare to charge the oncoming locomotive. "Quick, said the drummer, aren't you going to save the bull?"

"Magnificent animal," the farmer said, "Such courage!"

"I'm not worried about his courage," said the drummer, "I'm worried about his intelligence!"

But I felt reassured by my discussion with the Chancellor. So long as he and the non-political Board of Trustees of the Institutions of Higher Learning supported the cause, we would prevail.

(N.B.: Once policies had been established, Dr. Johnston and his colleagues served the medical school faithfully and well.)

Katherine Poynor Hardy was born on April 19, 1955, in the Memphis Baptist Hospital. Quite some years later one of our former residents, practicing in Eupora,

Mississippi, asked Weezie solicitously as to the health of our youngest (fourth) daughter. On being assured that she was fine, he told her that he had been an intern at Baptist Hospital and that he had had to deliver Katherine when her obstetrician had not arrived in time!

Accompanied by Arcola Sanford, the maid, the Hardy family moved to Jackson in June, 1955.

The Hospital of the University of Mississippi opened its doors formally on July 1, 1955. We clinicians had urged the Nursing Service to be ready to open on time. I pointed out that if the 81st Field Hospital in Germany could admit 170 patients in a 24-hour period, our University Hospital should absorb the 23 chronic patients from the small charity hospital downtown. They represented the three B's: Breaks (fractures), burns and bladders (prostate obstruction).

Within an hour or so after our opening, a call from the E.R. (emergency room) informed us surgeons that a patient had arrived with a strangulated, irreducible groin (inguinal) hernia and must be operated upon promptly. The operation was performed with every present surgical affiliate scrubbing up so he could place at least one stitch in the first patient operated upon in the University Hospital.

HOSPITAL PROCEDURES. Getting everything organized and straightened out did not happen overnight, partly due to inadequately trained personnel. For example, it was found that every time a venous pressure was taken (in the arm), the patient experienced a chilly sensation. Bacterial contamination was suspected. But it was eventually discovered that the hospital supply room was furnishing sterile tap water instead of isotonic saline. The

First Patient Operated Upon at University of Mississippi Hospital, July 1, 1955.
Patient: Jessie James, #22. Surgeons: Hardy and Caldwell. Assistants: Johnson,
Hulsey, Wolfer, Williams, Howard, Wofford, Gillespie, Harris.
Operation: Repair of Strangulated Hernia.

electrolyte-free fluid caused lysis of red blood cells.

The Emergency Room (ward) was in that era run by an intern and, as such, could be the hospital's Achilles heel. (In later years the E.R. came to be covered by full-time experienced physicians.)

One particular disaster occurred as a result of such lightweight coverage. One of Jackson's daily newspapers was consistently critical of everything that happened or was done at the U.M.C., and some of our physicians became somewhat paranoid over all the newspaper abuse. Well, one day a wife brought her husband in, saying frantically that he was having a heart attack. But the nurse on duty told her to sit down, that the doctor (the intern) was at lunch.

With this, the wife supported her husband back to the car and rushed him downtown to the Baptist Hospital. But he died on the doorsill.

At an emergency staff meeting held at the U.M.C. to plan the prevention of such tragic lapses in the future, one physician said that the event had been a put-up job by the enemies of the University Hospital. But another remarked dryly that "One thing's for sure. They're going to run out of volunteers."

Random unexplained infections continued to plague the clinical services. How could this happen in a spanking new, clean hospital? A nationally respected Boston specialist in such matters was consulted. He said that a new hospital often had more infections than an old one because of inexperienced personnel and the absence of long-established and well-tested procedures. He predicted that our infection problem would decline as our hospital settled into maturity. And it did.

POLITICAL INTERFERENCE. I had been warned by friends in Memphis that Mississippi higher education was riddled with politics, and that all professors were at the mercy of the next governor. Chancellor Williams had to acknowledge this reputation and said that he had been warned about the same thing when he accepted his current position. And hardly had he arranged his office in Oxford when he had received a call from a legislator. He was calling about the admission of a marginal student who had been denied, and that she was the daughter of one of his best supporters.

With this, Chancellor Williams said he was furious. That all the warnings about political influence flooded his mind.

But, having made his plea, the caller said, "Now, Chancellor Williams, I don't want you to *do* anything. I just want to be able to tell my friend that I called you!"

But we did experience some political harassment in Jackson. The first instance had to do with the contract for intravenous fluids which had been put out for bids. Dr. Robert Snavely, Chief of Medicine, and I and one other were appointed to analyze the bids and then make a recommendation to Dr. David Wilson, Hospital Director, and Dean Pankratz. This we did and turned in our analysis. The Baxter Corporation, located up at Cleveland, Mississippi, was not the low bidder.

But, heavens! What a commotion this produced. Baxter called Governor White, who had been instrumental in bringing Baxter to Mississippi. Governor White called Chancellor Williams and Chancellor Williams called Dean Pankratz and Dr. Wilson and asked that the specifications be changed so as to make Baxter the successful bidder.

I asked Dean Pankratz to omit me from the new committee.

When I told this episode to my brother John, a partner in Jones and Hardy, Building Contractors in Alabama, he had a story of his own. He said that Jones and Hardy had been bidding on Mississippi contracts for some years when one day at a bid opening Governor White had pulled him aside, put his arm around his shoulders and said, "Son, I hate to see you spending money to make bids on Mississippi construction. Frankly, no out-of-state bidder is going to get one of our contracts."

The two other instances of political harassment came from the legislature. The first was repeated demands that we inform them as to whether or not we kept the white blood separated from the black blood in the Blood Bank. We never kept them separated but imaginative broken field running was at times essential to maintaining our precarious position.

The third political skirmish was occasioned by the death of a young burn patient. When the University Hospital opened we began to get chronic burn patients from all over the state. Such patients require prolonged hospitalization and this was intolerable with the limited beds available for maintaining approval of the several different specialty programs. Moreover, it impaired the quality of learning of the medical students in our teaching "laboratory." Therefore, I had instructed my chief resident in general surgery to admit no more burn patients for the time being.

Well, a burned child was brought to the hospital that very afternoon, in my absence. The residents checked the patient, started intravenous fluids and sent her to a hospital in Vicksburg. Sadly the patient died in a day or so, probably from lung damage from having inhaled smoke.

In brief, some members of the legislature went on the warpath: Here we had a brand new state supported hospital that had "caused" the death of the child. A legislative committee was appointed to come out to the University Hospital and learn the name of the physician who had been responsible for sending the patient on to Vicksburg. With due respect, I steadfastly declined to give the name of my chief resident. I told them I myself had been responsible, for I had given the order to admit no more burn patients. The legislative group was quite incensed but finally departed. I certainly was not going to expose Dr. C. He was going into private practice in a few months, and I was well aware of what the constant newspaper animosity could do to his reputation.

Gradually the clinical service and the clinical teaching programs were falling into place. The teaching of the first two years of medical school had of course been transferred to Jackson and well established for many years.

A Very Special Patient: The Governor. We'd not been long in the University Hospital when Governor James Plemon Coleman came out for an examination, "referred" by his longtime friend Dr. Verner Holmes, a member of the Board of Trustees of the Institutions of Higher Learning. His chief complaint was that he often had indigestion after one of the "rubber chicken" dinners on the recent campaign.

Bob Snavely and I examined him separately, from head to toe. We then withdrew to a private conference room, sat down, and Bob asked me, "What do you think is wrong with him?" I replied that "If he wasn't the governor I would think he has gallstones."

"That's exactly what I think," said Bob, and this diagnosis was soon proven with appropriate X-ray studies.

He then had himself discharged and roared with his multiple Highway Patrol caravan back downtown to the governor's mansion. We thought we'd seen the last of the governor, but several days later he roared back. He said he had planned to go to the Mayo Clinic, but that he'd never had such a complete physical examination in his life; that he wanted me to operate on him.

Bob Snavely pressed me to ask one of the surgeons practicing in town to assist me, but I declined. After all, it was only a cholecystectomy, a relatively minor operation in my opinion. My two chief residents would be my assistants.

Just after I had scrubbed and was about to back through the swinging doors into the operating room, I said to Bob Snavely who was pacing in the hall, "Well, coach, any last words?"

"Look, buster, this had better be good!"

It was good enough and, just before he left, the Governor assured us that he would see to it that our U.M.C. budget would be approved by the legislature.

I hoped that the political significance of having this special private patient in the University Hospital had not been lost on Chancellor Williams.

The question arose as to whether or not I should send the Governor a bill. Between themselves, Chancellor Williams and Dean Pankratz decided that I should certainly send a bill, for the Governor's own protection—but that it could be a modest one.

ARTERIAL SURGERY. As noted previously, clinical arterial surgery blossomed in the early 1950s. Using the full thickness suture published by Dorfler of Germany, Alexis Carrel had used both arterial repair and arterial and venous grafting in animals in the early years of the last century, for which he was awarded the Nobel prize in 1912. His work was then to lie dormant until Robert Gross reported success in resecting a long segment of coarctation of the aorta in 1948 and replacing the defect with a cadaver aortic graft. But the modern surge of experience with arterial repair began in the Korean War. Even as late as 1950, injury to a major artery was usually treated by simple ligation of the vessel above and below the site of injury. Then the part, for example the leg, either survived or it did not. However, in Korea, some young American army surgeons practiced on dogs and then repaired arterial injuries in wounded soldiers with considerable success.

Then, in 1951, Charles Dubost of Paris successfully replaced a large abdominal aortic aneurysm using a graft from a cadaver.

Dr. Harwell Wilson and I had resected a large abdominal aortic aneurysm in Memphis and, after having set up there the process of preservation of aortic allografts with a freeze-dried method, I had brought two grafts with me to Jackson. Then one day, Dr. S. in Laurel, Mississippi, called me and said, "Dr. Hardy, I have a patient who I think has an aortic problem. Will you check him and, if you think an operation is necessary, I will send him to Houston to have it fixed."

"Dr. S.," I replied, "We are not in the business of processing patients for Houston. Let me make you a proposition. We will examine him but if after that he wants to stay here for an operation, will you be satisfied?"

"Fair enough, Hardy, but his brother recently had his abdominal aortic aneurysm resected by DeBakey in Houston. I doubt that you will be able to persuade him to stay."

The patient came and, would you believe it, his name was Houston!

We gave him the most complete physical examination imaginable, and then he returned to Laurel.

The next day Dr. S. called me and said, "What on earth did you fellows do to this man. He now says he will not have anybody else operate upon him but you!"

He returned to us and as our resident was making evening rounds before the operation, Mr. Houston said to him that he would like to ask him a personal question: If he himself was having this operation, would he have Dr. Hardy or "DeBecky" in Houston?

Dr. H. looked out the window for a few moments and then said, "Mr. Houston, don't you think it's a matter of personal choice?"

The operation was quite successful and the graft was still in place when I last examined him twenty years later. Our first ruptured abdominal aortic aneurysm was "referred" by our own Urology Service when we were consulted for bleeding into his scrotum. He was a very large and tall farm laborer from between Jackson and Vicksburg, and he continued to bring vegetables to the Hardy family for many years.

In late 1955, Dr. J. Englebert Dunphy called me and asked if I had the time to take on the job as Secretary of the Society of University Surgeons. I was flattered to be asked for it was a key step in the academic ladder of American surgery. I responded that if I were to be nominated and elected at the forthcoming annual meting in February, I would be honored to serve. (As with many or even perhaps most organizations, solid work as secretary can lead eventually to the presidency.) Through this post for three years, I came to know the young academic American and Canadian surgeons better than I ever would again. One became a "senior" member at age 45.

MEDICAL SCHOOL POLICIES: FURTHER COMMENT. The Student Promotions Committee. As the students in the two years at Oxford were settled into the four-year teaching program in Jackson, it became apparent that no valid set of criteria for medical school admission and especially promotion had existed at Oxford. It developed that no student had been dropped there for academic failure for the last eleven years. The inadequate student had simply been allowed to keep repeating a year until he finally got out and then transferred to one of the nation's four-year schools. I recall one student who had already spent six years in medical schools and had not yet got through the third year. And now Dean Pankratz had simply let him come to Jackson and enter our third year class.

Dr. James Rice, head of Pharmacology, and I pushed for a Student Promotions Committee. A committee consisting of three heads of departments would evaluate students in academic trouble and the composition of the committee would be rotated regularly. To my surprise, some members of the Executive Faculty objected, but the proposal squeaked by with a bare majority vote and became a lasting reality. Dean Pankratz still had the authority to reverse any decision, but I suspected that he was relieved to have some protection from the inevitable harassment by the family of a student who had been dropped for unacceptable grades.

The University of Mississippi was investigated by a national authority for its high rate of student dismissal in the first several years, but it was found that a number of the long-existing medical schools in the United States had an even higher rate of student dismissal. And soon we had established standards that guaranteed an acceptable standard of capability throughout the class.

THE FACULTY PROMOTIONS COMMITTEE. It soon became clear that faculty ranking had to be systematized to achieve and preserve the prestige of the rankings, even of full professors. Some departmental chairmen had been promoting willy-nilly without requiring any specific standards of productivity among the candidates for promotion. This of course resulted in significant resentment among members whose performance was judged and documented. Obviously, it diminished the prestige of the various faculty rankings of professor, associate professor and downward. Publications were the main basis for promotion of the preclinical faculty, whereas the members of the clinical faculty were often promoted with virtually no evidence of publication in refereed national journals. Obviously, salary and space were related closely to faculty rank. And I must confess that I too had promoted freely, first, so as not to penalize the members of my department under the circumstances or, second, to recruit and then retain scarce members of such specialties as anesthesiology and orthopedics.

However, after much debate and irregular progress, we finally did establish a rotating Faculty Promotions Committee that made recommendations to the Executive Faculty and they to Dean Pankratz.

THE TOWN-GOWN SHOWDOWN. 1956.

The Central Medical Society, composed of Jackson's Hinds County and surrounding counties had a rule that no physician's name could appear in a newspaper, since it would represent unfair advertisement.

But Dean Pankratz and Chancellor Williams wished to publicize the substantial amount of research money that was already being brought into the University Medical Center by the faculty. This was believed to influence the Mississippi Legislature to increase the budget allocated to the medical Center.

So, rather than expose individual grant recipients by announcing grant recipients singly, a newspaper announcement would display all the grantees and the amounts of each's grants.

This was done and it precipitated a visit by the Central Medical Society's Judicial Committee. These several members informed us that we would be censored at the Society's monthly meeting that evening. But between leaving Dean Pankratz's office and the meeting at 7:00 p.m. the committee decided to censor only Dean Pankratz (this unknown to us). At the meeting the committee moved to censor Dean Pankratz. But he was not in practice and everybody knew he would not hurt a flea.

Orlando Andy, just across the long table leaned over and said, "Did you hear that—only Dean Pankratz!" I realized instantly that the committee had made a huge blunder and I resolved to make the most of it. I asked for the podium and said all the things that should have been said over the past two years. I closed with the ringing declaration that "I cannot believe that medical statesmanship is dead in this town and I want a vote." Only two or three of the approximately 100 stood up.

The Central Medical Society Archives:
Dr. James Hardy expressed his convictions in defense of Dean Pankratz by saying the University Medical Center was going to be a first class Medical School and this was

the main goal of Dean Pankratz. In order to be a first class Medical School and have first class students, Research Funds were necessary, and publicity of such funds was necessary to impress students and grantors of the work that the University Medical Center was doing. Research is one of the prime objectives of the University Medical Center.

SEPARATE DEPARTMENTS?: ANESTHESIOLOGY, NEUROSURGERY AND ORTHOPEDICS. I had accepted as Chairman of the Department of Surgery with the clear understanding that all the surgical subspecialties would remain with the Department of Surgery (see Administrative Structure of the Department of Surgery, see page 232.)

Anesthesiology. Dr. Bittenbender had had a recurrence of the lung cancer and was increasingly ill. He wanted to achieve a separate departmental status as his final contribution to the specialty. I did not feel that an individual's health should decide an issue as important as departmental status and I opposed, at Executive Faculty and I prevailed, twice. However, I meanwhile had discovered that both the Hospital Director, Dr. David Wilson, and Bittenbender had written numerous letters to academic departments throughout the United States to the effect that anesthesiology was to be a separate department, as were a good many medical school anesthesia departments across the country.

Neurosurgery. Dr. Andy, head of the Division of Neurosurgery, had also lobbied with the administration for a separate department. This annoyed me more than with anesthesiology because, first, because anesthesiology did serve various functions outside of the Department of Surgery (e.g., Obstetrics and Gynecology). Second, Dr. Andy had at times gone to Europe in the summer for study with a brain group. He went without informing me and without providing staff coverage for his residents doing the neurosurgery. I would then have to call Dr. Charles Neill and his brother Dr. Walter Neill out in town and humbly ask them to at least cover the operations neurosurgery did.

Dr. Andy did prodigious research, on both man and monkeys, but as I had been warned in Memphis, he was less assertive in caring for the human patients on his service.

Orthopedics. Our hopes that the orthopedists in Jackson could be depended upon to cover the residents in that specialty were not realized, and within months of the University Hospital's opening we concluded that full-time coverage of the orthopedic service would be essential.

After considerable searching we were given the name of one Dr. William F. Enneking, who was just finishing his residency at the University of Chicago. He was said to be crusty but able. (But ominously, a friend of Dean Pankratz at Chicago called him and said that we would "rue the day" if we appointed Dr. Enneking.)

But we were in a very weak position. We could expect no help from the orthopedists in Jackson, and there were no other acceptable or willing academic orthopedists on the horizon. We offered Dr. Enneking the title of Chief of the Division of Orthopedics and Associate Professor of Surgery, but with the clear stipulation that orthopedics was to remain a division of the Department of Surgery and not a separate department.

Unfortunately, only a few months after his arrival in Jackson he began to maneuver for a full professorship. We felt we must, to retain him, and so the Dean and I conceded. However, that was not to be the end of his aggressive behavior. Now, he began to push for a separate department.

At about this time Chancellor Williams came down from Oxford on one of his periodic visits and I was one of the faculty who met with him in the Dean's conference Room. After greetings and a few felicitous remarks, he asked me how I thought things were going.

I told him that things were going fairly well but that there was the great need of planning, so that we would not just stumble from day to day.

Then he asked me abruptly, "Dr. Hardy, do you play golf?"

"No, Sir, almost never."

Then, "Do you cook steaks out in the backyard?"

"No, Sir."

"Well," he said, "That's all."

I left the little conference with the feeling that my capital with Chancellor Williams was badly depleted. One has political capital to varying degrees with everyone in his immediate association. I estimated that mine with the Chancellor was now no better than a five on a scale of from one to ten. He considered me a troublemaker.

And as confirmation of this, several weeks later he sent down from Oxford the directive that a Long Range Planning Committee be established. My name did not appear as a prospective member of this important committee.

It was clear to me that my authority over the Division of Anesthesiology had been undercut to the extent that I could neither influence it or be responsible for it. Thus I suggested that it be declared a separate department, to facilitate the recruitment of Dr. Bittenbender's successor.

As for Neurosurgery, nothing happened until Dean Pankratz resigned in 1960 to enter a residency in Psychiatry at the University of Tennessee in Memphis. But just before he left, it was announced that Neurosurgery was to become a separate department, with no communication with me. It was obvious that the decision had long been made but was delayed until Dean Pankratz's departure.

I was not surprised but I considered this action inappropriate. My problems with Orlando had been due, largely, to my insistence that he pay more attention to the patients on his service.

My perception was to be fully validated by events in the future.

As for Orthopedics, Dr. Enneking had once again threatened to resign, this time unless he was given a separate department. But this time Dean Pankratz had had enough. We had brought him as an Associate Professor right out of his residency at the University of Chicago. Then, under pressure promoted him to full professor within perhaps a year. And there remained the confidential warning from Chicago that we would rue the day that we had ever hired him. With all this background in mind, Dean Pankratz dug in his heels and said that he would accept Dr. Enneking's resignation. Dr. Enneking then moved to the University of Florida, but still without a separate department.

The State of Mississippi would be forever in debt to Dr. David S. Pankratz. It had been he, almost alone, who had criss-crossed the state tirelessly preaching the need for a four-year medical school. And we all knew him as a kindly man who tried to do his best by every one of his people.

Since Dr. Bittenbender's departure to spend his terminal illness from lung cancer in Houston, our anesthesia coverage abruptly became less than could be accepted for long, but we still had the corps of nurse anesthetists brought from Houston by Dr. Bittenbender and Dr. Jesse Mullins to staff them. Our intensive efforts to recruit a Chairman of Anesthesiology were rendered successful when we got Dr. Leonard W. Fabian from Duke University. He was a capable anesthesiologist himself, but provided only limited strength to our anesthesia services. For instance, he believed that nurse anesthetists would not be a part of his program and residency applicants were few. Even so, the overall function of his department was reasonably satisfactory until the advent of our **electrical anesthesia studies**.

In the course of studying the effects of chronic brain stimuli on water and electrolyte metabolism in dogs, we had found evidence that the brain stimuli appeared to produce an insensitivity to pain. (The electrodes were placed at specific sites by Neurosurgery.) The effect on fluid metabolites was minimal. The animals appeared to have no post-stimulus effects.

These observations, plus reports from elsewhere, suggested that a carefully controlled electrical current could be used as a general anesthetic. (Psychiatrists had used electroshock therapy for many years.) After careful studies in a great number of animals, the technique was extended first to minor biopsies in human patients, and later to operations in several volunteers who had far-advanced cancer. Extensive psychological and psychiatric monitoring was carried out.

In brief, the patients experienced a tugging sensation when tissue was placed under tension or retracted but had no pain. They remained awake throughout and had no significant sequelae.

BACK TO DR. FABIAN. We had invited him to join our group when we began the clinical phase of the electrical anesthesia research, and with our publication he began to be invited to speak at a considerable number of university medical centers. Always a fairly heavy drinker at parties, the inducements at the many commitments gradually led him to lose sight of his responsibilities at home. Thus, in the absence of his guiding hand, his department suffered. And, as his detachment increased, he resented any suggestion that he somewhat curtail his travel and stay home to run his department. But even when he was in town, he often failed to come in.

It finally came to a point where General Robert Blount, the current Dean, called Dr. Fabian in to counsel with him. As was usually the case with any advice, Dr. Fabian went up to his office and wrote a letter of resignation. He felt secure and safe in the current national paucity of anesthesiologists capable and willing to accept the financial strictures of an academic post. But soon another threat of resignation arose and this time Dean Blount said that he would not need a new letter. Reaching into a desk drawer, he assured Dr. Fabian that he still had his previous letter of resignation and that he now accepted it.

Basically, the dimensions and promise of electrical anesthesia had been the undoing of a team participant.

We were not able to bring electrical anesthesia up to a level that matched the long proven safety and effectiveness of ether anesthesia. Thus, when our electronics engineer was hired away by a national commercial concern, we discontinued the program.

Back to Anesthesia Coverage. After considerable search we hired a mature anesthesiologist at Western Reserve University in Cleveland, and he would be able to bring a young associate with him. But virtually the week he was to arrive he called to say that he could not come, after all. He being Catholic, we had assured him that he would not be expected to participate in female tubal ligations. But now, the Archbishop had ruled that he could not give anesthesia in any hospital where tubal ligations were done. He was embarrassed and sincerely apologetic.

His young associate did come but the responsibilities may have been too much for him. He was found dead on a sandbar in the Mississippi River, forty miles from Jackson, with his boat pulled well up on the gravel.

In this stark emergency I was able to achieve one of my greatest coups. First, we had always given our surgical residents an anesthesia rotation, because we wanted them to learn the problems of the anesthesiologist and, second, to have them as a ready reserve to actually give anesthesia in simple cases when needed. For example, we paid an extra stipend when a resident gave anesthesia for routine lung cases down at the tuberculosis Sanatorium, about 35 miles from Jackson. Second, I had learned that a Turkish physician learning lung transplantation had been an anesthesiologist in a university hospital in Turkey before changing to surgery. Third, Dr. Fikri Alican, who worked with us doing transplantation research for about ten years, knew a young trained female anesthesiologist in his university hospital in Istanbul who wanted to spend a year in the United States learning more English and anesthesia techniques in the United States. Finally, Dr. Akio Suzuki, who was with us in cardiac surgery, knew an excellent Japanese anesthesiologist at the University of Tokyo, who wanted to improve his English. And we did have one U.S. anesthesiologist who supervised the nurse anesthetists, Dr. Jesse Mullins.

But eventually we were able to recruit Dr. James Arens from the Ochsner Clinic in New Orleans. He, with several very able younger anesthesiologists, quickly developed a Department of Anesthesiology the likes of which I'd not seen since leaving Philadelphia.

Transplantation of organs is discussed in a separate chapter, but our early experience with lung transplantation and heart transplantation had attracted a steady stream of foreign visitors, and Weezie already had her hands full with our four small daughters. One Saturday afternoon, as I was helping Weezie get ready for a foreign visitor, I got a call from a Jackson physician who said that he had a patient with complete intestinal obstruction and would I please come down. Weezie was most put out, but what could I do? This was a genuine emergency. Upon arriving at the Emergency Ward, I found that his "patient" was his dog, who had swallowed a rubber ball. I was very annoyed, for he had taken advantage of me—he should have gone to a veterinarian. But, already there, I opened the laboratory, he gave ether

223

anesthesia and I removed the ball.

On another occasion we were having a Doctor O'Toole of Dublin to dinner but Weezie was concerned about cracks in the ceiling of the dining room of the rented house. I said, "Why don't we have a candlelight supper. Then the cracks won't show."

We did and the meal was progressing smoothly until Weezie said to Dr. O'Toole, "I am very fond of candlelight."

To which Dr. O'Toole, who had not looked up said, "Yes, and it hides cracks in the ceiling!"

We had one problem with our little girls on such an occasion. They would go around and place an admonition in each ash tray: "Smoking causes cancer."

RESIDENT ADDICTION. Addiction to prescription drugs is a constant hazard amongst medical personnel at all levels, nurses included. This is due to many factors which include constant stress, temptation, and availability. But my first confrontation came on July 4, 1960. A young surgery intern, who had just started his work on July 1, called me and said that he had to talk with me. He asked if he might come out to my home. He seemed agitated. I told him to come on.

His hands were shaking and he said that he could not handle the responsibility for taking care of sick surgical patients.

At this, I asked, "What responsibility? You just began your internship four days ago. Your job is to call one of the residents above you if some problem develops, pass the buck."

But he was insistent so I said, "R., you are just at the beginning of your career. It would look bad on your record if you dropped out now, only four days into your internship. Why not stick it out 'til mid-year. Then, if you still want to drop out you can do so without having major problems in finding an internship in another specialty."

He said he would try.

But some weeks later one of his fellow house officers chanced to see what appeared to be his injecting himself in the leg, this through the crack in the door near the hinges. He and another house officer then went to R.'s room and found syringes, needles and tourniquets in his bathroom drawer.

I called R. in. I knew that at one time he'd had a sympathectomy for hypertension and I thought he might be taking medicine for that. But R. denied taking any drugs, not even a barbiturate.

I remained concerned, though, and so I called Dr. Robert Q. Marston, our current Dean, to talk the matter over with him. He said that he and I had no experience in detecting addiction, and so he called the chief state health officer, Dr. Gray. He said he would send over his narcotics officer, formerly with the FBI. He met R. in my office and then left with him for a private treatment room.

They were back in my office in less than an hour and the agent told R. to drop his pants. There, boldly visible, were to be seen at least fifty needle puncture marks. R.'s modus operandi had been to volunteer to take the syringe of opiate solution from the nurses' station to the patient in need. But on the way he would duck into a treatment room, inject the medicine right through his pants pocket, and then take the syringe filled with isotonic saline solution to the patient. The patients complained that they got no pain relief from the "morphine" injections.

Dr. Gray recommended that he be sent to a jail-treatment center in Kentucky, but he warned that not more than 5 percent of addicts ever recovered completely or permanently.

(*Epilogue*: R. was released from the addiction center in Kentucky some months later, but subsequently was found dead from an overdose in his garage in northern Mississippi. He probably had lost his tolerance for large doses while in the treatment center.)

All in all, there were five known surgery residents addicted, over the years. Detection carried immediate and permanent dismissal from the program. There were at least three anesthesiology residents so afflicted.

THE FIRST OPEN HEART SURGERY IN MISSISSIPPI. The first successful open heart surgery using the heart-lung machine was performed by Dr. John H. Gibbon at Jefferson Medical College in Philadelphia. On May 6, 1953, he closed an atrial septal defect in an eighteen year old girl. But his complicated and expensive equipment he used for this monumental achievement was beyond the means of most cardiac surgery centers. This led the thoracic surgeons at the University of Minnesota—principally Dr. C. Walton Lillehei and Dr. Richard Varco—to search for a simpler method and this was provided by one of their assistants, Dr. Richard A. Dewall. He took advantage of the fact that carbon dioxide is released from the blood much more rapidly than is oxygen. Thus, using an inverted U-shaped piece of plastic tubing, he made holes at the very apex. Then he bubbled oxygen into the bottom of the tubing at the left lower side.

PULMONARY VALVULOTOMY-UNDER HYPOTHERMIA
Hospital of The University of Mississippi. January 27, 1959.
Patient, Lester "Sonny" Crow. Aged Two Years.
SURGEONS: Drs. James D. hardy, Watts R. Webb, Bryon E. Green, Jr.
Anesthesiologist, Dr. Leonard W. Fabian.
Intern, Dr. Walter P. Griffey, Jr.
Extern, Harris Van Craig.
Suture Nurse, Ellen C. Bozeman

As the oxygenated blood reached the apex, the carbon dioxide escaped through the perforations as the blood passed and descended down the right side, to be pumped into the patient, using the widely used DeBakey pump. This Dewall oxygenator spread rapidly throughout the United States, and I had prevailed upon the Mississippi Heart Association to send our appointed thoracic resident to the University of Minnesota to see the Dewall oxygenator in clinical use, work with it in the animal

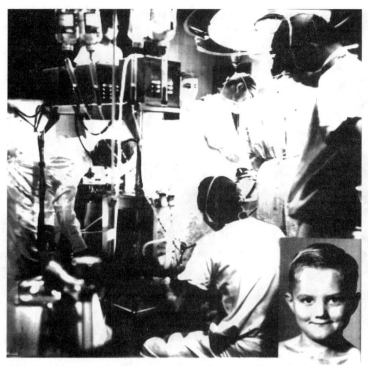

February 6, 1959
PULMONARY VALVULOTOMY-WITH PUMP OXYGENATOR
Hospital of The University of Mississippi
Patient, Danny Stringer. Age Six Years.
Surgeons: Drs. Watts R. Webb, James D. Hardy, Hector S. Howard &
　　　　　　　Bryon E. Green.
Pump Oxygenator, Dr. W. A. Neely, Mr. Don McNeil.
Anesthesiologist: Drs. Leonard W. Fabian, Doyle Smith.
Intern, Dr. john R. Montgomery.
Extern, Bob Earl McKee.
Circulating Nurse, Julia A. Corbett.
Suture Nurse, Ruby Nell Webster.

laboratory, and buy and bring back all the parts necessary
to establish open heart surgery in our animal laboratory.
(N.B. I happened to be on the membership selection of
the American Association for Thoracic Surgery when Dr.
Dewall's name came up for possible membership. There
was mixed discussion among our committee, and one

228

asked, somewhat testily, "So he invented the bubble oxygenator. What's he done since?"

To which another member said, "That reminds me of the cavemen members wearing bear hides and seated on rocks at the cave entrance. One says, "So he invented fire. What's he done since!"

After a great deal of practice in the animal laboratory, Dr. Watts R. Webb and I performed the first open heart operation in Mississippi on a five year old boy using hypothermia on January 27, 1959, and one week later we used the pump oxygenator to correct pulmonary valve stenosis in a second child.

Both children recovered promptly and their right heart outflow, the pulmonary artery, had been relieved of its obstruction.

THE CLOSED SOCIETY. 1961-62

So much has now been written about Mississippi's "closed society" that only a few highlights and accompanying details will be presented here. But the segregation fight had a profound effect on the progress of our medical school.

Ever since the United States Supreme Court decision in 1955 in favor of public school integration, the political forces in Mississippi had by an intricate series of maneuvers managed virtually to ignore the court order. Increasingly, Mississippi was indeed the "closed society."

Virtually all news sources were controlled by actual belief, or by social and economic coercion, to maintain rigidly the hard segregationist line. Almost every village and town developed its White Citizens Council, the purpose of which was to maintain segregation, ostensibly under law. Nonetheless, economic boycott and social ostracism were commonly the lot of those who exhibited even the slightest evidence of moderation in racial relations.[1]

For example, the story was told of a filling station owner who had a black employee who had tried to register to vote. This was of course a major offense against the establishment. The owner was informed by the Citizens Council that he must fire this worker. But the owner refused, saying that the black man had worked for him for over 20 years and was one of his most dependable employees. At this, observers were stationed just outside and took the automobile license tag numbers of cars that went into the filling station. Their owners were then looked up through the state registration, and it was suggested to them that they not use that filling station again. The results were obvious and effective. If the offence was considered extreme, the Ku Klux Klan might surface for more definitive persuasion of the recalcitrant citizen. In general, the members of the Citizens Council tended to be community leaders, with a substantial proportion of the Ku Klux Klan more on the order of enforcers.

Both the Hederman newspapers and the two television stations available at that time maintained the same defiance of the federal government and rang with the slogan *segregation forever*. Governor George Wallace was doing the same thing over in Alabama.

The negative effects of this policy were pervasive in numerous directions. For instance, when the most militant forces tried to close the public schools to prevent

[1] Silver, J.W., *Mississippi: The Closed Society*. Harcourt, BRace & World, New York, 1963, 1964

integration, many women banded together quietly and sought to prevent this disaster. My wife was among them and I was frankly uneasy about our safety.

THE FACULTY OUTFLIGHT. At the height of the integration struggle, Dr. Julian Youmans, deputy chief of Neurosurgery, stated that this worldwide noted conflict had cut down the academic frontrunners at our University Medical Center, and Dr. Artz voiced the opinion that if we did not want to die in Mississippi we'd better get out while we still could. Dr. Youmans soon accepted a chair of Neurosurgery in California and Dr. Artz became Director of the new Shriners Burn Institute at the University of Texas in Galveston.

In 1963 Dr. Webb accepted the post of Chief of Cardiothoracic Surgery at Southwestern Medical and Parkland Hospital in Dallas. Dr. Artz ultimately became chairman of the Department of Surgery at the Medical College of South Carolina at Charleston and Dr. Webb ultimately became Chairman of the Department of Surgery at Tulane University in New Orleans. And Dr. Bittenbender had become a victim of lung cancer.

Thus, the history of our enterprise had conformed to that of many or most professional organizations. Of the seven full-time mature clinical surgeons who had formed the original full-time cadre of the Department of Surgery, only one remained (J.D.H.). Neurosurgery, headed by Dr. Orlando Andy, had been given separate departmental status in 1960.

The replacements had been Dr. William "Gus" Neely, who had now finished our residency and was qualified in both general and thoracic surgery; Dr. Seshadri Raju, who had achieved his Boards in both General and Thoracic

ADMINISTRATIVE STRUCTURE, Department of Surgery

Chairman of Department and Surgeon-in-Chief to University Hospital

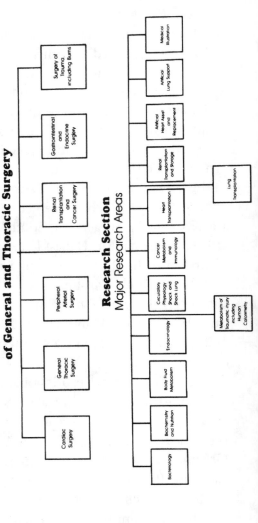

Divisions

Anesthesiology · Orthopedic Surgery · Urological Surgery · Plastic Surgery · Ophthalmology · Division of General and Thoracic Surgery · Otolaryngology and Communicative Disorders · Oral Surgery · Pediatric Surgery · Neurosurgery

Sections of General and Thoracic Surgery

Cardiac Surgery · General Thoracic Surgery · Peripheral Arterial Surgery · Renal Transplantation and Cancer Surgery · Gastrointestinal and Endocrine Surgery · Surgery of Trauma, including Burns

Research Section
Major Research Areas

Bacteriology · Biochemistry and Nutrition · Body Fluid Metabolism · Endocrinology · Circulation Physiology, Shock and Shock Lung · Cancer Metabolism and Immunology · Heart Transplantation · Renal Transplantation and Storage · Artificial Heart Assist and Replacement · Artificial Lung Support · Medical Illustration · Metabolism of Traumatic Injury including Human Calorimetry · Lung Transplantation

Surgery; and Dr. Hilary Timmis from the University of Pennsylvania in Cardiothoracic Surgery, who worked tirelessly to establish an Intensive Care Unit with well-trained nurses.

Dr. William O. Barnett remained aboard, but the signs of imminent departure were unmistakable: neglect of his teaching responsibilities, shedding the universally worn white coat in favor of new expensive looking suits and neckties, announcing that he was through with research and giving away his laboratories. Clearly, he fretted over the University policy of requiring that he return to the Dean's Office the money above a fixed limit that he earned from private practice but was not allowed to keep. He yearned to return to the earnings, the related emoluments, and the freedom of private practice, which he had enjoyed before joining our department full-time shortly after its development. So, he left.

But Dr. Barnett's going was a real loss. He was a fine teacher and clinician, and he was liked by the medical students. His research in the pathophysiology of small bowel obstruction had been widely recognized, and it had earned him membership in the Society of University Surgeons, the Southern Surgical Association and the American Surgical Association.

There sprang up overnight a multitude of private schools, many of which still exist today (2002). Our three oldest daughters finished at what had been selected for listing nationally: Murrah High School. But as Katherine came along, the federal law decreeing bussing had been enforced. She would be required to bus to three different schools over a period of two years, as I recall.

This disruption and waste of the daily travel time was

simply unacceptable, and we enrolled her in the new private Jackson Preparatory School.

The adverse effects of the segregation were pervasive. While "fires burned" up at the main University of Mississippi, at Oxford, where the 82nd Airborne Division had forced the enrollment of a black man, James Meredith, the medical school in Jackson had escaped major intrusion. But more subtle deleterious effects were felt. For example, for several years we received not one out-of-state application for our residency in surgery. Faculty members, often the frontrunners, accepted employment elsewhere, and it was almost impossible to import new faculty. Even if our proposition was attractive to the prospective male faculty member, his wife simply would not come to Mississippi.

I too received offers from elsewhere, but I elected to stay.

The police often suggested that one remove the Mississippi car tag when driving north, especially toward the midwest to include Detroit. And when this writer entered a famous hotel in Washington, D.C., the black bellhops refused to take our bags up to the rooms upon learning that we were from the South and Mississippi in particular.

The Society of University Surgeons had been scheduled for several years to meet in Jackson, but the organization now withdrew, citing that two members were black and would not be comfortable in Jackson.

One of the best things that happened to our University Medical Center in 1961 was that Dr. Robert Q. Marston came as the Dean and Director and, later on, became the Vice-Chancellor. With his arrival, all the previous political jockeying and bypassing had come to an end. True, he did not bring Orthopedics clearly back into line, since like most of the previous deans he apparently preferred to "let sleeping dogs lie," insofar as Orthopedics was concerned. There remained the uneasy university relationships with the orthopedists in town. They had little genuine association with the medical center, but things rocked along. Dr. Marston never tolerated for one moment the criticism of my administration by one of our surgical faculty members, without insisting at the same time that I be brought in. This policy effectively squashed ninety percent of the political problems that had been such a burden during the previous administration.

In another leadership role, one night, having gained Chancellor Williams' permission, Dr. Marston brought in a crew and tore down the wall that had separated the white and colored sections of the hospital cafeteria and all the drinking fountains in the building were stripped of the "white" and the "colored" signs.

THE FEDERAL GOVERNMENT AFFIRMATIVE ACTION PROGRAMS AND FULL COMPLIANCE. The federal government seemed to single out Mississippi and in particular the Hospital of the University of Mississippi as the strategic battleground to integrate hospital services. While the University Hospital had posed no problem for several years, focus turned to a nearby private hospital. There was a loophole in the Medicare law that permitted payment to noncompliant hospitals for emergencies. And it was said that the largest private hospital in Jackson had the largest number of "emergency" patients who did not actually represent an emergency.

In due course, Medicaid and Medicare, which had become the financial mainstay of many or even most hospitals—these agencies progressively squeezed until all hospitals were in compliance.

Affirmative Action. We ourselves at the University sought to acknowledge affirmative action. Mrs. Maurine Twiss, Director of Public Information, was making a tape for in-house projection depicting the early days of the Medical Center. She first interviewed me and then turned to a large, black, uniformed and armed policewoman, for both of us had been present from the founding of the hospital. "Officer Kelly," Mrs. Twiss began, with her best television smile, "You first had a career in our laundry. Would you please tell our viewers what influenced you to shift from your laundry career to assume your present career in law enforcement?" "Well, Miz Twiss, it wuz like this. Chief Wilson, he done come up to me and said, 'Look, the feds say we got to have two women on the force, one white and one black. You want the job?'"

Committee on Human Investigation. As human transplantation progressed, it became more and more apparent that not only did the patients involved need protection but the operating surgeon did also. For example, an experienced heart transplanter in a major city had made a limited attempt to find the brain-dead potential heart donor's relatives, but in the urgency of the situation had moved on, harvested the heart of the brain-dead donor, and had inserted it into another human who was doing well.

But news people, annoyed over being shut out—they instigated a search which was reported to have identified 28 of the donor's relatives in the same city. A lawsuit was in progress.

Thus, we asked Dean Marston to appoint a fairly large Human Investigation Committee which would include clinicians and basic scientists. This he did.

ARTIFICIAL PEARLS BEFORE GENUINE SWINE (NOT REALLY). A college professor was once asked what he considered his role to be and he replied, "To cast artificial pearls before genuine swine."

Since the beginning of the four-year medical school it had been the custom for the graduating seniors to put on a skit at an annual dinner just a day or so before graduation in June. This opportunity the students usually employed to poke fun, at times vicious fun, at members of the faculty. While I myself had generally been accorded gentle and at times outstanding treatment, one of my most able surgical colleagues was almost invariably ridiculed, as for example being awarded two horse shoes "as a suggestion." The previous year the class had dedicated the yearbook, The Medic, to me and this spring the class as a whole had voted me one of their outstanding teachers, along with several others. But in complete contradiction to the yearbook award voted upon by the class as a whole, the several students who had volunteered to put on the skit this year *nominated* me for the "vacuum tube"—one who had taught them nothing. The tube was actually awarded to someone else, but I was taken aback and my wife was mortified and humiliated. No one knew better than she the great amount of time I was putting on the medical school and its overall effort, and she felt that this attack by the medical students was out of bounds. As for myself, I had had infinitely more experience with criticism and its management than she, but the occasion of course not only annoyed me but it angered me in that Weezie's feelings had been hurt publicly. In general, such skits are best handled as stud affairs.

The main immediate problem, however, was that we had for some years invited the senior medical class to our home for a party on the Sunday afternoon after the Friday skit session. This clearly was going to be a very difficult party.

The next morning, Saturday, the representative of a group of the students called upon me to say that the skit had been a surprise to them, and that they wanted me to know that this certainly did not represent the attitude of most of the class, as witnessed by the yearbook award. My reply was that, in circumstances such as this, there had to be a certain corporate responsibility; that I appreciated his coming, of course, but that it had been a source of acute unhappiness to my wife.

Obviously, the party the next afternoon, though well attended, was more in the nature of a wake, for everyone concerned was embarrassed. Even the skit members had sobered up by this time, though most of them did not come anyway.

This was the last time we entertained the medical students as a class. Perhaps it was not the correct decision, but somehow the pleasure of having them in our home had been permanently impaired. And I did not ask Weezie, with four small children, to put it on again.

2531 EASTOVER DRIVE. We had moved into our beautiful, new home in 1960. We had built it on a cost-plus basis, on the recommendation of good friends who'd done so, but the costs seemed to balloon as it was being built. Weezie supervised and a Mr. W.E. Harrison was the builder. Mr. George Brock was our architect for the Georgian type building.

The run-overs were all legitimate. Mr. Harrison was a very capable and honest builder. But it was his added suggestions that came dear.

"Dr. Hardy," he would say, "You have four daughters and a wife who will find the architect's long driveway too narrow. It should be widened, against the time that the girls will be learning to drive. And, Dr. Hardy, when they are learning to drive they might run into the kitchen door from the carport. We must build an attractive stopper. And, Dr. Hardy, Mrs. Hardy wants an additional fireplace, in the family room. It will have to have a chimney."

But when he had finished I would not have changed one single item throughout the house.

PROGRESSIVE RECOVERY. RELATIVE TRANQUILITY. By 1968 the hassle that had followed our first heart transplant in man using a large chimpanzee donor—this prolonged criticism—had largely subsided. Not the seat of the soul, the heart was now accepted as being only a pump (though many years later it would be found to possess endocrine capabilities).

For the first time I, now 50, began to be tired upon occasion—something I'd rarely experienced before then. It was in this era that I served as an Elder in the Covenant Presbyterian Church for the six-year term.

STORM CLOUDS GATHERING (1971). The internal struggles in the Department of Surgery—first with Neurosurgery then with Orthopedics and twice with Anesthesiology—had inevitably taken their toll. Regardless of the merits of the case leading to a confrontation, each of the principals inevitably loses something in the exchange because both have friends and supporters, and the enemies generated by these conflicts tend to coalesce.

And true, I had been much in the public eye, too much so in many ways. My opposing Neurosurgery's becoming a separate department still rankled in some quarters, though ultimately my position here was to be vindicated. Critics said that Dr. Enneking had been "run off" in Orthopedics (though he had resigned) and that the head of Anesthesiology had been treated in the same manner—completely disregarding the fact that the latter had a separate and co-equal department of the medical center and that he had resigned.

Anticipating imminent attack, two of my senior residents, Martin McMullan and Joe Ed Varner, came to warn me privately that it was a precarious time and that I should try to pull back on all fronts. They said that some of the younger members of the clinical faculty, who felt that a change should be made in the leadership of the Department of Surgery, were meeting secretly. I had already been told of one meeting in which a perennial opponent in another department had suggested that two members of my own department, who were present at the meeting, should take over a segment of the operating activity that I had developed from scratch. This suggestion was quickly squelched by one of my staff who reportedly said, "Your suggestion just goes to show that you don't know Dr. Hardy at all. You just don't do that to him. He tries to treat everybody fair, and he expects the same in return."

Then a mid-level member of another department of

the medical center requested an appointment. Hardly had he sat down than he said abruptly, "We're going to get rid of you. You have served your time."

"That's a straightforward statement, to say the least, " I replied. "Fortunately, I work for the Dean, the Chancellor and the Board of Trustees of the Institutions of Higher Learning. I serve as the chairman of the Department of Surgery at their pleasure. Then there is of course the tenure problem, and it would take you a considerable amount of time to overcome that obstacle."

Thus the spring of 1971 was an unsettled period. It was clear that both clinical and political parameters needed to be strengthened. It was true that I had been much away from the University, though always with the permission of the administration. Also, in the 1960s we'd been on the front end of the learning curve for kidney transplantation and for open-heart surgery. We had lost the occasional kidney transplant, but this was due, in part, to the fact that we did not have timely blood dialysis and had to resort to peritoneal dialysis, which was not safe from infection or truly effective at that time. It was still a time when transplant surgeons chose to increase the anti-rejection drugs to a level that risked fatal infections, rather than to remove the failing transplant and save the patient by returning to hemodialysis.

Fortunately, the anesthesia problem had been wondrously solved by the recruitment of Dr. James Arens from the Ochsner Clinic in New Orleans.

Orthopedics continued to be covered by Dr. "Mike" Derian, who had been recruited by Dr. Enneking. He did not want an associate and we were in no position to press him, despite the risks of having a single man to man a division. In his absence, Dr. Donald Imrie of Vicksburg gave some coverage for the residents. The orthopedists in Jackson gave none.

On the evening of July 1, 1976, I was reading a manuscript at home when Vice-Chancellor Norman C. Nelson called to ask me to come down to his office right away. He would not say over the telephone what the problem was. I could not imagine what administrative problem could be of such gravity that he would neither mention it over the telephone nor let it wait until morning. Curious, I went right down to his office, where I found him, the university lawyer Carl André, the attorney William Winter (later governor), the Chief of Orthopedics (Dr. Derian), and the chief resident in Orthopedics, (Patrick Barrett). Dr. Barrett, representing the orthopedics residents, accompanied by Winter, had come to throw down a gauntlet: All eleven residents in orthopedics at the University of Mississippi Medical Center would resign immediately unless certain conditions were met. The principal condition proved to be that the chief of Orthopedics, the only full-time member of our orthopedic staff, must be relieved as Chairman of the Division of Orthopedics immediately. There was even discussion that he be fired, but this was completely inappropriate but also unrealistic, as he was a tenured professor. While there are grounds for firing anyone, a tenured professor is rarely released without considerable documentation and legal advice. Dr. Derian was accused of inadequate teaching and leadership in a wide range of activities.

The residents' move abruptly brought to a head a situation which I had long realized was an unhappy one, although I had not known the depth of the problem. Ever since the previous head of orthopedics had left, the affairs of orthopedics had been tacitly handled by the new chairman's direct communications with the current dean, rather than communications through departmental channels in the usual way. If this was the way the university administration wanted to handle orthopedics, it was the administration's privilege to do so. But I had sought clarification as far back as 1970. At that time I had written the current dean (Dr. [General] Robert Blount) that the previous dean (Dr. Robert E. Carter) had asked me to pay more attention to what Dr. Derian and his group were doing. I replied that, now learning that Dr. Derian had been in Europe for some time, I could not monitor what was going on in orthopedics without having all major items passed through my office. But that had never been done, nor had it been done under Dean Blount's regimen.

I said that thus I had neither knowledge nor responsibility as to what had been going on in orthopedics, but that I was ready to help in any way that I could.

It was a singular experience, it seemed to me, that the orthopedic residents had engaged an attorney (Mr. Winter) without first presenting their complaints to the University Administration.

The attorneys went into the Vice Chancellor's conference room and drew up an agreement. I did not see the agreement, but the sum of it was that Dr. Derian would step down as chairman of orthopedics and a new chairman would be brought on board as soon as possible. Dr. Derian agreed to this, to my surprise, but I sensed he realized that this course was the better of two unhappy alternatives. Moreover, at the time he was deeply distressed over an unrelated personal problem. The residents were to return the next morning and take care of their patients—whom they had abandoned.

As the meeting broke up, Dr. Derian said to Dr. Barrett, "Pat, you are still going to stand with me tomorrow, aren't you?"

"No way!" replied Dr. Barrett.

I then asked Dr. Derian what was the situation?

He said that his divorce before a judge downtown was scheduled for seven o'clock the next morning and that he had to have someone with him who would vouch for his character.

I said, "Mike, I'll delay my operating schedule in the morning and go down with you." At court, the judge had come early because of the persons and politics involved. Dr. Derian's wife was politically involved and later went with President Jimmie Carter to Washington as an assistant secretary of state. She had traveled widely the previous year or so, and Dr. Derian once told me that he had put up about $30,000 for her travels the previous year.

Before the judge, Dr. Derian wept and the judge said gently, "Take your time, Dr. Derian."

(Some months later Patt Derian married Hoding Carter III, of Greenville, Mississippi, who was later strongly prominent in the Carter administration in Washington.)

Meanwhile, the orthopedic residents failed to return to work the next morning, which they had agreed to do. Thus, as chairman of the overall department of surgery, on the instant I had become acting head of orthopedics. The members of the Mississippi Academy of Orthopedics met in urgent session and mailed a signed protest that the orthopedics division was being administered by a general surgeon (me). This while they well knew that any orthopedist available would be appointed on the spot.

Meanwhile, we on General Surgery covered orthopedics during the night. As a matter of fact, I'd had considerable experience with acute orthopedic problems such as bone fractures, for General Surgery had cared for virtually all the fractures at Penn: The orthopedists had been so heavily involved with tuberculosis of bone, acute and chronic staphylococcic bone infection, congenital deformities, and poliomyelitis disabilities, plus bone tumors—with all this, the Penn orthopedists were happy for the general surgeons to care for the acute fractures.

But the next morning none of our orthopedic residents appeared. Later on, if memory serves, they went on television to make additional demands, still ignoring the signed agreement which had been hammered out by the lawyers.

Thus it was clear that bad blood existed to the extent that other arrangements were going to have to be made. Therefore, I took two general surgery residents and surveyed every orthopedic patient in the hospital and discharged those who could safely go home. Likewise, since the orthopedic clinic was huge, we quickly went over this group over a period of several days and reduced it to an absolute minimum.

As noted, Dr. Donald Imrie had come back and forth from Vicksburg to give some assistance at the VA Hospital and the University Hospital. The orthopedists at the adjacent Methodist Rehabilitation Center were discreetly absent.

Meanwhile the orthopedic residents, apparently unsatisfied with the television attack on Dr. Derian, turned to the newspaper. Their accusations included 14 specific charges against Dr. Derian: failure to teach at operations, consistent lack of supervision in the clinic and elsewhere, continuous threats of dismissal of residents over trivial incidents, discouragement of residents wishing to do research, virtually total unavailability of Dr. Derian for night and weekend emergencies, failure to develop a dependable ongoing plan for the orthopedic education of the residents, refusal to allow any meaningful participation by qualified state and local orthopedic surgeons, failure to arrange visiting professorships to further orthopedic resident education, ineffective leadership and lack of interest in continuing orthopedic education on a state-wide basis, exorbitant amount of time playing tennis and engaging in other personal pursuits during duty hours, apparent lack of concern in keeping abreast of current orthopedic literature, unnecessary and uncalled for humiliation of residents, being required to record Dr. Derian as surgeon in all cases even though he was seldom present, inability of residents to discuss problems with Dr. Derian. Furthermore, Dr. Derian had been the only "faculty" in the department since the resignation in last June of Dr. Hugh Brown, a part-time attending.

This was of course a massive and bitter assault on Dr. Derian and its vehemence cut in many directions. For one thing, it appeared that Mr. Winter was no longer in control. The rock-like uniformity of the residents was impressive and indeed the residents themselves had been allowed to choose new residents coming in, with little input from Dr. Derian.

One thing one had to admire was the care with which the residents had prepared during the months before their ultimatum. For example, they had made a careful record of all the Medicare and Medicaid cases for which the surgery had been billed and collected, when Dr. Derian was out of town and, frequently, out of state. In another context, it was reported that they had obtained from the files at the River Hills Tennis Club the exact dates and times of day when Dr. Derian had played tennis, which appeared to be substantial.

Eventually Dr. Derian elected to practice in Virginia.

The orthopedic residents now proposed that they would return if accepted en bloc. This we would not do. We realized that they had taken on a bad situation with courage, but in their attacks by newspaper and television, their failure to honor the agreements made originally, by their hiring a lawyer without ever having voiced their complaints through normal channels—because of all this, we refused to accept all of them en bloc. However, we were prepared to accept them one by one.

The residents declined, and it developed that they had already lined up residencies elsewhere, so they left.

Dr. James L. Hughes of Johns Hopkins was recruited, and he soon developed one of the best Departments of Orthopedics in the United States.

Did Mississippi now have sufficient physicians? No.

This was brought home to me by a particular patient. A Mr. R. of Greenville, Mississippi, had had heart surgery in Dallas. Now he presented to the University Hospital with a ruptured abdominal aortic aneurysm. Following its resection, the patient sustained cardiac arrest several times in the intensive care unit, but was resuscitated quickly each time without having sustained serious brain or kidney damage.

He continued to come back and forth to Jackson for follow-up visits, a distance of about 100 miles, until one day I said, "Mr. R., it isn't really necessary for you to come all the way to Jackson. Get an internist there in Greenville and he will call me if he thinks I should see you."

Whereupon, Mr. and Mrs. R. exclaimed, "But, Doctor Hardy, we can't get a doctor in Greenville—our doctor developed a drug problem and retired and no one else will take us."

I replied, "That's ridiculous," as I tilted backward to reach the telephone. I called the office of a prominent internist in Greenville, told him the problem and asked if he would not take on Mr. R.

"Dr. Hardy, we are stressed out over here. I will take him on for six months but then he'll have to find another doctor."

Soon thereafter at Executive Faculty the question arose as to whether we should increase the size of the medical school classes. You can guess my vote.

Soon thereafter, our splendid maid (actually, she was far more than just a maid)—she said that she was a bit late because her grandchild had a bad toothache.

"S.," I said, "Why don't you take him to a dentist?"

She looked at me as if she thought I was a little slow and then said, "Dr. Hardy, you know no dentist in Jackson is going to treat a colored child."

Again, when the issue arose to determine whether or

not to establish a dental school, my vote was positive. (Prior to this, the state had paid dental schools in other states, especially Emory in Atlanta, to train the dentists for Mississippi, if memory serves.)

In 1970 I was King of the Carnival Ball in Jackson, perhaps the stellar social event of the season, under the auspices of the Jackson Junior League. But more about that later under The Hardy Family Chapter.

THE PHYSICIAN'S ASSISTANT PROGRAM. Following the lead of Duke and the University of Alabama, I applied to the National Institutes of Health (NIH) for support of a Surgical Assistants training program at the University of Mississippi Medical Center. But my application was not successful, on the basis that the experimental programs at Duke and Alabama were all that were needed at the time.

However, a year or so later the University of Mississippi was offered the NIH funds to conduct a general medical physicians assistants program and our Dean asked me to conduct the program, since I'd already had the experience with the unsuccessful more restricted surgical assistants program. I agreed to this and sought the collaboration of all the other clinical departments.

The program was effectively organized and executed, but several considerations resulted in its termination after one or two "classes" had graduated. First, the course had claimed so much teaching time that it was concluded that these "students" might as well have been formal medical students. Second, the President of The American Medical Association spoke at the annual meeting of the Mississippi Medical Association and came down hard against the training of these "half-baked" doctors. Our Dean was very impressed with the speaker's remarks. But, third, I had come to be concerned as to how well supervised the physicians assistants would be out in the rural areas of the state. For example, one general practitioner (who'd sent some bungled operative cases to us at Jackson)—he called me and asked when he could get a physician's assistant, that he wanted to leave his "gallbladder" (operations) to him while he took a prolonged vacation in Hawaii. He owned the small hospital, the only one in town. I had once called his son-in-law physician in Atlanta to ask him if he knew the situation with his father-in-law. He replied that he of course did, but that I must understand that there was nothing he could do.

But I cannot claim absolute purity. The physician had once sent me a lawyer, with a large abdominal aneurysm. As I was examining him, he said testily, "I don't know why Dr. X did not do this operation himself. He will tackle anything."

I admit that I dissembled and said, "I don't think Dr. X has the right instruments."

(After all, he *was* a referring physician.)

MISSISSIPPI CANDIES. My sole investment into local businesses was that of Mississippi Candies. It turned out to be painful but educational. Orlando Andy, head of Neurosurgery, had approached me about buying stock in this new venture. I first checked with the Mississippi Research and Development Center, which warmly endorsed the proposed new firm. It said that there was no other candy maker in Mississippi and that this proposed project was the most promising one "to come down the pike" in years.

I next checked with the Mississippi State Department,

which was charged with monitoring financial institutions throughout the state. I asked what would be done with our investment money while the candy factory was being put together. I was told that these funds would be held in escrow and that not a penny could be spent without specific permission by the appropriate officer in the Mississippi State Department.

With this reassuring research, I bought a number of shares of the stock for my estate and additional shares for our four children. My motivation in buying was that, first, I, now a Mississippian, would be participating in the financial affairs of the State, to a limited degree. Second, I wanted to show Dr. Andy that I harbored no ill will from our earlier battles with respect to the separate status of Neurosurgery as an independent element of the Medical School. Third, I hoped to interest our four children in Mississippi affairs. Fourth, I had been assured that this investment was fully justified and sound.

But what a bitter lesson I learned. I discovered a whole, vast demimonde of virtually no monitoring by the State Department and outright fraud. For example, the "director" of the project had used substantial amounts of escrow funds for his personal other enterprises. The "board" almost never had a quorum to vote, so that the "director" was left to do as he pleased. When I went myself to a board meeting (uninvited) I forced a frank analysis by the nationally prominent auditing firm, which had regularly issued favorable reports, when no candy had yet been made. When I challenged the auditing firm's representative, he admitted lamely that his annual reports had been misleading but that he had just wanted to help along a struggling enterprise (and, of course, keep the paying account).

It developed that virtually all the "escrow" funds had disappeared and that the stock was already badly oversold above what had been specified as the upper dollar limit. However, the fringe lawyer said that if he were given $1,000, he could get the upper limit raised (which he did, by whom, at what bribe?) I learned that the stock salesman, who actually sold the stock to me, had been investigated for stock fraud in the past. I learned that the Department of State monitoring was virtually a farce: the sole department financial officer (for the whole state of Mississippi, apparently) came in to his office about ten o'clock and left for home at about two o'clock.

But no candy had yet been made.

By this time, however, the word had got around and Mississippi Candies collapsed.

It was a painful lesson for me. I never invested in another local enterprise.

THE MISSISSIPPI SURGICAL FORUM. After we had established the medical student and housestaff education, we sought to initiate postgraduate education for practicing surgeons. Dr. William O. Barnett was to spearhead this project. For the first session we invited two nationally known surgical speakers, with the other slots being filled by local talent in our own University Medical Center. We had mailed programs to surgeons in Mississippi, Arkansas, Louisiana, Tennessee and Alabama. The attendance was disappointing. Shortly thereafter I participated in such courses at The University of Minnesota and U.C.L.A. (meeting at Palm Springs, CA). At Minneapolis Doctor Richard Varco explained that they ran a program in which the teaching material was

The University of Mississippi Medical Center circa 1998.

changed each year and that, if a physician came regularly, he would over the course of about four years be exposed to most of the current knowledge and management of the current spectrum of a wide variety of pathologic conditions. The Minnesota program had developed a solid corps of regular applicants, which guaranteed a respectable audience for the multiple nationally known invited speakers.

At the U.C.L.A. session I mentioned our small attendance the previous year to Dr. Wiley Barker, that our effort in Jackson the previous year had been disappointing. He then said that he would bet that we had sent our brochures to only surgeons in our immediate region, that U.C.L.A. sent out thousands of their flyers throughout the United States and Canada.

I returned home and told Dr. Barnett that we too would rotate the subject matter of our programs, mail out several thousand brochures, invite multiple nationally known speakers, pay them expenses plus a decent honorarium, and charge a reasonable admission fee. We would put up ten thousand dollars for the session, which would be supplemented by the "students tuition."

The results were spectacular! Over 400 physicians came the next year, a capacity crowd. As an inducement for repetitive attendance, we had a graduating ceremony for those who had attended for 5 years and, later, those who had attended 10 years. With "Pomp and Circumstance" being played in the back of the hall, the honorees came forward in alphabetical order. I announced to the membership the name and home state of each recipient, and Dr. Barnett handed him his certificate for framing.

It was great fun.

THE ENT-PLASTIC SURGERY BATTLE. (1979) Prior to the 1970s, our Otolaryngology (ENT) service and our Plastic Surgery service had existed in fairly good harmony, and the national struggle between the two specialties for which would operate on what pathologic conditions had not been a problem. But now, with full-time heads and approved residency programs, the turf protection and new claims became one of my principal administrative concerns. Ear infections, infected tonsils, and sinus problems had been so common and serious for so many years that the ENT specialists had had all the work they needed. But with the increasingly effective antibiotics, operations for the above problems were vastly reduced and ENT began to invade what had long been the turf of Plastic Surgery and General Surgery.

My responsibility was to preserve a corpus of patient material for each specialty that would be essential to maintaining residency approval in all three disciplines.

But the ENT staff and residents were never satisfied. Each of the periodic meetings to agree upon allocations of turf resulted in a loss for Plastic Surgery. I began to make a tape recording of each session, so that neither side could come back later and claim "foul." The final straw came with face-lifts. This was the quintessence of Plastic Surgery, and it had been agreed that the ENT residents would not try to claim even these. Neither one of our full-time staff members in ENT had ever done face-lifts and did not wish to do them.

Once again, though, I found that the ENT residents were doing face-lifts under false appellations on the operating schedule, usually on Saturday mornings when fewer observers would be around. Still worse, it was alleged that they had brought in a surgeon from Memphis to assist them, who of course had no formal operating privileges in our hospital (we had offered to pay ENT residents while they rotated through a plastic surgery service out in the city of Jackson).

Needless to say, this ENT resident activity was beyond the pale. I told the operating room staff not to set up for anything the ENT residents scheduled that might be masking a face-lift.

The Deputy Director of the ENT Division, Dr. Myron Lockey, took the stand that if his residents were not allowed to do face-lifts in the University Hospital then he and all the ENT residents would resign. The Chief of the ENT service was at the point of his retirement, and did not want to get involved. Dr. Lockey asked to present his case to the clinical staff of the University Hospital. Even though sorely vexed, he gave a comprehensive and temperate appeal. I was proud of him.

But I was supported twice. Dr. Lockey resigned and all the ENT residents departed for residencies found at other institutions. I was truly sorry, for they were a fine bunch. As the last one was leaving, he stuck his head inside my office door and said, "Dr. Hardy, you are the Mohammed Ali of survivors!"

Meanwhile, the ENT physicians across Mississippi had attacked me, the Dean, the Chancellor and the Board of Trustees of the Institutions of Higher Learning in Federal court and had all signed the manifesto. This proved to be a fatal strategic error. Clearly, *exhaustive* depositions of each of the large number of Mississippi specialists who had signed the lawsuit would need to be taken, at a very considerable expense. It was this expense that caused the lawsuit to be dropped by the ENT specialists. The expense of the University's defenses were of course paid ultimately by the state treasury.

I took no pleasure in this. Meanwhile, as upcoming president of the American College of Surgeons, I was embarrassed by the threat that several thousand of the ENT members would resign if the Board of Regents did not censure me.

Fortunately, we were soon able to recruit Dr. Winsor Morrison, Chairman of ENT at the University of Tennessee Medical College in Memphis. He quickly restored the residency and brought in additional staff as well.

CHAPTER 11

Books: The Teacher's Teacher

(The reader should be alert not to be seduced by the following discourse penned by an utterly incurable bookaholic.)

This chapter will deal with two separate sections. The first has to do with my (expensive) hobby of collecting medical history books. The second has to do with selected examples of the twenty-two books I either single authored or co-authored, or edited or co-edited.

THE MEDICAL HISTORY COLLECTION (TO HAVE AND TO HOLD, FOR A TIME)

The Genesis. My first interest in medical history began when a medical student in our dormitory at the University of Alabama brought into our college sophomores pre-med room and said we should read it— Lloyd C. Douglas' *Magnificent Obsession*. This was of course not hardcore medical history—it was a novel. But it made a lasting impression on me and I still have it after these sixty-five years.

The second medical history book I received was a Christmas gift from my parents—*The Life of Pasteur*, and it too made such an impact that I was able to use a quote from it at a major address at the dedication of a new building at Milwaukee, Wisconsin, in 1966.

The third book, also given me by my parents, was the *Life of Madame Curie*. The author was her daughter Eve Curie and both of them won Nobel Prizes for radiation discoveries.

From this point, for many years, I had no money to buy other than the necessary textbooks, but I did keep a lookout for inexpensive medical history volumes.

I should note at this point that my interests were catholic, largely biographical, and would remain largely so through the life of my collection. However, in later years, surgical historical figures received preponderant attention. The collection eventually reached approximately 800 volumes.

Two additional external stimuli should be cited. Dr. David Reisman in Philadelphia gave us one or two talks on medical history when we were medical students. Then, some years later when I was a resident in surgery, Dr. Ravdin at times admitted the portly Dr. Abraham Rosenbach for toe infections secondary to his diabetes. So we surgery residents had got to know him fairly well. He was a world-class rare books collector and dealer.

One evening Dr. Ravdin had invited several of us residents down to his home on Delancy and his neighbor, Dr. Rosenbach, came over for a free wheeling gabfest about the exciting career of the rare book dealer. For instance, if he were to learn that a major book collection in Great Britain was to come at auction, he would jump on a ship (later a plane) and speed to examine and perhaps to buy at the sale.

I began to go down to the huge O'Leary bookstore in downtown Philadelphia and browse about looking for inexpensive volumes but worthwhile ones for the collector who was just beginning.

Purchasing. There are several authoritative books available that offer guidelines for buying medical history books. Suffice it to say that the low or medium-priced book collector may have the special pleasure of the independent search. Here not a lot of money is at risk. In brief, the value of a book is determined largely by its scarcity, its intrinsic worth and its condition. First editions and ones signed by the author add value.

But if a major purchase is contemplated, for a book priced at $1,000 or more, it is wise to have formed an alliance with a knowledgeable and reputable rare medical history book dealer. He may have an identical copy at a lesser price, or he may offer to find one for you. My principal consultant was Terrance Cavanaugh, the rare medical book librarian at Duke University. When I had to go up the east coast, to Washington, the N.I.H. or still farther north, I would leave Jackson early and drop off at Duke. Terry would then leave me in his home with his collection, and I would select the items to buy.

(Incidentally, it is necessary to have an understanding and forgiving wife as the buying proceeds.)

Rare book dealers are just like the rest of us, some are more "forthcoming" than are others. But some are special. A dealer outside Boston saw my list for sale, and called to ask if I realized the value of a certain book. I had not, for I had paid a reasonable price for it in a regular used bookstore. He said that it was among the one hundred most valuable medical books in existence. He offered to pay "up to" five thousand dollars, depending on its condition. He paid $4,000 after he had received and examined the volume. Question: How many other dealers would have done this? The last thing they often want is for the inexperienced seller not to know the value of each of the individual books offered for sale.

Protection of the Collection. As soon as the collection has reached financial significance it should be insured. The principal hazards are water (burst pipe in the attic) or smoke-fire conflagration in the kitchen. Of course, recovering the financial loss is welcomed but a far greater loss is the damage to one's special library, gathered together with such care over the years. This writer had a colleague whose library was virtually destroyed by water. We had a major fire in the kitchen during the early morning and the house was quickly filled with smoke so thick that one could hardly see his hand before him. The firemen arrived in minutes and placed a very large fan at the front door and blew the smoke out of the house. And, fortunately, the door to my study had been closed. After wiping off each of the eight hundred or so history books, it was found that only minimal smoke damage had occurred.

Direct sunlight will over time deface your books and it should be avoided.

Catalogue the books from the outset. Keep a record of when, from whom, and how much you paid for the volume. All this will be required later for tax purposes.

Very special or expensive books should be wrapped. Consult your librarian for the best current method.

Prevent any new markings in the books. In the advanced stage of my wife's illness, she began to write, "This book is the property of James D. hardy and Louise S. Hardy"—this in every book she could reach. Thus, the medical history collection had to be protected with lock and key.

The Louise Scott Sams Hardy Collection. One day I told Weezie that I wanted to do something lasting for her: Would she like another scholarship at Agnes Scott College in Decatur, Georgia, founded by her forebears? Or, would she prefer a substantial gift of the best books in my medical collection donated to the Rowland Medical Library of our University of Mississippi Medical Center here in Jackson?

She pondered over the choice for several days and then decided for the library contribution. She said that

Dedication of the Louise Scott Sams Hardy Rare Medical Book Collection. Left to right: Bettie Winn Hardy, Louise Roeska-Hardy, Louise Scott Sams Hardy, James D. Hardy, Katherine H. Little

we'd spent the better part of our adult lives here. I was very pleased, for many reasons.

Thus, I asked Dr. Julius M. Cruse, our most appropriately knowledgeable faculty member, to come to our home one morning early. I would depart, leaving him to select the best one hundred seventy-five items. This number was all that the library could accept at one time and place in an attractive display inside locked panels. The door was left open for future contributions when more space became available.

The University planned and mounted a splendid reception for the occasion. Vice Chancellor and Dean Wallace Conerly and Dr. Cruse first addressed the large attendance. I then conveyed to Dr. Conerly that Weezie wanted to say a few words. He was apprehensive but I assured him that I had written the remarks she wanted to read. I would stand beside her at the podium and, if she faltered, I would take over seamlessly and conclude the few remaining remarks.

But my assistance wasn't needed. Weezie read her material in a clear and firm voice beautifully.

Sadly, the collector knows that one day his beloved volumes must pass to other hands. And again be wafted around the world on the winds of the market.

What did I get out of my hobby, almost an avocation? First, it was my diamonds, the value of which need not be explained—again, to have and to hold and to enjoy, even with my very limited knowledge of French, for example. Second, it afforded me pleasure to hold in my hands a publication written by the great French physiologist Claude Bernard over a century ago. Third, it gave my thoughts and lectures greater dimensions and a certain freshness despite its age. Fourth, a respect for the authors of yore who helped advance medicine to its current status—kindred spirits. Fifth, many hours of special search through the catalogues of half a dozen rare medical history dealers. Sixth, a whole special life and acquaintance with these book colleagues. Seventh, a hobby to pursue in bookstores wherever. One of my surgical colleagues rushed to see the cathedral in whatever city we were. Another's hobby was to learn more about the physicians on the frontier and even farther west— often portrayed by Hollywood as drunkards, failures in the East, bereft of family and capable only of sobering up with pots of coffee to a point where they could operate on the kitchen table and save the damsel in dire distress.

What was the downside? At times the books received on order were by no means in the fine condition suggested by the catalogue. For example, when the time came that I must sell, the potential buyers complained that the identical books they had sold me twenty years earlier were in poor (unchanged) condition.

And one should not expect to enjoy financial appreciation. Without the mailing list of the professional book dealer, the solitary dealer may find it hard to locate buyers.

But perhaps the most egregious event was when a dealer offered me only $250 for a book that I had bought from him ten years previously for $1,200. I declined but proceeded anyway at $500, for we had to sell because of the occupancy contract deadline.

Therefore, would I do it again? *Of course!*

Books which JDH either Authored or Co-authored or
Edited or Co-edited

PROFESSIONAL BOOKS (JDH)

This writer single authored, or co-authored, or edited or co-edited some twenty-two books having to do with surgical physiology, operative surgery and surgical complications. There follows a brief synopsis of the genesis of some of these.

Surgery and the Endocrine System. The W.B. Saunders Company, Philadelphia, 1952. This slender volume derived from my perceived need for more accurate and complete information in teaching advanced "Physiology of Surgery" to a group of graduate nurses who came from all over the east to participate at Penn. For example, I found that the "bible" of human anatomy stated that all four parathyroid glands together weighed scarcely more than a gram (1000 milligrams). In the autopsy room, I found that each weighed about 30 milligrams, or approximately 120 milligrams for the four.

I proposed to Dr. Ravdin that I write a monograph and he endorsed my letter with a "Go Ahead."

At the time of its publication I asked John Dusseau, Editor, how many copies of such a book would have to be sold for the Saunders Company to recapture costs. He said, "If we sell 5,000 we break even; if we sell 7,500 we will make some money; if we sell 10,000 we all go out and get drunk!" The book sold well enough that Saunders recovered expenses and paid a small honorarium.

(Actually, some best sellers sell little more than 10,000 before going into paperback.)

Fluid Therapy. Lea and Febiger, Philadelphia. This modest sized volume was written in response to two considerations: First, it was solicited by the Lea and Febiger Company on the basis that no surgical fluid book had been published since Carl Moyer's book, which was now out of date. It was a simple project for me to undertake, for I was deeply immersed in water and electrolyte physiology at the time. It got excellent reviews and paid quite acceptable honoraria. But, despite repeated entreaties from the publisher, I did not prepare a second edition. (Most medical books require a revision about every four years.) By this time I had moved on to more frankly clinical surgical arenas, and wished to establish myself as an operating surgeon.

My most vivid memory of Fluid Therapy is that of a shocking mistake despite the multiple proof readings. I received a letter from a surgeon in Canada that discussion of HCl (hydrochloric acid) and $NaHCO_3$ (sodium bicarbonate) was erroneously reversed on page (X). Stunned, I quickly looked and found he was right.

In telling this to Dr. Warren N. Bell, a Canadian in charge of the hospital laboratories, he laughed and said, "I bet I can tell you who the correspondent was. It is his hobby to scour new books and write the author if he can find an error."

Complications in Surgery and Their Management. The W.B. Saunders Company, Philadelphia. Associate editor Robert Rowan had come to Jackson, along with other medical school cities, seeking potential authors and topics for new books. At dinner I brought up the fact that I knew of no books dealing with the inevitable complications that will occur no matter how perfect had been the operation itself. I noted that a book by Max Thorek of Chicago was long out of date. Bob Rowan immediately embraced the idea and asked if I would develop such a book. I replied that I was already overburdened but that, if my colleague Curtis Artz would take on responsibility as first editor (of the multiple authored book by specialist contributors) I would take on the responsibility as co-editor. Curt Artz promptly agreed enthusiastically and the book was successful immediately and throughout several new editions. There were those who commented that I was foolish to have the name "Hardy" become synonymous with "complications" and at times I had misgivings myself. At a meeting of the American Medical Association, an unknown physician, noting my name badge, came over and said, "Dr. Hardy, I would never have dreamed that one surgeon could have as many complications as you've had."

Even so, the "pain" was eased by the handsome royalties I "toted" to the bank.

Critical Surgical Illness. W.B. Saunders Company. This equally successful book by multiple contributors was quite as popular as Complications. I took the assignment because I wanted myself and my department in Jackson to gain stature on the national scene. It sold well from the beginning.

There was one problem at the outset: It had to do with the title. Francis Moore of Harvard had published a book entitled Critical Care of the Surgical Patient. The issue was whether or not I could the word "critical" without causing offense. But Dr. Moore said he had no objections.

Pathophysioslogy in Surgery. Baltimore, Williams and Wilkins, 1958. This substantial single author volume filled a special need at the time and was quite well received, with solid royalties. But despite repeated entreaties by the publisher, I did not prepare a second edition because I had moved on, out of active membership in the American Physiological Society and into the more clinical arenas.

Surgery of the Aorta and Its Branches. As a minor editor of one of the J.B. Lippincott special features, I undertook to write a chapter (I believe each month) about vascular surgery. When the series was finished,

Lippincott proposed that I refurbish the (five?) chapters and form them into a book. The book received decent reviews but, with vascular books sprouting all over, it had limited sales.

Hardy's Textbook of Surgery. Philadelphia, J.B. Lippincott Co., 1983. (Most people recognize only the "final" truth, being unaware of the circuitous route by means of which "truth" was arrived at.)

My experience with the Lippincott textbook of surgery began with a telephone call on Christmas day, perhaps 1980. Jonathan E. Rhoads was asking me, once again, to join the editorship of the Lippincott Textbook of Surgery, the surgical flagship title of most major medical publishers at the time. Of the four original authors of Allen, Harkins, Moyer and Rhoads, two—Harkins and Moyer—had died. Gerald Austen of Harvard and Massachusetts General Hospital had agreed to fill one vacancy and I was wanted to fill the other. Thus far, I had declined but, with Jonathan's comment that unless I joined to push it the new volume would not see completion, I reluctantly agreed. The first joint editorial board meeting was to be held at the Lake Placid Club ("comfort without ostentation"). It was there that Dewey had developed the Dewey decimal system for storing library books. An editor of the Lippincott Company was also present, our families were invited, and Dr. Terry Rhoads was most attentive to playing tennis with Bettie and Katherine and doing other things to keep them from being bored. Weezie did not play tennis.

The four original authors had taken turns spearheading the preparation of each new volume, and this year it was Garrott Allen's time to do this.

But Allen seemed to be at loose ends. Each morning we would meet for several hours and decide specific issues. But the next day Allen would propose that we discuss exactly that which I thought we had settled yesterday. After such days, I suggested to Dr. Rhoads privately that the situation seemed to be hopeless under the current leadership. Jonathan agreed but expressed the hope that at the forthcoming meeting of the Society of University Surgeons in New Orleans in February, we would find Allen in firm control. It was a very delicate situation.

But in New Orleans things were no better and clearly Lippincott was becoming deeply concerned.

Next, at the (spring) meeting of the American Surgical Association at the Century Plaza Hotel in Los Angeles, Lippincott asked for a meeting with a representative of the publisher at breakfast in the roof garden. No sooner had we finished the meal than the Lippincott representative, George Stickley, said bluntly that Lippincott wanted Allen and Rhoads to drop out. (Austen was not present and had withdrawn from the editorship). At this stunning turn of events, Jonathan looked across the table at Allen and said, "Gary, it looks like they don't want us anymore."

Stickley continued that Lippincott wanted me to take over the book as a sole editor.

What an awkward moment. I of course said that I would find it unacceptable to take over under these circumstances and that I must withdraw along with Drs. Rhoads and Allen. Needless to say, it was no longer a very convivial breakfast, and we shortly disbanded.

That night Mr. Stickley called me in my room and asked if I wouldn't reconsider. I replied that I'd known the book had very serious problems with Dr. Allen in the leadership role, but that Jonathan and I had been good friends for many years.

About one year later, Lippincott came to me once again, and by this time the dust had settled and bruised feelings had largely healed. I had given a lot of thought to a possible textbook, and this time I asked Jonathan if he would be offended if I undertook the proposed project and he said he would not.

Hardy's Textbook entered the field against formidable competition. Schwartz's with McGraw-Hill had been splendidly developed and was immediately popular. *Sabiston's Textbook of Surgery* with W.B. Saunders had been a bastion of surgery for decades, with multiple successive editors.

Our book got fine reviews and it sold well. But it did not exceed, even through a second edition, the success of its competitors.

CHAPTER 12

❧

And Gladly Teach

Before going to college at the University of Alabama I, like perhaps even most high school graduates, was undecided as to what career I should embrace. Of one thing I was certain, I did not want to continue in the lime business after what I had seen during the Depression. I liked farming but this occupation didn't seem to have much intellectual challenge. Then I began to consider teaching, perhaps of English. There was a long tradition of teaching in Mother's family.

My first teaching experience began in several directions during my sophomore (middle) year at Alabama. The first was the tutoring of a football player in English Literature. The professor asked me if I would tutor this student because he already had a job coaching if he could just get out of college. I replied, cautiously, that all I did was to feed back his own lecture material. He then said that if the football player could feed back anything near the same thing he would pass. (He did.)

Additional teaching experiences are presented in Chapters 1, 3, and 7.

SURGICAL RESIDENT TEACHING. The teaching opportunities and responsibilities of the resident in surgery were not dissimilar to those of the medical resident but with two major additions: the operating room and the weekly quiz sessions. Each of the surgical residents was assigned a quiz section of the students on the surgery rotation. I seem to recall that it was late on Friday afternoon. The purpose was to quiz the students on the reading assignments during the week, but also to give the moderator the opportunity to embroider the information with his clinical experience. Although the students were assigned to a particular resident or staff member, some would steal away and go to Dr. Julian Johnson's session. As chief of both thoracic surgery and a service of general surgery, he of course was able to discourse authoritatively on most surgical topics, spiced with clinical anecdotal experiences.

But my quiz section held up well. Incidentally, a tall lanky student on the back row I kept for last: If no other student knew the answer I called on Reemtsma and he unfailingly had the correct answer. He was later to become a luminary in the surgical firmament. Another bright student was named Waksman and, if memory serves, he was the son of the Waksman who won the Nobel prize for discovering streptomycin. This drug was the first truly effective for the treatment of tuberculosis, and this agent ultimately initiated the death toll for most tuberculosis sanatoria all over the world.

As a rule the student liked his experience in the operating room, even if he or she was not interested in embracing surgery for a career. The resident would take the time to allow the student to tie a few knots.

One former student, now a prominent radiologist, told me recently that he'd had not the slightest interest in surgery but that he'd elected the surgery rotation solely to be able to say that he had operated with me.

THE MEDICAL COLLEGE OF THE UNIVERSITY OF TENNESSEE, AT MEMPHIS. As noted previously, in Chapter 10, in addition to the usual ward teaching, I gave all the general surgery lectures four times the first year that I was there. I was the new and only full-time surgery staff member and the medical school was under the quarter system with another class graduating every three months.

THE UNIVERSITY OF MISSISSIPPI MEDICAL CENTER, JACKSON. As professor and chairman of the Department of Surgery, I now had the complete responsibility for the student teaching program in surgery. The lectures were given by all members of our staff, but for my small group teaching I elected to use the Socratic method on rounds or in small classes. I would first ask the question and then look at all the assembled students, allowing each to think hard before called upon, then I would ask a specific student for the specific answer. If the student answered immediately, well and good. But if it was obvious that the student did not know, I would quickly give the answer myself before there was time for embarrassment. And, in general, the students went along with this format.

But not always. One student froze and could utter not one word, but several months later she was ready and unloaded. Another student wrote, long after she was in surgical practice in South Carolina, that she had dreaded having to stand up in class; that Thomas Jefferson was barely able to address an audience. But this fine person was in double jeopardy. I had "appointed" her to monitor

273

the use of the various forms of the verb "to lie."

The most memorable contretemps came from another female student. The quarterly examination was just ahead and, to review the material covered during that period, I elected to take the principal topics and write each on a slip of paper which also bore a student's name. The student was to stand up and speak for two minutes on his or her topic. I stood at the door and passed these out as the students filed into the small classroom. If a student faltered, I immediately plunged in both to instruct and to avoid student embarrassment.

Well, when I called upon a young lady on the front row she turned ashen and said vehemently, "I won't do it."

So, to smooth over what had become an awkward situation, I quickly said that I could discuss anything for two minutes. Instantly, she stuck her head out of her shell and challenged, "Discuss Baroque art!"

"Well," I said, "There's been much discussion about Baroque art over the years but, since Professor Baroque and I were never close, I will discuss the French impressionists Renoir, Monet and van Gogh." Which I proceeded to do.

Another objective of our teaching program was to accustom students to take oral examinations, against the time in the future when they faced oral examinations in passing practice Board examinations.

On patient rounds I did "look" rounds. I would not let the intern or resident tell me what was wrong with a new patient until I had looked at him silently for a few moments. Then I would recite what I saw and what I thought was wrong with the patient. I was right more often than the housestaff expected, but I had the

Classroom Teaching: The professor, the student speaking, the class, the patient, and the X-rays on the viewbox.

advantage of longer experience than they.

At other times I stressed that it was important to get some idea as to what the patient did for a living, what home support we could expect when we discharged him. Thus, one day I walked over to a person unknown to me, to demonstrate. "Mr. Smith," I asked, "What do you do for a living."

"Why, Doctor, I am the beaver control officer for Leake County."

"Good heavens, are there that many beavers in Leake County?"

"Yes, Doctor, there's lots of beavers!"

"Well, I am impressed. How do you catch the beaver?"

"Doc, you don't catch the beavers, you blow them up. What you do is put dynamite in the hut they build in the water and then lead the control wire out into the nearby woods. Then you beat a dishpan to make a big racket, the

275

beavers run out of the woods and into their underwater house, and then you explode the dynamite."

"Well, Mr. Smith, it looks like you get them, all right."

Then he motioned me to come over close to him and he whispered, "Doc, don't kill 'em all, or you'll be out of a job!"

SURGICAL RESIDENT TRAINING. The development of a competent surgeon takes a long time, usually five years, plus two more if cardiothoracic training is achieved. And it proceeds seamlessly and continuously, with increasing responsibility each year. In addition to countless patient rounds, we have tried to be sure that each resident had operative experience with all the usual procedures. But these procedures change year by year and the young surgeon must be prepared to learn and advance with the new advances in his or her field.

I have also endeavored to have each more senior resident complete a short research project, write it up after statistical assessment and give it at a regional or national surgical meeting.

And, over all, this program has been reasonably successful. But there *have* been some awkward situations. For example, for some years I was active in the Southern Society for Clinical Research and I was unhappy that there was no discussion of each paper given, leaving the essayist wondering if his paper had been that bad. So, at the business meeting I proposed that next year each moderator be instructed to ask questions himself if there were none from the floor.

Well, one of our residents was to give a paper on this rather high-class program and I had rehearsed him time and again. At the meeting in New Orleans he read his ten-minute paper flawlessly. I was proud of and for him.

Then the moderator, as instructed by the Council, called for questions to the essayist from the large audience, and there were none.

So, the moderator began by asking our man what was the error of his method. We had been over this in Jackson, but our man said he did not know. The moderator again asked for questions from the audience; there were none. So, the moderator turned back to the essayist and asked, "Doctor, did you use any additional method to measure blood volume?" Our man said he had not. Then, desperate to ask some question that the essayist could answer positively, the moderator turned toward our essayist but, before he could utter another word, our essayist blurted out, "Doctor, I never thought much of this work myself!"

POSTGRADUATE EDUCATION. We realized that, after student and resident education had been established, we were obligated to continue the lifelong re-education of our surgical offspring.

To achieve this in part, we initiated the annual Mississippi Surgical Forum, (see Chapter 10) and also brought in a series of Visiting Professors. The institution of Visiting Professor is dealt with further in Chapter 16.

CHAPTER 13

The Transplantation of Organs and the Artificial Heart History

The possibility of replacing worn-out individual organs has challenged human imagination throughout the ages. Consider the imagery of the Greek chimera, the Minotaur and the wings of Daedalus and Icarus. But now this dream has been realized.

It would be hard to impart to beginners, at this late date, the huge excitement and challenge the pioneers of human organ transplantation felt in the 1950s and 1960s.

The beginning of modern transplantation may be said to have begun with the work of Father Gregor Mendel in Czechoslovakia in the middle of the 1800s. By crossing different colored peas in the monastery garden, he worked out the genetic laws of inheritance, the Mendelian laws of genetic inheritance which still hold. The genetic difference between a human donor and the human recipient of the organ determines the intensity of the immunologic rejection reaction in the recipient. Identical twins accept each's organs without rejection.

A contemporary of Mendel's was Charles Darwin of Great Britain, whose monumental work regarding the

Father Gregor Mendel, who developed the laws of genetic inheritance by growing different colored peas in the monastery garden in the middle of the 1800s.

origin of species was published and continues to be challenged today.

A next major advance was the discovery of human blood groups (A, O, B and AB) by Landsteiner at the early years of the 20th century. For this work he received the Nobel prize in 1930.

A next major scientist who contributed to transplantation development was Alexis Carrel. During the closing years of the 19th century and the early years of the 1900s, he and Guthrie transplanted organs in animals, especially the kidney in cats. They used the suture method of Dorfler of Germany, who had shown that vascular anastomoses using full thickness vessel wall were commonly successful. But the transplants between the unrelated (genetically different) cats failed in days or weeks. For his work in the general transplantation field, Carrel was awarded the Nobel prize in 1912. On the occasion of the republication of some of Carrel's work in the Journal of the American Medical Association, I was invited to contribute a companion article (J.A.M.A. **250**:954, 1983).

Enter Peter Medawar in the 1940s in England. In caring for burn patients during World War II, much skin grafting was required. However, the skin grafts from an unrelated donor failed after days or weeks or months. It had of course long been known that autotransplanted skin (from one site to another on the same donor) survived permanently. Medawar's group began investigations using mice. They concluded that the rejection was immunologic in nature, that the host's immune system could recognize between self and non-self. This theory was strengthened by the fact that a second graft from the original donor was rejected more rapidly than the first (the "second-set" phenomenon).

I had a forthcoming speech in London and had secured a letter of introduction to Professor Medawar at the University College of London. But when I introduced myself to his secretary, she said that the professor was frightfully busy and would not be able to see me.

Rising to leave, I happened to mention that I had this

Alexis Carrel, Nobel prize in 1912 for work in the field of organ transplantation.

Karl Landsteiner, Nobel prize in 1930 for his discovery of the human blood groups.

Joseph E. Murray, Nobel prize for demonstrating absence of rejection reaction between identical twins. Reproduced by permission of the University of Pennsylvania Press. (Memoirs)

Peter B. Medawar, Nobel prize in 1960 for demonstrating that allotransplant rejection was caused by immunologic attack between genetically different partners.

letter.

"Oh", she said, "just a minute." She disappeared behind a cloth screen and I heard whispering. Suddenly, a tall, handsome man in a white coat appeared, introduced himself and we chatted an embarrassing length of time about the status of transplantation in general but particularly in the United States. When I said that he and his group were considered the best theoretical unit in the world, he repeated again, "Oh no, my dear fellow, I must enter an immediate disclaimer, we've done nothing here."

He urged me to visit the British museum and the National Art Gallery. It was raining, so he seized an umbrella and escorted me out to a taxi.

I next spoke at the Royal College of Surgeons and began return to the United States the following day. While awaiting my flight from Atlanta to Jackson in the early morning hours, I picked up a newspaper and on the front page read "Medawar wins Nobel prize". I read on and it was indeed my Medawar. I immediately sent him the message: "Magnificent lifetime prize. No further disclaimers accepted here. Congratulations."

I received a handwritten note from him a week or so later. He had had no warning before a Swedish reporter arrived and began beating on his door. He had shared the prize with Sir Macfarlane Burnet of Australia (1960).

By this time transplantation research was performed in academic laboratories throughout the world, but it remained to demonstrate finally the absence of rejection if the human donor and the recipient were identical. This was done by Joseph E. Murray and his team at the Peter Bent Brigham Hospital of Harvard University in Boston in 1954. A kidney was transplanted from one identical twin to her identical sister who was in renal failure. There was no rejection. Murray was awarded the Nobel prize.

Tissue Typing and Immunological Therapy

TISSUE TYPING. The basic immunological barrier to allografting having been defined, it remained to search for ways in which to abrogate this barrier. Clearly the greater the genetical disparity, the greater the rejection reaction. Thus, it was pertinent to obtain donor tissue from a close relative who shared many chromosomes-genes-antigens with the prospective recipient. However, since a close and willing relative would not often be available, it became desirable to develop tissue typing—similar to ordinary blood typing but infinitely more complex—so that an unrelated donor whose tissue was reasonably compatible with the recipient might be found. A leader in the United States has been Terasaki at U.C.L.A. in Los Angeles.

Meanwhile, the major role of the thymus in providing the immune capability was discovered.

STORAGE. But living donors were limited in number and attention was turned to the use of cadaver organs. Hence the need for effective organ storage (preservation) capability became paramount. Numerous methods were variously employed, but continuous perfusion under cold conditions became a preferred method and that of Belzer of Wisconsin University became a gold standard in the United States. Cold temperatures were used for short periods of storage. With the use of cold perfusion methods, the useful life of cadaver donor organs was extended from a matter of several hours to days. This permitted shipping the organ or organs to distant transplant centers. But it raised a further host of ethical and moral problems already associated with organ transplantation in man.

Meanwhile the drugs and other modalities available for reducing the vigor of the rejection reaction between unrelated pairs began to improve. And so did the overall transplant success rate.

ETHICS AND MORALITY OF TRANSPLANTATION IN MAN. Organ transplantation was beset by ethical and moral questions from its inception, in contrast to skin allografts in the treatment of burn patients, which had been used for decades. There was a natural reluctance of the patient to have an organ from (to him) an unknown donor, reluctance of relatives to permit use of their deceased member's organs, and some religions opposed transplantation as well. Finally, the transplanters themselves were stressed when the prospective recipient asked what success he might expect, for they did not know themselves. When you enter a swamp, you don't expect to find paved roads.

Are Transplants Morally Wrong?

THE COMMERCIAL APPEAL, MEMPHIS

SUNDAY MORNING, MARCH 15, 1964

Reproduced by permission of the University of Pennsylvania Press. (Memoirs)

However, the success rate gradually improved, and the public experienced imagination and general acceptance. The more successful an operation becomes, the less immoral it is perceived to be.

THE EARLY WHOLE ORGAN TRANSPLANTERS IN THE UNITED STATES. It is always risky to pinpoint who did what first, but amongst the early North American transplant surgeons some individuals have stood out.

The Kidney. The transplantation group at the Peter Bent Brigham Hospital in Boston must surely be counted amongst the earliest clinical kidney transplanters. One of this group, Joseph Murray, received the Nobel prize.

The Liver. Both Moore of the Brigham and Stuart Welch, also of Boston were among the first to transplant the liver in man, but it was Starzl at the University of Colorado and, later, at the University of Pittsburgh who truly established liver transplantation as clinical therapy.

The Lung. The first lung transplant was performed by Hardy and Webb and team at the University of Mississippi Medical Center in Jackson. Substantial success was achieved only after Cooper and associates at the University of Toronto improved the technic of bronchial anastomosis. Today, lung transplantation is a routine therapy for end stage respiratory insufficiency in a variety of lung diseases.

The first **heart transplantation** in man was performed by Hardy and associates at the University of Mississippi Medical Center. This and the first lung transplant will be presented in some detail later.

The Pancreas and the Small Intestine. Considerable success has been achieved in the transplantation of these organs, but as yet neither organ transplant has achieved a dependable long term survival rate.

Selected Personal Experiences
With Transplantation (JDH)
(Plus Six Mississippi Firsts)

It was my good fortune to grow up surgically during the modern advent of vascular suturing and anastomosis for vascular problems, cardiac surgery and whole-organ transplantation.

As noted previously, Dorfler of Germany had reported the supremacy of full-thickness sutures in achieving consistently successful vascular anastomoses. And Carrel had been awarded the Nobel prize in 1912 in part for his extensive experimental work with vascular anastomoses in animals, including successful kidney transplantation and transplantation of the heart to the neck vessels. However, his work remained largely unused until Gross of Harvard in 1949 reported the successful use of aortic hemografts (now "allografts") for replacing long segments of the coarcted aorta.

The author has drawn liberally from his review in *The Chimera*, Vol. 8, No. 3, pp. 5-13.

Transfer of Vena Cava to Aorta in Pigs. As recorded previously, my first transplantation experience began when during my thoracic surgery residency (1949-1951) at the Hospital of the University of Pennsylvania, I was assigned a research project by Dr. Julian Johnson, Chief of the Service. I was to operate on twenty-five pound pigs, remove a segment of the infrarenal vena cava, then close the right flank wound, then roll the pig over, make a left upper thoracic incision and insert the vena caval segment into the thoracic aorta just distal to the left subclavian artery.

287

Transplantation Considerations in Memphis. Leaving the University of Pennsylvania in 1951 to add strength to the research activity at the University of Tennessee College of Medicine in Memphis, I found that a large number of burn patients were admitted to the John Gaston Charity hospital. These patients required skin grafting, but skin grafts from genetically different persons survived only weeks to months on the recipient.

This led to skin graft studies in rabbits, though these experiments of limited scope were never published. However, this work brought me into the transplantation field of research. Thus when I was appointed Chairman of the department of surgery at the new four-year medical school being developed in Jackson, Mississippi, I decided that a major segment of research at the new University of Mississippi Medical School would be devoted to the new field of organ transplantation.

The general field of organ transplantation was covered previously and thus only our personal experiences will be covered here.

Six Mississippi Firsts

Our department has been variously credited with having been the first in the United States or the world to perform the following transplantations:

1. Kidney autotransplantation in man for High Ureteral Injury. Report of first case. (J.A.M.A., 184:97, 1963)

2. Lung Homotransplantations in Man: Report of the initial case. (J.A.M.A. 186:1065, 1963)

3. Heart Transplantation in Man: Report of the first case. (J.A.M.A., 188:1132, 1964)

4. Adrenal Autotransplantation in Cushing's Disease. (Ann. N.Y. Acad. Sci., 120:667, 1964)

5. Intestinal Transplantation: Laboratory experience and report of a clinical case. (Am. J. Surgery, 121:150, 1971)
6. Replantation of the Uterus and Ovaries in Dogs, with Successful Pregnancy. (Arch. Surg. 92:9, 1966)

KIDNEY AUTOTRANSPLANTATION FOR HIGH URETERAL INJURY. Our group had begun kidney transplantation in the laboratory and the hospital of the University of Mississippi Medical Center in the late 1950s. Essentially we were following the lead of the kidney transplantation group at the Brigham Hospital in Boston.

For several years we had asked the urologists to refer to us any patient whose ureteral injury was so high that the remaining segment attached to an otherwise normal kidney would not reach to the bladder. To be sure, occasionally the severed end of the ureter was anastomosed to the opposite, healthy ureter. However, this procedure was rarely successful and it also jeopardized the function of the opposite (healthy) kidney and its ureter. Thus, urologists commonly simply removed the kidney and ureteral remnant on the side of the ureteral injury, if the opposite kidney was present and had good function. The length of life with only one normal kidney is almost that of the person who has both normal kidneys.

In 1962 we ourselves caused a high ureteral injury on the right side. The patient was a man in his 60s who had had lower aortic surgery elsewhere in 1956 for occlusive disease. The fabric graft placed at that time had now become aneurysmal. This was long before truly safe and durable fabric materials had become available. Aortic allografts had proved reasonably successful, but these

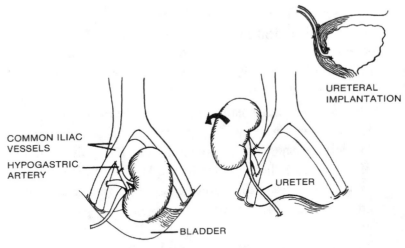

COMMON ILIAC
VESSELS

HYPOGASTRIC
ARTERY

URETERAL
IMPLANTATION

URETER

BLADDER

Autotransplantation of the kidney for the management of high ureteral injury. From Hardy, J.D.; Timmis, H.H.; Weems, W.L., et al., "Kidney Transplantation in Man: Analysis of Eleven Cases," Annals of Surgery 165 (1967): 933. Reproduced by permission of the University of Pennsylvania Press. (Memoirs)

were in short supply in 1956. Dacron eventually proved to be a dependable fabric graft substitute.

In August, 1962, the patient came to our University Hospital with a large aneurysm of the graft at its lower anastomosis. At operation the distal portion of the right ureter could not be identified in all the dense old scar tissue and beneath the aneurysmal aortic graft. However, it proved possible to expose a short segment of the right common iliac artery. This was swept clean of overlying tissue and a vascular clamp closed down on it. But unknown to us, at the 1956 operation the right ureter had been placed behind the fabric graft and it was severed along with the right common iliac artery. This accident was suspected several days later and demonstrated by radiological procedures.

What to do?

The left kidney exhibited hydronephrosis caused by compression of the left ureter by the large aneurysm. There were several possible methods for management of the severed right ureter: (1) leave the nephrostomy drainage tube in the right flank permanently to permit ready egress of urine from the right kidney? (2) anastomose the severed end of the right ureter to the left ureter near the left kidney? (3) simply remove the right kidney? or transplant the right kidney down to the pelvis on the right so that its shortened ureter would reach to the bladder?

Our urological consultants had deep reservations about transplantation but, I argued, if transplantation was not successful the right kidney could still be removed.

Incidentally, the ureter has its own intrinsic innervation which will propel urine toward the bladder when all other nerves have been severed.

Inasmuch as the patient was on our service, I elected to transplant the kidney. The transplantation was immediately successful since we had transplanted self to self. (Pasteur: *Fortune favors the prepared mind.*)

THREE VIGNETTES OF RENAL TRANSPLANTATION IN MAN. The early transplanters experienced numerous unusual experiences and surprises. Three of ours will suffice here.

I.M., a black female had undergone kidney transplantation after a long period on dialysis before a successful kidney transplant. One night very late I got a call from her home in Laurel, Mississippi, about 100 miles from Jackson. The physician said, "Irma just had a baby." I replied, "That is ridiculous. We've just seen her in the clinic and she is not even pregnant." He replied, "Doctor Hardy, I'm holding the baby right now!"

The fact was, Irma had gained a lot of weight but we thought it was due to the steroids she was taking to prevent rejection of her kidney transplant. She brought her boy to see me occasionally until he was a perfectly normal teenager.

Another patient, a dairyman in his early thirties was referred to us by the Ochsner Clinic in New Orleans, for they had not yet begun kidney transplantation. A live donor, a prisoner at the state penitentiary, had volunteered to give a kidney. Governor Barnett agreed to it, but promised nothing in return. (Such prison donors had been accepted in the United States at that time.)

We did not have tissue typing available then, but when it became available from Terasaki at U.C.L.A., the donor and the recipient were found to be a poor match. Even so, the transplanted kidney functioned well from the outset. (And someone spotted the prisoner on the street in Jackson only weeks later!) Some time later the patient stopped all his immunotherapy for months before telling us about it. At that time a renal biopsy disclosed very limited rejection, but he was induced to reinstitute his immunosuppressive therapy regimen.

The third vignette displayed the problems that may arise in getting a donor. The patient was a fourteen-year-old boy who was stabbed in the chest with something like an ice pick in a Jackson school hall amidst a group of other boys. He initially felt little, but on going downstairs to his locker, he saw that there was blood on his shirt over his heart. He suddenly collapsed on the floor, and by the time he was finally brought to our University Hospital emergency room, he appeared to be dead. Although he was resuscitated, with a beating heart and functioning kidneys, there was no evidence of brain function. He was declared brain dead by the neurologists and neurosurgeons. We asked the parents, both school teachers as I recall, if they would donate the boy's kidneys for transplantation. They said, "No, Doctor, we are opposed to having his kidneys used."

I replied that I could certainly understand.

When it became clear several days later, I told them that we had done everything we could but that he would probably die that night.

About four o'clock in the morning the hospital called and said that the boy's parents wanted me to come down. I remonstrated mildly, since I had already done everything possible and had explained the situation to them, but when they insisted I got dressed and went down. "Doctor," the father said, "We want to give our boy's kidneys for transplantation."

"That's certainly generous of you," I said. They went through the formality of signing the consent forms.

As I was about to walk away, the father said, "Dr. Hardy, don't you want to know why we changed our minds about giving the kidneys?"

"Why, yes, I do."

"Doctor, his mother and I were afraid you wouldn't work quite as hard with our boy if you were waiting to get his kidneys."

Lung Homotransplantation in Man. Investigations of lung transplants were begun in the second half of the 1950s. Performed and published were experiments dealing with, first, the reimplanted lung, usually in dogs but in a variety of other animals as well. These studies included operative techniques, respiratory function of the transplanted lung, regeneration of lung lymphatics, regeneration of nerves (histologically and as reflected in the return of the Hering-Breuer reflex) the effect on respiration of the differential division of the structures of the pulmonary hilum, allotransplantation (including relief of induced pulmonary artery hypertension), and growth of the reimplanted lung in puppies.

THE FIRST LUNG TRANSPLANT IN MAN. Deaths associated with pulmonary failure are common in all general hospitals. The commonest causes are emphysema and lung cancer, both almost always caused by cigarette smoking. In early 1963 Dr. Watts Webb, my colleague in doing the thoracic surgery in the University Hospital, and I approached the Dean-Vice Chancellor, Robert Q. Marston, presented our extensive research over a period of seven years using hundreds of animals, and requested permission to transplant a lung in man if the appropriate clinical-ethical-moral opportunity should present. Two patients in our sister V.A. Hospital could have met these requirements. One of these aspirated vomitus into his lungs and was almost surely going to die if remedial therapy was not successful. It was clear, within hours, that he would die soon, but we had no donor and he died. The second patient had extensive bilateral alveolar cell lung cancer and only a very small residual functioning lung tissue. He was in terminal pulmonary insufficiency. But we had no donor and he died.

However, these two patients showed that lung transplantation would be clinically and ethically feasible at some point in the future.

REPORT OF THE FIRST LUNG TRANSPLANT IN MAN. On April 15, 1963, a 58 year old dyspneic white man was

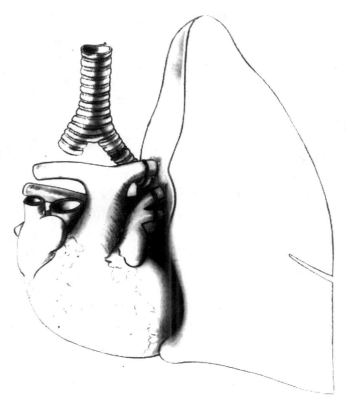

Operative technique used for transplantation of the first lung in man. Hardy, James D., Webb, Watts R., Dalton, Martin L., Jr., and Walker, George R., Jr., J.A.M.A. 1963; 186:1065-1074. From Hardy, J.D., "The Transplantation of Organs," Surgery 56: (1964): 685. Reproduced by permission of the University of Pennsylvania Press. (Memoirs)

admitted to our University Hospital with the history of repeated attacks of pneumonia which antibiotic therapy had failed to halt. A heavy smoker, he had lost 26 pounds since December, 1962. Chest X-ray revealed virtual opacification of the left lung and advanced emphysema in the right lung. Bronchoscopy with biopsy revealed almost complete occlusion of the left main-stem bronchus by squamous cell carcinoma, with distal suppuration. Even so, the left lung was supplying a limited amount of his reduced respiratory capacity. His chronic renal disease prompted a percutaneous renal biopsy which was interpreted as revealing chronic membranous glomerulonephritis.

After extensive further laboratory studies and discussions among our team members, we agreed to offer the patient a lung transplant at the time the diseased left lung was removed to excise the cancer and to cure his pneumonitis and abscess formation. His renal function was marginal, but consultants believed it was adequate to support the proposed operation. The patient and the family accepted the proposed transplant.

Thus, on June 11, 1963, a donor left lung became available, the patient's left lung was excised despite the fact that the tumor had invaded the parietal pleura, and the donor lung from a man who had just died from a massive spontaneous intracranial hemorrhage was inserted into the recipient.

Both surgical teams, the one harvesting the donor lung and the one removing the left lung of the recipient, functioned superbly. The transplanted lung performed immediately, as demonstrated by the oxygen content of the pulmonary artery ("venous" blood) and the pulmonary veins ("arterial" blood).

As Dr. Webb and I approached the entrance to the surgery suite, we were told that the civil rights leader Medgar Evers had just died in our emergency room from a gunshot wound to the chest. (It was actually voiced in some quarters that we had used one of his lungs for the transplant donor.)

In brief, the transplanted lung remained expanded and functioned as an effective organ of respiration until his death at 19 days from renal failure and general debility. The immunosuppressive therapy had consisted of azathioprine, prednisone, and radiation to the thymus gland. Histologic study of the transplant revealed only minimal evidence of rejection.

Clearly, lung transplantation would eventually provide effective therapy for otherwise fatal pulmonary insufficiency.

THE FIRST HEART TRANSPLANTATION IN MAN. The transplantation of hearts in dogs was begun by Webb in our laboratories in 1956 and short survival was published in 1957 (Surg. Forum, 1957; 7:302). Following the first lung transplant in man in June, 1963, Webb and I again approached Dean-Vice Chancellor Marston. We presented the data achieved in the laboratory and were given permission to proceed with a heart transplant in man if the appropriate clinical and ethical requirements were met.

Many potential recipients were evaluated, but in each instance it appeared that the patient might survive with non-operative management; or, if the patient was clearly terminal without a heart transplant, no donor heart was available. It was not acceptable at that time, in 1963, to remove a still beating heart, even from a brain dead donor. Head injury patients were considered the ones most likely to provide a suitable donor heart.

As time passed, it became increasingly clear that a circumstance where the acceptable prospective recipient and the no longer beating heart from the prospective donor would occur at the same time was unlikely. Our

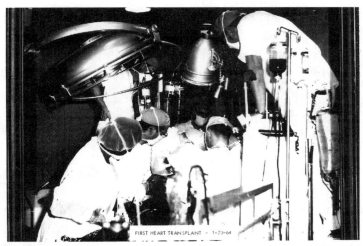

FIRST HEART TRANSPLANT - 1-23-64

Reproduced by permission of the University of Pennsylvania Press. (Memoirs)

plan was to gain permission to insert femoral artery and venous catheters and thus to perfuse the heparinized donor while a thoracic incision was made and the heart removed when death occurred.

Meanwhile, it was difficult to get kidney donations, and I had visited Keith Reemtsma at Tulane University where he had achieved remarkable early results with the transplantation of chimpanzee kidneys into a series of human patients. Thus, we bought four chimpanzees for possible transplantation in man when no suitable cadaver kidney was available. (Dependable long-term renal dialysis was not yet available to us.)

On January 21, 1964, a 68 year old white man was referred to our surgical service with gangrene of the lower portion of his left leg. He had had hypertensive cardiovascular disease for many years, for which he had been taking digitalis and diuretics. Two nights earlier he had been admitted to his community hospital in a comatose state and with no detectable blood pressure. At that time rapid atrial fibrillation had been recorded, and vasopressor drugs in high doses had been required to elevate the blood pressure to a systolic level of 100 mm. Hg. By the following morning, however, it was possible to maintain his blood pressure level with minimal drug therapy. His sensorium had cleared slightly.

This was his overall condition when he arrived at our University Hospital. The gangrenous portion of the left leg was quickly amputated on January 22, without noticeable effect on the patient's general condition.

By January 23, 1964, however, it had become clear that the patient would not survive, and the opinion of the cardiologist was as follows: "From the cardiovascular standpoint, the situation is unequivocally critical due to myocardial failure and apparent multiple emboli arising from the left atrium or ventricle: By all rules, life expectancy can be measured in the case by hours only."

With terminal cardiovascular collapse so imminent, we considered heart transplantation. The patient had not truly regained consciousness, but the family was well aware of his years of decline and their representatives signed for heart transplantation if a suitable donor heart became available. In fact, a brain dead trauma victim lingered on in the I.C.U., but we knew that no organ harvesting was acceptable at that time until the heart itself had stopped beating. Thus, we began to think of the largest of the 4 chimpanzees, for it had long been known that chimpanzees were far more closely related genetically to humans than were other lower primates such as the baboon. In fact, chimpanzees and humans share approximately 98% of the same chromosomes. And we had first-hand knowledge of the early success of the

*The First Heart Transplant in Man. Hardy, J.D., et al,
J.A.M.A. 1964; 188:1132-1140.
From Hardy, J.D.; Chavez, C.M., "Transplantation of the
Heart," in Hardy, J.D., ed., Human Organ Support and
Replacement (Springfield, Ill.: Charles C Thomas, 1971).
Courtesy of Charles C Thomas.*
Reproduced by permission of the University of Pennsylvania Press. (Memoirs)

Tulane group with the transplantation of chimpanzee kidneys into humans.

At approximately six o'clock in the evening the prospective recipient went into shock and further delay was out of the question if there was to be any hope of successful transplantation. In brief, the patient was rushed to the operating room, the chest opened and cardiopulmonary bypass instituted. Meanwhile, the largest chimpanzee had been anesthetized. But at this point serious constraint developed among the five members of our transplant team. Should the chimp heart be used, even though the patient was at the point of death and supported only with the heart-lung machine? The

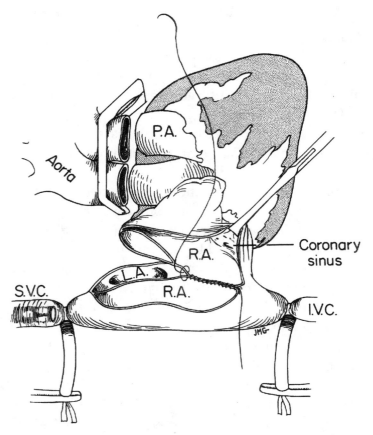

*Operative technique used for transplantation of the first heart
in man. Hardy, J.D., Chavez, Carlos M., Kurrus, Fred D., Neely,
William A., Eraslan, Sadan, Turner, M.Don, Fabian, Leonard
W., and Labecki, Thaddeus, D., J.A.M.A. 1964; 188:1132-1140.
From Hardy, J.D.; Chavez, C.M.; Eraslan, S.; et al., "Heart
Transplantation in Dogs: Procedures, Physiologic Problems,
and Results in 142 Experiments," Surgery 60 (1966): 361.*
Reproduced by permission of the University of Pennsylvania Press. (Memoirs)

head injury patient in the I.C.U. continued to exhibit
effective heart action. I was well aware, from the "first
lung" experience, that the transplantation of a heart

would prompt a world-wide sensation; and to use a "monkey" heart would cause even greater criticism. Accordingly, I polled each member of the transplant team. Four were in favor of proceeding with the chimpanzee heart. The fifth abstained but did not oppose.

The harvesting team in the adjacent operating room harvested the chimpanzee heart as we excised the human heart. It was an awesome sight to contemplate the empty space that the patient's greatly enlarged heart had occupied. The chimpanzee heart was sutured in place in about 45 minutes, with the same operative technique that we'd used in the laboratory. The condition of the donor heart had been preserved by the retrograde perfusion of cold, oxygenated blood through the coronary sinus, as we had done with heart transplants in calves. A forceful beat was restored and supported a blood pressure of 90 to 100 mm. Hg. for about 90 minutes. However, the chimpanzee heart was too small for the large man, and his metabolic condition was deeply impaired by preoperative periods of shock.

But much knowledge was gained by this first heart transplant in man. First, the heart could be readily transplanted in man and a forceful beat restored. It was clear that the transplantation of a healthy human donor heart, when transplanted into a human being in reasonably stable metabolic balance, might well provide additional years of life.

THE AFTERMATH TO THE FIRST HEART TRANSPLANTATION IN MAN. The publicity, the outcry, the criticism were enormous. Public media reporters seemed to come out of the woodwork. We hunkered down and waited it out. However, there were redeeming moments. While the

Mario S. Barnard
(S. Afr. Med. J. <u>41</u>, 1967):

"Hardy and co-workers had in 1964 transplanted a chimpanzee heart into a man...a regular forceful beat was restored...the feasibility of cardiac transplantation was now irrefutable."

Barnard war nicht der erste*

*Bernard was not the first

Diesen Mann kennt die ganze Welt: Prof. Barnard. Er nahm Ende 1967 in Kapstadt die spektakuläre Herzverpflanzung an Louis Washkansky vor

Diesen Mann kennt keiner: Dr. Hardy in Jackson. Kollegen warnten ihn im Sommer 1963: »Bei einem Mißerfolg sind Sie ein toter Mann«

From Jurgen Thorald, Die funf Patienten.

criticism in the United States among physicians was often stringent, this was not true in Europe. When I traveled there I was frequently asked why we had not already done another. The answer was that I could expect the

University Administration to protect me just so far. And I had noted that when one loses his academic post, for whatever reason, he is not likely to get another one of comparable significance. I decided to wait until Shumway and his group transplanted a heart in man.

By 1966 the criticism had begun to subside. My old Chief of Surgery at Pennsylvania said, "Jim, there's been enough of the criticism, it's time for the counterattack."

This was reminiscent of the legend of the report of a committee of the French Academy of Science sent to Lyon to explore the report that the surgeon there had performed a colostomy successfully. They found that he had. Their report was "It is often sufficient to know in the large that a thing may be possible" (Littre, Royal Academy of Science, Paris, 1710).

And, finally, there was the toast of Professor Vichnevsky in Moscow in 1971 upon the awarding me two medals, one for the first lung transplant and one for the first heart transplant. "Dr. Hardy, a lot of water has passed under the bridge since you transplanted the first heart in 1964. But remember this, 'No words can ever be taken from a poem, nor notes from a song.'"

> # "IT IS OFTEN SUFFICIENT TO KNOW IN THE LARGE, THAT A THING MAY BE POSSIBLE AND NOT TO DESPAIR OF IT AT FIRST SIGHT."
>
> LITTRE, ROYAL ACADEMY OF SCIENCE, PARIS, 1710

James Daniel Hardy (1918–)
Professor of Surgery, University of
Mississippi

Richard Rowland Lower (1929–)
Professor of Surgery, Medical College
of Virginia

Norman Edward Shumway (1923–)
Professor of Surgery, Stanford
University

Christiaan Barnard (1922-2001)
Professor of Cardiac and Thoracic
Surgery, University of Cape Town
Courtesy of Mrs. Owen D. Wangensteen

The Origianl Heart Transplanters in Man

HUMACKER, H.B., EVOLUTION CARDIAC SURG.

Scientific Programme

FRIDAY MORNING, June 6th 1969

SITE: Man and his World, Auditorium Ste-Hélène
9:00—GENERAL SESSION
"THE WORLD'S EXPERIENCE"

Chairman: James D. Hardy, M.D.,
University of Mississippi, Jackson, Miss., U.S.A.

Panelists

1 GROOTE SCHUUR HOSPITAL, Cape Town, South Africa.
  Christiaan N. Barnard, M.D.
2 STANFORD UNIVERSITY, Palo Alto, Calif., U.S.A.
  N.E. Shumway and E.B. Stinson, M.D.
3 TEXAS HEART INSTITUTE, Houston, Texas, U.S.A.
  Denton A. Cooley, Grady L. Hallman, M.D.
4 MEDICAL COLLEGE OF VIRGINIA, Richmond, Virginia, U.S.A.
  Richard R. Lower, Eric Kemp and Walter H. Graham, M.D.
5 BROUSSAIS HOSPITAL, Paris, France.
  Charles Dubost and J.P. Cachera, M.D.
6 MONTREAL HEART INSTITUTE, Montreal, Canada.
  Pierre Grondin and Gilles Lepage, M.D.
7 UNIVERSITY OF SAO PAULO MEDICAL SCHOOL,
  Sao Paulo, Brazil.
  E.J. Zerbini and Luiz V. Decourt, M.D.
8 METHODIST HOSPITAL, Baylor University, Houston,
  Texas, U.S.A.
  Michael E. De Bakey, M.D.
9 GUY'S HOSPITAL, London, England.
  Donald Ross, M.D.
10 UNIVERSITY HOSPITAL, Ann Harbor, Michigan, U.S.A.
  Donald R. Kahn, J.A. Walton and Herbert Sloan, M.D.
11 UNIVERSITY OF TORONTO, Toronto, Canada.
  W.G. Bigelow, M.D.

The first world conference on heart transplantation.
Reproduced by permission of the University of Pennsylvania Press. (Memoirs)

ADRENAL AUTOTRANSPLANTATION FOR CUSHING'S DISEASE. In 1962 we had to reoperate on a patient upon whom we had performed subtotal adrenalectomy for Cushing's disease. The right adrenal had been totally removed, but a small amount of the left adrenal had been left, attached to the central vein. But now she had recurrent Cushing's syndrome. We had been reluctant to risk adrenal crisis in this particular patient by performing total (bilateral) adrenalectomy, lest she fail to manage her cortisone replacement therapy. At the second operation we transplanted the residual segment of the left adrenal

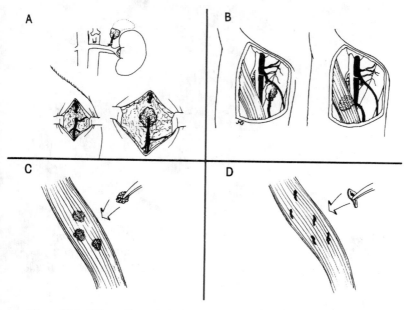

Virtually all the adrenal slices in the right sartorius muscle survived, and in one patient each slice formed a small "tumor." One patient developed recurrent Cushing's disease from these nodules. A small tumor of the anterior lobe of the pituitary was later excised.

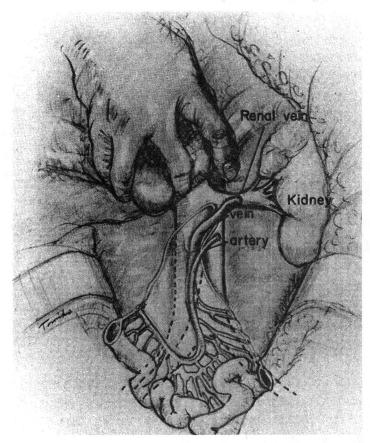

Alican, F., Hardy, J.D., Cayirli, M., Varner, J.E., Moynihan,
P.C., Turner, M.D., and Anas, P., Intestinal transplantation:
Laboratory experience and report of a clinical case. Am. J. Surg.,
121:150, 1971.
From mother to small son who had lost virtually all his small
bowel by volvulus and whose intravenous access sites were
exhausted. The inferior vena cava was thrombosed up to the
renal veins. Note that the artery of the transplant was sutured
to the aorta and the vein to the left renal vein.

gland to the right thigh. Biopsy under local anesthesia showed that the transplant was viable, but its function was not sufficient to allow discontinuation of all oral steroid therapy. In a subsequent series of patients, however, we implanted multiple slices of the excised adrenal tissue into the sartorius muscle in the right upper thigh, this after total intraabdominal adrenalectomy. Virtually all these slices of adrenal tissue in the thigh survived, and in most instances oral cortisone therapy could be discontinued. In fact, in one patient each of the adrenal slices became a small tumor and caused recurrent Cushing's syndrome.

Eraslan, Sadan, Hamernick, Robert J., and Hardy, James D., Arch. Surg. 1966; 92:9-12. Reimplantation of the uterus and ovaries in dogs with successful pregnancy. (This study was prompted by a gynecologist as to whether we could transplant these organs in a newly married young woman whose pelvic organs had been removed earlier for questionable indications.)

However, eventually improved radiological advances permitted the demonstration of a small tumor of the anterior lobe of the pituitary gland and it was surgically removed.

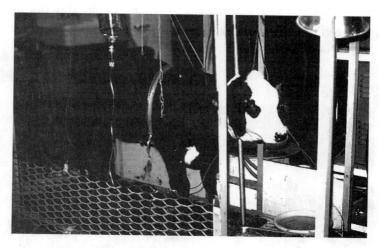

Alice. A calf at one month after total artificial heart replacement. Akutsu, T., et al. 1967.

CHAPTER 14

The Nitty-Gritty of Surgical Practice

This chapter is devoted to the everyday problems and concerns of the practicing surgeon. Included are:

1. The surgeon enters the operating room with many things on his mind.
2. Five illustrative cases which depict major everyday surgical dimensions.
3. Complications and their Management
4. Setting the charges.
5. Whom to "sign out" to.
6. Amnesia: traumatic and anesthetic.
7. The Hospital Director's Problems.

THE ACADEMIC SURGEON ENTERS THE OPERATING ROOM (some of his check-list items, not necessarily in order of significance):

The overall success of an operation can be influenced by the operating room personnel who have sterilized the instruments improperly, who pass the wrong solution up to the sterile operative field, or report a sponge count as correct when it was incorrect, or even by personnel far removed from the operating room itself: (Over my 55 years I have seen or know of each of the mishaps listed.)

- Pharmacy: Delivers incorrect fluid, or the correct fluid but in the wrong concentration. Or two look-alike drug bottles and the circulating nurse passes up the wrong one without reading the label.
- The Supply Room: "Out" of a major routine need. Someone did not place a timely order.
- The Record Room: The old chart cannot be found to allow the surgeon to learn what was done at a previous operation (as with the abdomen).
- Radiology: The wrong films (chest) or the two sides mislabeled. (Check by teeth.)
- Laboratory: Incorrect data, especially potassium (heart needs) or prothrombin levels (in the patient just weaned off Coumadin).
- Patient transport: Bring the wrong patient.
- Physical examination: Hernia recorded on the wrong side.
- And so on. Note that the anesthesia and its conduct has not yet been cited above. But it will be, below, for the anesthesia is the major hazard in most routine operations. It would be hard to cause major, life-threatening damage in the repair of a simple groin hernia, but poor anesthesia management in that same patient could cause major injury and even death. For many years the patient's blood pressure measured with the arm cuff was the principal gauge available to the anesthetist. Then came continuous intraarterial instrumentation. Next, repeated measurements of the arterial blood gas values, and the continuous

electrocardiographic monitoring.

In sum, the elements that maintain the normal blood pressure are the pump (heart), something to pump (blood volume) and something to pump against (peripheral resistance provided by normal tone and contraction of the small vessels at the periphery). The roles of the heart and the blood volume are obvious but the maintenance of the peripheral resistance is more complex. This poor peripheral resistance can result from hypoxia or systemic infections.

Judgment. This is the precious quality which can be achieved only through experience. The superior clinical surgeon knows when to operate and when not to operate. Or when to stop while he is still ahead. When to call in a colleague to assist in the control of, or the avoidance of, massive hemorrhage that could prove fatal. It takes a certain type of courage to admit that one needs more help but I learned from my chief of thoracic surgery in Philadelphia. A master surgeon himself, he would have called in the janitor if it would render him successful in his "fight for the patient's life."

FIVE ILLUSTRATIVE PATIENTS.

E.C. A victim of Hospital Jealousy. This late middle aged patient came to me in the following way. I received a telephone call from the director of a hospital about one hundred miles from Jackson. He said that he was calling from an outside telephone booth and that it could cost him his job if it became known that he had called me. But that he simply could not in all conscience stand by and see a patient in his hospital die from intestinal obstruction and probable dead bowel. No surgeon there would tackle the challenge, but they did not want the patient sent to

Jackson. Would I take him?

"Yes," I replied, "Just give his family a note to present at our emergency room, stating that I am to be called immediately."

Well, when I saw him I could certainly understand the surgical reluctance in his home city. His greatly distended abdomen exhibited what appeared to be multiple loops of dead intestine that would shortly erode through the tissue-paper thin skin. All this was secondary to an abdominal operation he'd had many years before.

In brief, we waded into this daunting situation and after many hours we managed to salvage a few feet of normal small intestine, to provide food absorption.

His postoperative course was marked by coma, a cardiac arrest in the I.C.U. which was reversed by an alert resident, renal failure that required dialysis, and massive gastric hemorrhage that required an emergency subtotal gastrectomy while he was still comatose.

I told our residents that if they managed to get Mr. C. out of the hospital alive I would take the whole crew to a steak dinner.

Well, Mr. C. finally recovered. We had put so much time and toil on him that I actually escorted him out to his family waiting in the car. As we walked I said, "Mr. C., we are going to have the 'C.' memorial dinner tomorrow."

"But, Doctor, I thought that memorial ceremonies were for patients who had not made it."

"Mr. C., you were so close to death, so many times, that I think we can just fit you in!"

K.H. The value of debulking the tumor in this instance.

"Debulking" a malignant tumor is often fraught with

serious complications and the patient is of course not cured. But K.H. had been diagnosed at a distant hospital as having hyperinsulinism, presumably due to a tumor of the pancreatic islets which secrete insulin. The patient had to take in food every three or four hours and at times his wife would find him passed out below the refrigerator door where he had sought to drink orange juice.

The local surgeon explored the abdomen and found that the patient did have the suspected tumor, but it was malignant and had a rich blood supply. Having encountered serious hemorrhage, the operator backed out and referred the patient to our University Hospital. With a far more adequate blood bank than the operating surgeon, I explored again and assessed the situation. The cancer that was producing excessive amounts of insulin involved the major vessels of the upper abdomen (portal vein, vena cava and aorta) and had involved the liver and retroperitoneal spaces. Cure was impossible, but by excising as much tumor as feasible, we were able to diminish the hyperinsulinism repeatedly at five operations over a period of fourteen years.

L.D. The value of the operations to reduce morbid obesity. I had long declined to honor requests that I perform one of the operations developed to reduce morbid (health threatening) obesity when all counseling, diets and "Weight Watcher" programs had failed. But one of my applicants was a professional's twenty-something daughter in Jackson. Finally, after talking with surgical colleagues throughout the country who had already chalked up considerable experience in the field, I decided that I would perform the most commonly employed small intestine bypass procedure in ten patients and then assess this experience before proceeding onward.

The first patient was the young lady cited above, and the results were remarkable. After losing about 100 pounds, she became truly beautiful, got a job she had wanted, and became engaged. There were no detectable effects on her general health.

Without recounting further details, let it be said that hypertension and diabetes (type 2) receded along with the weight loss. There were no deaths but one patient exhibited impending liver damage and thus the normal continuity of the small intestine was restored at a second operation. Another developed intestinal obstruction which had to be relieved at a second operation.

But back to L.D. She was a huge black woman, quite tall, the wife of a cordwood cutter out from Natchez and weighed about 400 pounds. She had seven children. She had been unable to lose weight with the limited facilities available to her. She was so fat and large that she could not reach to clean herself.

I asked her, "Who would take care of your seven children when you were here in the hospital?" She said, "I done taken care of that. The oldest daughter, ten, will cook for the family. Then each of the others will look after the one just beneath."

We did the operation, and she gradually lost about 150 pounds over the following eighteen months.

When she returned to follow-up clinic she was all smiles. "Dr. Hardy, I can now keep myself clean and, for the first time in years, I can go places with my family!"

Baby X. My worst case. Quite some years ago I was asked by Professor Philip Sandblom of Lund, Sweden, and Lousanne, Switzerland, to contribute my "worst case" to a book he was planning to compile. I declined but I have thought a lot about it over the decades since then. And, of the countless operations in which I participated, the second operation on this little boy may have been the "worst."

The little two-year-old boy had been operated on by us at birth for coarctation of the aorta. But now the size of the opening achieved at the first operation was too small to permit adequate blood flow to the lower part of the body. He was the parents' only child.

At this second operation I told the thoracic resident that he should open the chest and gain good hemostasis, but then, under no circumstances was he to approach the previous operative site on the aorta. Because of scar tissue and friability of the aorta, extreme caution and delicacy would be required. I told him to call me up in the animal experimental laboratory the minute he had the chest open.

But the next thing I knew was the message of one of our most experienced scrub nurses: "Dr. Hardy, come quick!"

The resident had disobeyed my instructions, dissected down around the aorta and got into potentially fatal hemorrhage unless the bleeding could be controlled: Just picture the situation: First the little patient's total blood volume was perhaps 300 cc. We could not put him on the pump from our position. The anesthesiologist was frantically trying to get an additional venous route for transfusion. Every time we retracted the left lung to visualize the site of hemorrhage (currently being controlled with firm thumb pressure), the heart faltered and threatened to stop. The pediatrician came in every few minutes to ask what he could tell the parents.

To sum up, it took us all afternoon and far into the night to control the hemorrhage with fine sutures and maintain an open lumen in the aorta. The patient survived.

I said nothing to the resident at that time. Recrimination could wait—we needed to save the patient.

But about twenty years later he sidled up to me at a medical meeting and thanked me for not "eating him out." He said that he was already "bleeding" over his transgression and that no further reminder was needed. But while doctors may forgive, they don't forget.

S.T. Large Painful Aneurysm of the Thoracic Aorta Eroding the Spine. Trust.

I had just told this elderly black man that we would operate the next day. But he called me back. After looking at me silently with his one eye for a few brief moments he said, "Doc, we ain't talked much but I'se countin' on you."

And trust is the only milieu in which successful and happy surgical practice can be carried on.

COMPLICATIONS. No matter how perfectly the operation itself was performed, complications will at times occur: For example, heart attack, stroke, or pulmonary embolus. Possibly the most careful of surgeons I have known used to say that he did not want a surgeon who had never had a postoperative complication; that he wanted a surgeon who had had the inevitable complications and knew how to get out of them. But most non-medical people rightly view the development of a major complication as a threat to life. When my first private patient, referred to me for a cholecystectomy, after I finished the general surgical residency, asked me what

James D. Hardy

my fee would be. While I was trying to think of a proper fee amount, she blurted out, "Doctor, I mean unless complications set in, then I know it would be more."

But I was thinking, "Dear Lady, if complications set in I probably would pay you to leave town!"

The number of postoperative complications that occur can be diminished by careful preparation of the patient for operation.

HOSPITAL DEATHS DUE TO MEDICAL ERRORS. There has recently been renewed effort to assess how many deaths from medical errors occur in the United States each year. There has been a wide range of conclusions and we are not prepared to take a firm stand here. However, all physicians know of one or more such untoward events. And those that occur on surgical services are often the most visible. Some have resulted in justifiable lawsuits and others may have passed quietly into history. The

319

cause of death is assessed firmly at the surgical mortality conference in most university hospitals and the death assigned to ED, ET, PD, EAM, EJ, EM, UC (see Chapter 5). Unfortunately, the surgical mortality conference in perhaps a majority of hospitals in the United States is not as searching as it could be.

SETTING THE CHARGES. My first experience with the need to do this occurred with the patient who was to have the cholecystectomy. After a college degree, medical school degree, two plus years in the Army and the equivalent of seven years surgical residency—after all this I should expect the patient to pay me?

Hearing my uncertainty out in the hall Miss Lucas, the office manager and a marvelously capable person, called me into her little office, put her feet up in a chair, lit a cigarette, and said, "Dr. Hardy, sit down and let me give you the facts of life. These are private patients and they want to make arrangements for their coming hospitalization. I will give you the reasonable charges that the other members of our staff make for each type of surgery and then, if the case proves unusually difficult or prolonged, you can adjust your fee accordingly. And then there are those who have little except their pride, and these we charge less."

I always charged moderate fees, and then Medicare and other forms of third party modified many or most billing policies throughout the country.

WHOM TO SIGN OUT TO? Having been a hybrid who had passed his boards in general and in cardiothoracic surgery, I was limited in that the responsible surgeon had to be able to handle general surgery including major trauma, plus cardiothoracic cases. Thus, after Dr. Watts

Webb had accepted the chair of cardiothoracic surgery at The University of Texas Medical School in Dallas (Southwestern), I had limited staff that I could call upon.

But when one is signed out to another surgeon, the substitute is instantly responsible for one's patients. Hopefully, the substitute will call you if any serious problem develops in a patient, but this is not always the case. One particular occurrence comes to mind. This elderly lady had come in by ambulance for massive gastrointestinal bleeding. Since the blood was bright red and gastroscopy was non-revealing, we took the patient at once to the radiology department to try to identify the bleeding site. But the bleeding was so brisk that blood obscured the site of the bleeding vessel. We then turned to barium enema and arteriography, but it was soon obvious that immediate operation was imperative. However, as is all too often the case, once inside the abdomen, it was not possible to identify the level of the bleeder using the usual maneuvers. Therefore, we resected most of the colon and anatomosed the terminal ileum to the upper reaches of the rectum that could be cleared by inspection.

The patient did well thereafter and I went on to an N.I.H. commitment. I left explicit instructions that I was to be called at any time, night or day, if any complications developed. Well, about the third postoperative day she began to run a moderately elevated temperature, not a surprise under the circumstances. Full antibiotic therapy had been initiated during and following the operation.

At this point the resident reminded the staff man, several times, that I wanted to be called about this private patient at any time. The staff man said that, no, he was now in charge and that he would operate immediately.

The suspected leakage at the ileo-rectal anastomosis did not exist but the staff man selected maneuvers that were ill-considered and resulted in the patient's hospitalization for weeks on end.

Needless to say, I never signed out to this staff surgeon again.

LAWSUITS. That a debilitating lawsuit may lurk behind every major operation is never far from the American surgeon's mind. In fact, the current litigious psyche in the United States extends far beyond medicine. (Lawsuits are far fewer in Canada and Western Europe.)

This writer has had a wide variety of lawsuit threats but was never actually sued in court or settled a case out of court. This is not to imply that there weren't cases where I could have been sued, justifiably and successfully.

SEVEN ILLUSTRATIVE CASES FOLLOW.

Case 1. The Good Samaritan, Legal and Penalty Hazards Therein. The patient was an early middle-aged pharmaceutical representative upon whom a colleague had performed a weight-reducing operation several days previously. Just as I was leaving the University Hospital around six o'clock one afternoon I heard myself paged. Picking up the phone, I learned from an associate that he was tied up in the operating room but that a nurse had called to say that his fat-bypass patient was clearly very ill and that he should be seen at once. Dr. S. asked me to see the patient and then call him in the operating room. Remonstrating mildly that I was leaving for home, I did see the patient. He was obviously very sick, and I told Dr. S. that I thought he had peritonitis and must be operated upon. Dr. S. said that he had to remain in his operating room for several more hours and that, as head of the Department, it was my duty to operate on the patient.

At operation I found that most of the small intestine was necrotic, having herniated through a space created by the fat operation itself.

After several hours we managed to anastomose two or three feet of probably viable small bowel to the colon.

Postoperatively his survival was in question. I had been scheduled to go on vacation but I felt morally bound to see him through his precarious state of recovery. However, I told him and his mother that he remained Dr. S.'s patient, that I would be a consultant.

After several touch and go weeks he had "turned the corner" and I felt free to depart on vacation. However, for some inexplicable reason, I wrote the patient and his mother a formal letter and delivered it myself. It said that he had always been Dr. S.'s patient and that I was finally to go on vacation.

At this the patient and especially the mother thanked me profusely, saying that I had saved his life (which I had). They promised never to forget me.

They didn't. Almost to the day that the "statute of limitations" was to expire, two lawyers entered my office and handed me a summons. The patient was suing because of a weakness in the fourth and fifth fingers in one hand. The accusation: That I had placed him on the operating table inappropriately.

The case dragged on for two or three years but was finally dropped, probably because the involved fingers had regained normalcy.

Case 2. Sponge Left in Wound. The patient was a man with tuberculosis who'd had the first stage of the standard three-stage thoracoplasty for this disease. There'd been nothing unusual about the operation I had done and the sponge count had been "correct." But when a day or so later a chest X-ray was taken to see how much the removal of the first four ribs had achieved, the radiologist called me to say that I should come down to the X-ray department and see the film. I told him that I was very busy and that I would take his word for it. But at this he said, "Jim, I think you're going to want to see this film yourself."

Alas, despite the "correct" sponge count following what was always a somewhat bloody operation, I had left a sponge in the wound, as seen by the wire that all the sponges contained.

But, fortunately, there were two remaining stages to be performed. (The second stage would ordinarily be done at two to three weeks, but in this case the second stage was performed uneventfully at one week.)

Case 3. "Where There's Death There's Hope." This patient was a 79 year-old black man who was brought down from the Delta in an ambulance for a very large and probably leaking abdominal aortic aneurysm. He was very thin and we placed him on an electrical warming blanket on the operating table to prevent excessive cooling during what could be a prolonged operation.

The large aneurysm was not ruptured and its excision proceeded briskly. However, during the operation I felt the heating blanket through the sterile drapes, something I had not experienced before. The resident across the table agreed. So, I asked the anesthesiologist, twice, to check the temperature of the blanket on the gauge that he was following. Each time he checked the dial and pronounced that the temperature of the blanket was satisfactory.

The next morning the residents meet me at the door and said, "Dr. Hardy, there's something in the I.C.U. that you must see."

In brief, the patient had sustained third degree burns (would have to be grafted) on the pressure points, both shoulders and over the sacrum.

It was found that the maintenance contract on the electrical blanket had long since expired, and that a small set-screw that controlled the temperature had fallen out.

I called our chief of Plastic Surgery immediately and he made plans to skin graft the sites of third degree burns (which was readily accomplished satisfactorily).

This patient of course had a solid legal complaint and it was promptly forthcoming. He mowed the lawn of a lawyer!

This case had dragged on for some many months, but at a Christmas reception I encountered one of the University's lawyers. I asked, "What is happening to the back burns case?"

He replied, "We've heard nothing lately. The patient was 79, wasn't he? Doctor, where there's death there's hope!"

Nothing else was ever heard from this legal action.

Case 4. Trial By Jury. This concerned my acceptance to testify for the University of Kansas Medical Center in Kansas City. The patient had been working on an oil derrick in Western Kansas when his right (?) arm was pulled off at a level just below the shoulder. Called about it, the surgeons in Kansas City instructed that the arm be placed in ice and it and the patient be flown immediately to their University Hospital. In brief, the arm was reattached successfully. The oil company had instructed that the patient be placed in a private room with around-the-clock private duty nurses. The first several days were uneventful and the arm was clearly viable. However, it was the week of Thanksgiving and private duty nurses were simply not available. But the unattended patient remained far down the hall, far from a room near the nurses station. And to make matters worse the patient's "Doctor" (the third year medical student) had left for the holidays.

During one night, the patient became disoriented and tore loose some of the sutures in the arm, with hemorrhage and loss of the arm, as I recall it.

A lawsuit resulted, claiming that the patient's personal physician (the medical student) had abandoned him.

The patient had been willing to accept $35,000 but UK decided to defend.

At the trial I was not much help, I felt. I pointed out that such an operation had only rarely been attempted; that the third year medical student had not been the patient's personal physician; that his true physicians, the surgeons, had numerous notations on the hospital chart. (The jury awarded something over $100,000 to the plaintiff.)

But at noon recess as I sat in a restaurant with the University's battery of four lawyers, I posed a case "that I knew about" and asked their opinion. At this the elderly "dean" of the group reached across the table and patted the back of my hand. "Son," he said, "You know too much about that case for it to have been 'elsewhere.' If I were you I'd settle tomorrow morning for $100,000!" (It was one of my colleague's cases.)

Case 5. One Half Needle Left in Chest. One day I

received a call from a physician in Meridian. He'd had a chest X-ray made on a patient who was to undergo a breast operation. It showed part of a needle behind the heart. She'd been operated upon by us almost a decade before for a dissecting aneurysm of the thoracic aorta.

I remembered the case. A needle had broken and, when we simply could not find the pointed half, we had brought in a metal detector and still could not find it. And, to our dismay, it had gone unnoted on a postoperative film.

Her current calling physician said she had no thought of suing me, that she was just grateful that we had saved her life at that time.

Case 6. Sovereign Immunity. The patient involved was a relatively young female with a mass in her (left?) small breast. At operation by a senior resident who was shortly to enter private practice, several liberal biopsies were taken but none showed cancer on immediate frozen section. Accordingly, the breast wound was closed and she was advised in writing to return in three months for further evaluation.

Meanwhile, though, she had moved to Texas, where a new biopsy there disclosed cancer.

I was sued, even though I'd had had no knowledge of the patient or of the operation biopsies in the clinic.

But our University lawyer appealed to the Mississippi Supreme Court, pointing out that, while I was surgeon-in-chief to the hospital, I'd not even known of the patient.

The Supreme Court took the position that I could not be present for every minor operation by my residents; that since I'd not known of the patient and had sent no bill, I would be accorded Sovereign Immunity.

Case 7. Routine Splenectomy. Failure to Wake up

327

Promptly after Operation. This patient had been referred by the hematologists for splenectomy. It was a "routine" procedure and I had never lost such a patient.

But after the operation he did not readily wake up. And it was to be seen that urine output was limited. At this point I told the residents that if he became jaundiced, indicating severe liver damage, that in all likelihood he had been inadequately ventilated during the operation. And, consulting the anesthesia record, it was found that no arterial blood gas measurements had been done. Ventilation had been maintained by simply squeezing the bag manually, eschewing the use of a mechanical ventilator.

The patient never woke up satisfactorily, went into renal failure and died at about six weeks.

Some weeks later the patient's wife and daughter came to see me in my office. Mother asked, "Tell us, Doctor, what happened? It was supposed to be such a routine operation."

Here I ask you, the Reader, what reply would you have given?

There had been no problem with the "routine" operation and I was virtually certain that anesthesia had been defective. But I had no proof.

My lame answer was that, "He did not tolerate the anesthesia satisfactorily."

N.B. No operation that requires general anesthesia should be looked upon as "routine."

INTERNAL AUDIT OF SURGEON'S RESULTS. On April 5, (1979?), the Executive Committee of the Hospital Staff of the University Hospital met to review and audit a thorough investigation of the operations performed by the Chairman of Neurosurgery. The data submitted by the subcommittee charged with evaluating the work, plus a remarkable volume of material submitted by lawyers in the city of Jackson and surrounding areas, resulted in the suspension of his hospital privileges beginning immediately. This seemed to me a very harsh decision but over the years he had simply not paid attention to his administrative leadership duties, and now it had come down to this. Someone at the meeting said loudly to me, "Dr. Hardy, he was once in your department. Why didn't you do something about this sort of thing?"

My rejoinder: "I tried, but what happened was that the administration gave him a separate department."

The next day the individual concerned came down to my office. He asked that I tell him frankly what I assessed his position to be.

I noted that, since his hospital admitting privileges had been suspended, he could no longer function as chief of the neurosurgical service, which was essential if he were to remain as chairman of the Department of Neurosurgery. I opined that he probably would, at some point, regain his hospital admission and operating privileges but that he would not regain his position as Chairman of the Department of Neurosurgery and Chief of the clinical service.

He left expressing his determination to regain all that he had lost.

He did recover hospital privileges but not his Chief of Neurosurgery Service and Chairman of that Department.

THE HOSPITAL DIRECTOR'S PROBLEMS. As we neared the end of our first decade, petty crime and misdemeanors forced new hospital policies. For the first time all hospital personnel had to wear name and photo badges. Women were molested in parking lots as shifts were changed at eleven o'clock at night. Thefts in the parking lots became a significant problem. Insider thefts were facilitated by loose management of pass keys. The police force mushroomed from two or three to a formidable number.

To give a specific reference number: One hundred bed sheets were numbered and sent down to the laundry, but only 12 of these ever returned to the patient floors.

CHAPTER 15

National and International Responsibilities

Time Tithing

The Academic Surgeon can have many "outside" calls upon his time, but he must continually see to it that his work and responsibilities at home are not neglected.

But on the other hand, the Chairman has an obligation to go to his national meetings and to bring home new ideas and procedures. Sir William Osler termed the attendance at one's professional meetings as "brain dusting." And if the Chairman attends and participates in his specialty meetings consistently, his knowledge of his specialty will not only remain current but he may become president of the society, which affords his medical school department additional national and international prestige. It also enables him to help place trainees, helps trainees obtain positions for further training at other universities, and it facilitates the application for research grants.

I was away from Jackson a considerable number of times, but I always tried to travel both ways as rapidly as possible, and commonly at night. And I rarely did a high risk operation the day of my departure.

Therefore, to the people of Mississippi I will say, "I did it for you!" As Governor Herman Talmage of Georgia was reported to have said to his constituents when he was speaking at an outdoors rally, "Yes, I stole, but I stole for you!"

There follows a brief sketch of some of my professional societies:

ALPHA OMEGA ALPHA (1942). This is the "Phi Beta Kappa" (scholastic society) of medical schools. I was one of five new members of my 130-140 class elected at the end of my junior year and was then elected as president to serve during my senior year.

PHI BETA KAPPA (HON.). I was elected as an honorary member of the University of Alabama chapter and gave the principal address the following year. My title was "The Nature of Discovery." This was especially gratifying in that I had failed of election in college because of a failure in freshman math.

AMERICAN PHYSIOLOGICAL SOCIETY (1950). This organization was always exciting, and at that time the annual meeting was held in Atlantic City. There I gave my first truly national paper. It had to do with the use of heavy water (D_2O) in determining the body water and fat content.

THE SURGICAL BIOLOGY CLUB (FOUNDING MEMBER). This group was taken up in Chapter 8. It was established under the leadership of Francis D. Moore of Harvard. It was to provide an opportunity for "exchange without piracy" on the Sunday immediately preceding the annual meeting of the Clinical Congress of the American College of Surgeons. The rough and tumble discussions represented a true cutting edge of the physiological surgery to come, and later on many or most of the members became chairmen of departments of surgery in the United States. Again, the Zollinger-Ellison peptic ulcer syndrome was born in this group.

THE INTERNATIONAL SURGICAL GROUP. In 1959 I was called by Jonathan Rhoads who was joining the American complement of Americans, to combine with Western European surgeons to establish an International Surgical Club that would meet every two years to reestablish the communication that had existed prior to World War II. He invited me to be one of the 25 American members, to join with the 25 Western European members for a biennial meeting that was to alternate between the two continents. I was flattered to be asked, for I was far younger than many or most of the proposed members.

The first meeting was held in Edinburgh, hosted by Sir John Bruce, Head of Surgery at the University of Edinburgh. The meeting went well, but two changes were requested: First, brought forward by Jonathan Rhoads, it was suggested that the "Club" appellation be changed to "Group"—to diminish the possible interest by the Bureau of Internal Revenue. The second suggestion, by John Gibbon (inventor of the heart-lung machine), was that a meeting be held every year, to establish and preserve continuity. A third (but unspoken) agreement was that no German surgeons would be included. WWII was still too fresh in memory. (But after some years this stricture was dropped.)

I confess I was far from a regular attender. I had voted for a biennial meeting, not an annual meeting. I gave several papers but the necessary time required to make the trip, usually in late August or September, was just too much in that our medical school year was just beginning.

THE SOCIETY OF UNIVERSITY SURGEONS (SUS). Membership in the Society of University Surgeons is a first major achievement in the career of an American Academic Surgeon. And when this writer is asked to evaluate the curriculum of a candidate for specific academic advancement, the presence or absence of SUS membership is an important consideration. This, plus Alpha Omega Alpha and, to a lesser extent, Phi Beta Kappa, when combined with a solid bibliography, will usually carry the day.

I was elected to the SUS in 1952. As noted in Chapter 9, a couple years later I received a telephone call from Dr. Englebert ("Bert") Dunphy, a leading star in the American surgical firmament. He was calling to learn whether or not I could take on the job as secretary of the Society of University Surgeons. It would entail a lot of work, for in those days virtually everything about the organization was carried on in the office of the secretary. (In later years this was all "farmed out.") I was surprised but I well knew that the secretaryship of many if not most organizations was a road to the presidency. I accepted at once and it was a rich experience.

I served as President in 1961. But upon hearing my nomination for President, I had sprung up and was hastening up the aisle toward the podium when that imp, Bert Dunphy (presiding) said with puckish humor, "Wait a minute, Hardy, you've only been nominated. I must solicit nominations from the floor!"

One of my proposals, that our SUS meet periodically with our British colleagues, was acted upon with a meeting in London several years later.

SOCIETY FOR SURGERY OF THE ALIMENTARY TRACT. This was another organization in which I had early membership status. Its birth came about as follows. Dr. Robert Turell, a prominent proctologist in New York City, wrote to Dr. Warren Cole, Chairman of Surgery at the University of Illinois in Chicago, pointing out that the colon was being inadequately represented in the scheme of things, and he proposed the formation of a Society for Colon Surgery with Dr. Cole as its first president. Dr. Cole thought the proposal a useful one, and he enlisted Drs. John Waugh of the Mayo Clinic and Harwell Wilson, Chairman of Surgery at the University of Tennessee Medical College in Memphis. Dr. Cole then appointed me as chairman of the first program, to be held in Miami. If I recollect accurately, the meeting was to last two days.

But I found it difficult to develop a program on just the colon, aside from what was already known and in practice. For instance, there was very little new information regarding the physiology of the colon. I did my best but it was a pretty "tame" session.

Meanwhile, I had written Dr. Cole suggesting that the "Surgery of the Alimentary Tract" be substituted for "Surgery of the Colon." If this change was accepted by the membership, then the program chairman would have the opportunity to develop a rich program, that would include additional organs such as the stomach, esophagus and the gut tributaries, the liver and the pancreas. This was put to a vote and it passed. I was again named Program Chairman and was elected President at the 1969 meeting.

THE SOCIETY FOR CLINICAL SURGERY was founded by Harvey Cushing at Harvard's Peter Bent Brigham

Hospital and George Crile who founded the Cleveland (Crile) Clinic. The stated objectives had to do with visiting member surgeons in their own clinics and operating rooms, instead of the format of most surgical meetings held in some hotel where only prepared papers were used.

In general, the members arrived in the host's city on Thursday, then watched operations on Friday morning from about seven until noon, then papers largely by members of the host's staff, then a dinner-banquet that evening (often in the host's home), and then additional papers from nine to twelve on Saturday and then adjournment.

We had the Society come to our "shop" in Jackson. During Friday morning I took two operating rooms and resected a large abdominal aortic aneurysm in one operating room, then closed an atrial septal defect on the heart-lung machine in the other room and then did a closed mitral valve commissurotomy back in the first operating room. My assistants were opening and closing the wounds, and I was out of the operating room in time to begin the "papers" session at ten.

One other thing. I was twice elected Vice President. The nominating committee obviously had forgotten my first term and, when I mentioned it to Jonathan Rhoads he chuckled and said that obviously I had served so well the first time that the Committee remembered it! (The reader should know that the vice president has absolutely no duties.)

THE SOUTHERN SURGICAL ASSOCIATION. My first intimation at the meeting in Florida (it alternated between Hot Springs, Virginia, and Florida) was Harwell Wilson's question, "Where is Weezie?" I replied that we'd just returned from Brazil and that she was at home getting ready for Christmas.

"You'll be sorry," he said.

And at the business meeting I *was* elected president (1972).

The President has little to do except to prepare his Presidential Address. All other business is conducted by the Council, on which he becomes a member upon the election of the next president.

I chose the title "She Is Risen." I reviewed the South's academic, educational and financial progress since the Civil War. It was pointed out that of the 36 fully established medical schools located in the southern and border states which supplied 75 percent of the membership of the Southern Surgical Association, the chairman of surgery had received his medical school and residency training in one of our member schools in only eight instances. All except two of the eight were educated in border states. Three of the eight were from Johns Hopkins.

I pointed out that the educational levels in a state are a reflection of its general wealth, and that approximately the one-third black segment of the population pulled down the overall per capita income level.

And then I introduced a "no-no" topic. I said that as long as the Southern Surgical Association remained 100 percent white, when there did exist fully qualified black candidates, we had to consider our organization as only a club.

I closed my address with:

When I was a boy, my grandmother used to tell us about how the Federal troops had burned everything

The department of surgery, 1984. Front row, left to right: Karen Morer, Lamar Weems, Samuel Johnson, Richard Miller, Martin Dalton William Neely, JDH, William Hart, Winsor Morrison, Seshadri Raju, Ojus Malphurs, Judson Farmer, Ching-Jygh Chen. Second row: Don Turner, Scott Houston, James Maher, Fred Rushton, Keith Smith, Connie McCaa, Ralph Didlake, Steve Isbell, Barry Newsom, Douglas Godfrey, David Crawford, Alex Haick, Jeff Budden, Bill Owen, Howell Tucker, Mukadder Cayirli, Stephen Bayne, Barry Sauer, Hunt Bobo, Maxine Eakins, Jim Pennington, Luther Fisher, Bill Mayo, Swayze Rigby, Jeff Cook, Joel Knight, James Peck. Third row: John Tomasin, Joe Moore, Vinod Anand, Ron Krueger, Jim Cotter, Twatchi Yamcharern, Kathy Jackson, Vickie Gerken, Mark Barraza, Lyle Zardiackas, Kirk Banquer, Ron Graham, Marc Aiken, Todd Sherwood, Greg Fiser, DeAnn Smith, John Petro, Ped Hooper, Gray Buck, Jay Miles.

Reproduced by permission of the University of Pennsylvania Press. (Memoirs)

when they came through during the Civil War. And men would say, "Hang onto your Confederate money, boys, the South will rise again."

Gentlemen, she is risen.

This was unacceptable to perhaps a majority of the southern segment of the membership. The Council met all the afternoon to decide whether or not to approve my address for publication in the Annals of Surgery, along with all the other papers of the meeting as usual.

Finally, Harwell Wilson was dispatched to come to my room and require that I drop mention of race. I replied that the national audience had already heard my address; that I would agree to have the line say all qualified candidates, omitting the word "black." This was accepted by the Council.

At the banquet the last evening, my daughters, seated just below the head table kept motioning to me. I had introduced the twenty or so other people at the head table but not my wife! I finally caught on and did it so smoothly that it appeared to have been planned that way.

The Doctors Leslie and Paddy LeQuesne of London were our special guests, and he spoke briefly about the current status of the health care system in Great Britain.

After toasting the President of the United States and the Queen, I toasted the ladies:

> *"They do an awful lot of scrubbing,*
> *But they never use a knife*
> *As with sunlight and chlorophyll,*
> *Their sunshine is resplendent in the tender growing edge of*
> *our children.*
> *In truth, they make everything else worthwhile.*
> *Gentlemen, to our wives!"*

The LeQuesnes traveled with us to Jackson. Avid bird

watchers, they recorded 28 species around Eagle Lake, if memory serves.

The following year I and two other members proposed a black candidate but the Council rejected him. Two members of the Association resigned in disgust. Meanwhile, the proposed member had become president of the American Cancer Society, a member of the American Surgical Association, and later, secretary of the American College of Surgeons.

Thus, when two Virginia members asked me to join them with a new membership proposal, LaSalle Leffall was elected a member of the Southern Surgical Association.

THE AMERICAN SURGICAL ASSOCIATION. This society represents the "priesthood" of American (and Canadian) surgery. President Eisenhower joined the President's Dinner in Washington and, as he entered, he noted that all the wives were sequestered in an adjacent hall. He refused to speak until chairs were brought in and all the ladies welcomed.

I had not served as an officer in any capacity and had no dream of being President. There *were* tantalizing little comments there at the Chateau Frontenac Hotel meeting in Quebec, Canada. For example, Zolly (Dr. Robert M. Zollinger) passed Weezie in the hall and said "You'll be very happy tomorrow." "Jim," she asked, "What could he be talking about?" I said that I had no idea, which I hadn't. Then the next (last) morning, Jonathan Rhoads saw me paying my bill and said, "You're leaving?" I replied that I would attend the business meeting just after lunch, but then Weezie and I had to scuttle to make it to Jackson that night.

The Nominating Committee's report came last. The

AMERICAN BOARD OF SURGERY
1963-1969

*Reproduced by Permission of the University
of Pennsylvania Press. (Memoirs)*

Chairman read off all except the nomination for President. Then, as the Chairman proceeded to read in detail all the accomplishments of the candidate to be named, it began to dawn on me that he might be describing my own career. And shortly, I heard Harold

341

Barker, seated just behind me, say to his neighbor, "By golly, I believe it's going to be Jim Hardy."

AND IT WAS! I had never seen a single hard bitten surgeon fail to quail when nominated for the American Surgical Association presidency, and I was no exception. I was escorted to the platform by Claude Welch and Leo Eloesser.

I don't remember my acceptance remarks, but Robert Sparkman of Dallas recorded them for me.

Thus, I had to remain in Quebec to run the afternoon program, but Weezie went on home.

To conclude, my first responsibility was to prepare for the late January meetings and these were conducted at the Holiday Inn Downtown in Jackson. For my President's Dinner I chose to begin with cocktails in our home; then buses to the Old Capitol museum where an historian stood and spoke from the very podium where Mississippi had declared war against the North in the Civil War; and lastly to the University Club's roof dining hall. Chancellor Porter Fortune had come down from Oxford and spoke of William Faulkner and showed a movie of the geographical areas which had provided the background for the novels that had won him the Nobel prize.

My gift to each member of those national surgeons was a silver cup which bore the ASA designation and contained a fully opened cotton boll.

This was perhaps the University Club's first dinner of such national import, and the maitre d'hotel kept coming behind me at the head table and whispered, "How are we doing?"

And I whispered back, "Just great! Keep moving."

Truly, Mississippi did us proud that evening. I later

overheard one guest say to another, "This has been the best of these I've ever attended."

And from time to time in subsequent years, someone would tell me that it was the first time he'd ever seen a cotton boll. And that it still remained on display in his office.

The full meeting came later, in the Spring, and my presidential address was entitled "American Surgery—1976."

THE AMERICAN COLLEGE OF SURGEONS. This is a very large organization embracing approximately 45,000 members in the United States and from chapters in other countries. The main requirement is that the candidate for membership must have passed the qualifying boards in his or her specialty. I had served in many capacities and programs over the years when Director of the College, C. Rollins Hanlon, called me out of a committee meeting to tell me that I had passed successfully all the hurdles to the Presidency, and that I would be nominated at the business meeting on Thursday. I was of course enormously pleased, for I had been on the nominating committee myself some years previously, and I knew the great care taken to nominate for president a surgeon of true gravitas, who had labored faithfully in the ACS vineyards over the years, and whose character was considered by his colleagues to be impeccable.

This election entailed attendance at a number of chapter meetings in the United States and several in Europe. Special events were attendance at a reception and then a dinner meeting where President Reagan joined the Irish Surgical Society in honoring Dr. Loyal Davis, Nancy's stepfather. Virtually every cabinet member was at

Left: James D. Hardy, M.D., President of the American College of Surgeons. Right: Sir Alan Parks, President of the Royal College of Surgeons, England. Reproduced by permission of the University of Pennsylvania Press. (Memoirs)

the Irish embassy during the afternoon, and Mrs. Annenberg, Ambassador to the Court of St. James, leaned over and asked, "Who's keeping the store?"

That evening I found myself seated beside Edwin Meese, who had accompanied Reagan from California. Making conversation, he asked me what I thought of Jimmie Carter's carrying his own bag. He said that on arriving in Washington they had decided to reflect a bit more formality. What did I think? I said, "Mr. Meese, I am hardly the one to ask. Frankly, I'm running for knighthood!"

THE AMERICAN ASSOCIATION FOR THORACIC SURGERY. This meeting was often the most exciting one of the year. It was a period in which new procedures and results of cardiac surgery were catalogued regularly and open-heart surgery was being established in every major academic center.

I served on the Council in 1975. However, I was not pure, in that I also did a considerable amount of general surgery. I did not expect to advance up the hierarchy and I did not—despite my having transplanted the first heart and the first lung in man.

THE INTERNATIONAL TRANSPLANTATION SOCIETY. I was an early member of the transplantation society. I served on the ethics committee, the chairman of which was a Nobel prize winner. I was on the Arrangements Committee for a meeting in Rome and was a vice president. The meeting of the arrangements committee for the meeting in Rome met in Professor Leslie Brent's laboratories at the University College, University of London. Professor Cortesini was the local chairman of arrangements in Rome, and he arrived in London with the good news that the Pope had agreed to participate in the opening ceremonies. At this, I asked Dr. Cortesini about the Pope's position on the ethics of organ transplantation in man, that some religions still opposed transplantation. Dr. Cortesini replied, "Dr. Hardy, the Pope is for anything that works."

And then Cortesini said that he and his committee in Rome needed an additional allocation of funds. At this a Briton asked why not get the funds from the Vatican bank. To which Cortesini replied, "It is blessed."

THE INTERNATIONAL SOCIETY OF SURGERY (SOCIETÉ INTERNATIONALE DE CHIRURGIE). Here I had progressed through the lower offices of the United States Chapter to the Presidency. Perhaps my major contribution was to mount an Herculean effort to clean the Augean stable of the chaotic membership rolls.

In any case, I advanced to the Presidency of the United States Chapter, then to the Council of the International Society and ultimately to the Presidency of the International Society, presiding first at the Parisian meeting and, two years later, at the meeting in Sydney, Australia. One of my major contributions was the resuscitation of our "World Journal of Surgery" when the previous editor had abruptly resigned because the Council would not yet vote to have 12 issues a year instead of six. Manuscripts were submitted in various languages by surgeons all around the world, but all had to be reduced to English. Professor Maurice Mercadier of Paris provided summaries in French. My editorial board grew to represent a number of major countries.

Left: Louise ("Weezie") Hardy. Right: JDH
Meeting of the James D. Hardy Surgical Society, London, The
Savoy Hotel, The Queen's Room. (Note bust of Winston
Churchill in background.)

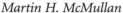

Martin H. McMullan   *Richard L. Yelverton*

THE JAMES D. HARDY (SURGICAL) SOCIETY. After several aborted attempts, the James D. Hardy Society was established by Martin H. McMullan and Richard L. Yelverton and the first annual meeting was held in Jackson in 1992. Thereafter the meeting was held in Sandestin, Florida; Heidelberg-Paris-London; Sandestin; Istanbul-Athens; Amelia Island (Florida); Venice-Florence-Rome; San Antonio; Jackson; and Biloxi. The general format has been for the members to present papers and for the host hospital's staff to present papers—all with unlimited informal discussion. At times a distinguished foreign surgeon was a guest speaker throughout the three days of the meeting.

Gradually, a solid corps of regular attenders developed, and the Hardy Surgical Society has proved to be a valuable, enjoyable, and cohesive force for our surgical resident alumni.

347

TIME TITHING

The chairman of a department of surgery in the United States can be expected to serve on national boards of one sort of another. The individual is usually not paid for his or her time but travel expenses are paid.

EXAMINING BOARDS. In brief, my major commitments along these lines were examining boards for medical students and for surgery residents who were applying for Board Certification for the practice of surgery. The service on the Board of Medical Examiners consisted of meeting with four other surgeons in Philadelphia to prepare questions for medical students to take. Each of us prepared an assigned number of questions, five as I recall, and then we five sat around a table and tried to "shoot down" the others' questions—true or false, or multiple choice. My special memory of these sessions is that how hard it is to formulate a question that can have but one answer. We were preparing questions to add to the general pool, so that the National Board questions would be fresh but would have only one "right" answer.

While I was there one day, a German unit was deciding whether or not they should buy questions for usage in their country.

THE AMERICAN BOARD OF SURGERY. This body was and remains the principal examining body which certifies the finishing surgical resident for the requisite surgical training and knowledge for safe surgery. It is not a legal body but passing the written and the oral examinations is essential if the surgeon seeks to be a member of the American College of Surgeons and other prestigious surgical societies. However, some surgeons never manage to pass the Board examinations but are free to practice surgery anyway.

348

The term of service for me was six years and I served as vice-chairman for a time. I would leave Jackson on Sunday afternoon, examine candidates at some hospital, medical school or hotel on Monday and Tuesday, and fly back to Jackson on Tuesday night. There were six or so trips of this type each year. Miraculously, not once over the duration of my term did I fail to return to Jackson in time to operate Wednesday morning. Each candidate met with three pairs of examiners during the day, and each pair had been given the list of organs and diseases to examine for. In this way the whole range of the body was covered.

For years after my term had been completed some young surgeon would come over to me at some national meeting and say, "Dr. Hardy, you examined me on the boards." And I wondered how I had treated him.

Dr. Olga Jonnason and I were examining a candidate who was so bright that we had used up most of our questions in the first fifteen of the allotted thirty minutes. (I was glad he was not examining me!) At this, Dr. Jonnason said that she was going to have to go to the bottom of the barrel. I asked, "What do you mean?"

She replied that she was a minister's daughter and when he had not had time to prepare a new sermon for Sunday, he reached way down into the barrel to get one that he hoped the congregation had forgotten.

The whole group of examiners met together late Tuesday afternoon and discussed each candidate of the session. Since the location where the candidate had trained was unknown to the examiners, we all looked forward to learning who was the "high man" and where he had trained.

I was very pleased with a comment I heard from one examiner to another. "He may be from Viet Nam, but I examined him, too. And I'll bet he's a Hardy man. His guys know how to stand on their feet and deliver."

Editorial Boards
Advances in Surgery, Year Book Publishers
American Journal of Surgery
American Lectures in Surgery
(Charles C Thomas, Publishers (1972-73)
Journal of Surgical Research (1961-72)

Surgery
World Journal of Surgery, Editor-in-Chief
Hardy's Textbook of Surgery

World Journal of Surgery

Official Journal of the Société Internationale de Chirurgie and of the Collegium Internationale Chirurgiae Digestivae

1983

EDITOR-IN-CHIEF

James D. Hardy, M.D.
Jackson, U.S.A.

CO-EDITORS

EDITORIAL BOARD

CONSULTANTS

Reproduced by permission of the University of Pennsylvania Press. (Memoirs)

351

CHAPTER 16

The Visiting Professor and Selected Honors

The advent of the jet airplane substantially increased the calls upon the time of Departmental Chairmen and others deemed worthy of the term Visiting Professor. And the siren calls from many quarters to come and perform can constitute a serious hazard to the otherwise stable employment of the academician. It is not possible to examine here in detail and depth the genus and species and academic life expectation of the unsophisticated young chairman. This has been achieved with laser accuracy and scintillating wit by Eiseman and Thompson (New Eng. J. Med. <u>296</u>:1977).

Therefore, this writer will simply confirm, through his own Visiting Professor experiences, the basic principles which delineate the visit.

The invitation is commonly extended by telephone, and thus the solicited Visiting Professor is caught without his commitments calendar at hand. Under this circumstance the recipient is perfectly free to ask for all the details in a letter. The exact dates, every appearance the visitor is expected to make, the topics to be discussed, a banquet speech?, are expenses paid (and are the wife's), the airplane schedules, tuxedo?, lodgings, and so forth. Most speakers would prefer the isolation of a hotel to the host's home.

The host will often propose a three-day stay on campus, but this visitor gradually whittled it down to two days, with the travel to and from at night when possible. Of course, when the Visiting Professor's presence is part of a postgraduate course the host institution is offering, time schedules will have to be arranged accordingly.

How much time away can one's department (or university officials) tolerate? One example: The writer was at one of this country's great surgical clinics and we were discussing "time away." My friend said he felt quite secure. He said that he was away from his "shop" lecturing around the world almost three fourths of each year. However, he had his department so well organized that it ran just as well when he wasn't there.

I returned home and told my wife, "Our friend is in an hazardous situation." (N.B. He was relieved of his Chairmanship within the year.)

RECIPROCAL VISITS. But, if I wanted to bring in major luminaries in American and world surgery (for the edification of our students, residents and staff), I had to be willing to go to their universities.

For example, once I had been appointed a Distinguished VA Physician (a post of substantial merit), I was called by the Chairman of a Department of Surgery in California. I felt that my new appointment should have rendered me immune from Visiting Professor stints. But as I began to explain that I now worked full time for the VA and that the VA frowned on outside commitments,

Bill said, "Wait a minute, Jim, I came for you!"

"Oh, yes, Bill, what do you want me to do?"

But I found most of my Visiting Professor commitments both interesting and educational.

And since the Visiting Professor visit commonly included some named lecture of the year, I shall treat the Visiting Professorship and the named Lectures as one. Selected honors will follow.

Until legal liability suits became commonplace, the visiting surgical professor was often asked to operate. I always did during the first years of my chairmanship. And, indeed, what disease condition I was to operate for at times appeared in the printed program if there was an associated meeting—sometimes when I'd not been even asked if I would operate. However, the chairman of the department always saw to it that I had first-class assistants and scrub (suture) nurse.

I select here ten of the more than eighty occasions that I served as Visiting Professor-Lecturer over the duration of my departmental chairmanship. The selections are chosen as ones which may be of particular interest to the reader.

The Da Costa Oration of the Philadelphia County Medical Society, 1962. This invitation had of course important overtones, for I had spent thirteen years at the University of Pennsylvania Medical School and University Hospital.

Even so, though "Da Costa" had been an "household" surgical name in Philadelphia, I realized that I knew little about him. So if the moderator at the Society meeting did not offer the usual felicitous remarks about the honoree, it would fall to me to produce them. And I vividly remembered such an occasion at our medical center when a new building was being dedicated. At the close of the keynote speaker's address he had invited questions from the floor. At which the first question was, who *was* the Honoree? And the speaker had not a clue!

Therefore, I left Jackson early in the day and visited the National Library of Medicine in Washington. (Incidentally, the Lieutenant Frank B. Rogers who'd taught us logistics at Carlisle Barracks in WWII was to become Col. Rogers and director of the National Library of Medicine.)

I found reams on Da Costa and one of his remarks bonded us as kindred spirits: "Many men, when called to a post, say that they were called by the Lord. But most of the time they were called by the Board."

Dr. John H. Gibbon (inventor of the heart-lung machine) was president of the Society, and from several possible topics I had submitted to the Program Committee, the "Complications of Gastric Surgery" had been selected. The oration and dinner went well.

Dr. Ravdin, my chief of surgery at Penn, had had a longstanding commitment with the mayor of Philadelphia regarding a proposed new Children's Hospital. However, he had had Miss Lucas, his invaluable office manager, call me several times during the day as I visited other hospitals. I was to come by his home, only several blocks from the Philadelphia County Medical Society's building, for a drink before I took the midnight plane back to Jackson.

Therefore, after the meeting's adjournment, a friend and I walked over to Dr. Ravdin's home on Delancy Street. There were no lights on downstairs, but we pressed the button several times and Dr. Ravdin's daughter appeared at the door. Upon identifying us, she called up the stairs and said, "Dad, it's Jim Hardy!"

He came down in a house robe and exclaimed, "Jim Hardy, what are you doing here in Philadelphia in a tuxedo at this hour of the night?"

Sadly, his memory declined steadily and he died in an institution at age 76.

THE ALPHA OMEGA ALPHA (AOA) LECTURE AT COLUMBIA AND PRESBYTERIAN MEDICAL CENTER, NEW YORK 1962. This lecture is selected because I had accepted with a special purpose in mind. My topic was "The Transplantation of Organs," and I was to sample opinion outside of Jackson relative to transplanting major organs in man, especially the lung and heart.

The talk was well attended and at its close I invited questions and comments from the audience.

Near the close, I asked for a show of hands as to how many would accept a kidney transplant: Most would. Then a liver transplant: Fewer but still a significant number. Then a lung: Far fewer but still positive votes. But for the heart: Absolutely none.

Clearly, if these soon-to-be physicians felt as they did about lung and heart transplants in man, we could expect to precipitate major controversy. (And we certainly did.)

THE WILLIAM MITCHELL BANKS MEMORIAL LECTURE AT THE UNIVERSITY OF LIVERPOOL, 1963. (In association with the annual meeting of The Surgeons of Great Britain and Ireland.)

Professor Charles Wells and I had discussed on the Atlantic City boardwalk a year before the possible topics I might choose for this, his department's showpiece of each year. He had waved off everything until I mentioned "The Transplantation of Organs." At this he said enthusiastically, "Hardy, that's it!"

I had flown to Heathrow Airport in London and took the train to Liverpool. Inadvertently, in the diner I overheard the deliberations of the Nominating Committee for the Presidency of the Association during the coming year.

The opening of the meeting the following morning found me still far from over the jet lag. However, I had been assigned to discuss a paper on leg ischemia, and I had also been informed by mail that presentations at the meeting must be "talked," not read.

Meanwhile, the integration fight in Mississippi was visible on every newsstand, and Charles Wells was glum and doubtless wished he'd invited his speaker from anywhere but Mississippi.

Well, I arose and strode to the podium to discuss the previous speaker's paper. There was nothing but steely stares to be seen on the faces of the large audience.

I began: "Before I discuss this fine paper, I would like to bring you the best wishes of our faculty at Mississippi; also of the Dean of our Medical School; and of the Chancellor of our University.

And I would have liked to bring you the best wishes from our governor, but relations are strained."

At this, the audience was all smiles and rapped on their desks as they often do instead of clapping.

Then I discussed the previous speaker's paper. And as I sat down beside Charles Wells he too was all smiles, "Hardy, that was brilliant!"

The William Banks Memorial Lecture was to be held

that afternoon at four o'clock. The "platform" party marched into the auditorium in single file, in full academic regalia, but my mortarboard kept slipping on my head. I was still "dopey" from lack of sleep and jet lag, and I chose to read my address, "The Transplantation of Organs." (Reading was permitted at the oration.) But it was late in the day, and there were no lights except for a small one on the speaker's lecturn. The audience was becoming restless and Charles Wells' showpiece was threatening to be a disaster. Something different had to be done.

Closing my manuscript with my two hands, I turned to the slides and began to speak as I might at Grand Rounds in Jackson. The interest of the audience quickened, and I soon had solid attention. I showed a movie demonstrating lung transplantation and heart transplantation in dogs.

I then asked for all the lights. And I concluded with, "Gentlemen, these operations will be performed in man in the early future."

There was splendid applause, and years later Professor Witold Rudowski of the University of Warsaw told me that it was the best such an address that he had ever heard.

I've always considered the William Mitchell Banks Memorial Lecture one of my best efforts. For I'd had to change my plan and delivery in midstream, as it were—but successfully.

THE FIRST BEARDSLEY PROFESSORSHIP AT BROWN UNIVERSITY, R.I. 1965. This occasion is selected because it was the only one, of many operations away from home, that entailed open-heart surgery. It was for the closure of an atrial septal defect. The chairman of the department ran the pump! All went well.

My lodging was in an "ancient" club associated with Brown University. The campus bookstore offered an astonishing array of diatribes against the South and, most especially, Mississippi. One author presented herself as a Southerner who knew the South and its complexities from birth. But, on close inspection, it was to be seen that, while she *was* born in New Orleans, she had lived there only a few months.

INVITED PROFESSOR AND LECTURER TO THE NATIONAL HEART ASSOCIATION OF AUSTRALIA, 1966. The site of this meeting was Perth, for it coincided with the annual meeting of the Australasian Surgical Society and the Research Society. Weezie and I lodged at a "Sleepy Rue" motel that was just down the hill from the University Hospital. I spoke at both the formal meetings and many times at the Medical School-Hospital. The commitments there lasted three weeks, and from there we went to Bombay where we had a speaking commitment at the Seth Edward Hospital and Medical School. Our sponsor there was Dr. P.K. Sen, who had spent two years doing research with me at Pennsylvania. What I remember best is the hordes of people, sacred cows in the streets, and the high quality of the surgical team that Dr. Sen had assembled in Bombay.

THE 17TH ANNUAL ALFRED A. STRAUSS LECTURESHIP AT THE UNIVERSITY OF WASHINGTON IN SEATTLE, 1966. This was indeed a memorable assignment for many reasons. First, Henry Harkins, one of my best "older" friends in American surgery, had extended the invitation. He explained that Dr. Strauss was a former All American (?) on the University of Washington football team who had been eminently successful in his surgical practice in

360

Chicago, and Dr. Strauss always came to one of the University football games and that his financial contribution was what made the Lectureship possible. He alluded deftly to the "restrained attention" that the lecturer might be expected to show Dr. Strauss. All the surgical residents, plus the Lecturer, would be expected to accompany Dr. Strauss to the football game.

Well, when I got to Seattle it was very cold, with snow on the ground. For some reason, I had had the idea that Seattle had balmy weather due to a warming breeze from the Orient. I had brought only lightweight suits and I shuddered at the thought of having to sit through the football game. So I told Henry Harkins my concern but he answered, "Not to worry. I have a 20-year-old raccoon coat that will go down to your ankles."

And so the stay began. Each evening there would be a formal dinner and Henry would provide me with small cards that told me the origins and interests of the dinner companions on each side of me. One evening I found myself seated beside the President of the University of Washington and he was chortling over stealing a string quintet from the Philadelphia Orchestra.

I gave the lecture Friday evening in tuxedo. Title: The Transplantation of Organs. An acquaintance said that it was the best such lecture he'd ever heard in Seattle, but the reader should know that I take such compliments with a grain of salt. However, the lecture was well attended and was a success.

Meanwhile, it was learned that Dr. Strauss had pneumonia, in Chicago, and that his coming was in doubt. At this, I quietly checked plane schedules and found that I could fly directly to Dallas and be home a day earlier, if Dr. Strauss did not come and I could escape

361

from the football game.

And Dr. Strauss did not come!

I was torn over indecision. Should I beg off and fly home? Or should I keep the bargain and go with Dr. Harkins and his residents to the football game?

It was a hard decision but I decided that unless Henry mentioned it himself, I would not try to leave early.

By the way, Washington, the underdog, defeated Stanford that afternoon.

That evening as Dr. Harkins was driving me from my hotel to his home where he was giving a buffet dinner for all his staff and residents and their wives, he said to me, "Jim, I've always thought a lot of you but my estimation has absolutely soared this day. Many a guy would have tried to 'bug out' of here when it developed that Dr. Strauss was not coming."

"Thank you, Henry," I replied meekly.

RIO DE JANEIRO. 1972. The invitation to Rio was to serve as visiting professor to the major city hospital and to participate in a postgraduate course given for surgeons from all over Central and South America. On hand was a remarkable commercial language interpreter group.

As Weezie and I got off the plane, we were met by a young couple who were to be our shepherds to all the commitments of our stay. The young surgeon had a fair command of English, but he could understand Weezie's English better than he could understand my English. We were whisked through customs and, on the way to our hotel, he asked me if I would operate for the assembly, to be shown on a large screen in the lecture hall. I replied that I of course did not speak Portuguese and would not be able to communicate with the scrub nurse. "No problem," he said, "I will give you the names of the common instruments—knife, scissors, forceps, etc.—and I will be standing behind you in any case."

Somewhat doubtful, I asked what operations he had in mind. At this he presented the program for the meeting and it read that Dr. Hardy would perform a cholecystectomy, a subtotal gastric resection with vagotomy, and resection of a thoracic aortic aneurysm!

Not to be outdone, I did do the cholecystectomy the next day and the gastric resection the next. However, I declined to resect the aneurysm and then leave the postoperative care to others. But it would have been a simple matter to resect it: It was of moderate size and located just at the middle of the thoracic aorta.

The meeting was attended by a huge audience, and I presented several papers during my stay.

But I look back on the Rio visit with mild unhappiness. I had always recorded the names and addresses of those who attended me, and written the "thank you" letter immediately upon my return to Jackson. But I somehow lost the names and addresses of our young couple and procrastination extended to "too late" for a graceful message.

THE FIRST JULIAN JOHNSON LECTURE, 1974. The reader will remember that it was Dr. Johnson who had trained me in cardiothoracic surgery. Thus I felt much pride that he had chosen me to speak on this auspicious occasion.

My lecture was entitled "Lung and Heart Transplantation." The audience was large and enthusiastic, for I was already known to many members attending.

The Lecture was followed by a formal reception at the

University's Museum.

PETER BENT BRIGHAM HOSPITAL, 1976. For several years Dr. Francis D. Moore, Harvard Professor of Surgery and Chief of Surgery at the Brigham Hospital, had invited me to serve as Professor Pro Tem, but always some other commitment interfered. But this year, he reminded me, was his last year in the Chair with the privilege of inviting me. And also, he noted, our daughter Julia would soon be graduating from the Harvard Medical School. (The reader will recall that Dr. Moore had founded our Surgical Biology Club (I), and that he and I had been early users of heavy water for the measurement of total body water.)

We stayed with the Moores for the first several days but then moved to a small hotel near Julia for the rest of the week. My participation involved actual operating with the residents, participating in numerous conferences, attending evening affairs, and in giving a formal talk on Saturday morning. In speaking on a transplantation topic, I felt like I was bringing "coals to Newcastle," for the Brigham was at that time the fountainhead of organ transplantation in the United States and the leader of the kidney group, Joseph Murray, was later to win the Nobel Prize. However, my topic was the usual Lung and Heart Transplantation and no one at the Brigham was involved with such investigations.

THE MARNOCH LECTURE IN ABERDEEN, SCOTLAND. In the mid 1960's a number of departments of surgery in the United States were asked each to provide an honorarium for one British speaker who would be coming to the February meeting of the Society of University Surgeons. I was assigned a Professor of Surgery at the University of Aberdeen, Dr. George Smith.

Time had fled and I suddenly realized that, to get a respectable audience at our school, I better had post some notices. I called him and it was late night in Aberdeen. He offered two topics: Ischemic Neuritis and the History of Medicine.

We've got a problem, I said to myself. I knew little about ischemic neuritis and medical history was always a "hard sell." Nonetheless, I put up the notices about the hospital, threatened susceptible students and others and prepared for a minor disaster.

He appeared at the airport in a black suit, black shirt and black hat. Not a promising appearance, I thought to myself.

But at his first lecture, on ischemic neuritis, we had a decent audience who heard a splendid presentation of a (largely) new subject to us. By his medical history talk the next day, the word had got around and the full house audience was treated to a truly captivating dissertation on medical history.

Several years passed by before I heard from him again after his thank you note.

But then he wrote to invite me to come over and deliver the annual Marnoch Lecture on any topic having to do with neoplasia. I chose the title "Systemic Effects of Non-Endocrine Tumors." I had remained interested in this vein of neoplastic pathophysiology since I had told Dr. Ravdin, on the first day of my surgical residency in answer to his question as what did I plan to investigate: CACHEXIA.

But this trip was ill-starred from the outset. Honoring obligations at home, I had planned to fly to Aberdeen the day before the Lecture was scheduled to take place in the early afternoon. But my plane in New York was delayed for many hours and I reached Glasgow only on the morning of the lecture. Then I had to take a helicopter to catch the plane to Aberdeen. Thus I arrived there literally about two hours before the oration. By this time Professor Smith must have been at his wit's end and, would you believe it, he was called to an emergency in the hospital and I was left, essentially, to introduce myself to the restive but substantial audience.

"Strung out," I did the best I could, but it was not an unmitigated triumph. As the audience was leaving, an elderly gentlemen lingered behind and said, "Son, that was a good talk but next time don't try to tell so much in one hour." (Alas, Weezie had not been with me to tell me to cut the slides.)

I stayed with the Smiths in their home, but my suitcase had been left somewhere behind in my mad dash for Aberdeen. On about the third day Professor Smith asked, "I say, Professor Hardy, what are you sleeping in?"

My reply, "About what you'd expect."

He presented me with a pair of pongee pajamas, which I retained for many years.

During hospital rounds, I was introduced to the Doppler instrument's monitoring of pulses that are too weak to be palpated, as in the foot. The Doppler effect is employed as a fish finder. (Professor Doppler's statue stands in the covered courtyard of the University of Vienna's medical school.)

One patient was sitting straight up and appeared to be in cardiac failure, probably due to mitral valve stenosis, but he was being treated for a leg problem. So I asked why he had not been operated upon for his heart condition. The reply was that no such surgery was done in Aberdeen and that they had not yet gained permission to move him to a heart hospital.

Even though it was June, it was very chilly, bordering on cold, in Aberdeen. Mrs. Smith, from Ohio I think, having met Professor Smith when he was visiting Johns Hopkins, said that she expected never to be warm again.

The bag had not come, but I flew to London where I was scheduled to moderate a session on heart valves. I remember well the heavy criticism directed at Alain Carpentier of Paris who was developing methods for preserving human heart valves from cadavers. Many had failed. However, he persevered, studying one storage procedure after another, until the use of human valve allografts became almost routinely successful.

The night before I was to leave for home, I got a call from the Heathrow Airport. They had my bag and would send it out in a taxi. "No," I said, "I will myself come out and retrieve my bag, for I am leaving England in the morning." This I did. (N.B. Despite my travels all around the world, despite many delays and misdirections, I never actually lost a bag permanently.)

APPOINTED DISTINGUISHED VA PHYSICIAN

At some point in approximately 1984 I was asked if I was interested in being appointed a Distinguished VA Physician. This special VA category was comprised of about 12 persons. A single person represented his specialty, such as internal medicine, psychiatry, anesthesiology, and so forth. I would represent surgery.

I still had several years before mandatory retirement from the University, but a number of considerations had to be factored into the making the decision. First, it would

Veterans Distinguished Physician.
Sites of VA Hospitals visited during three year tenure.

afford me a more leisurely pace before total retirement. Secondly, it was an appointment of substantial merit, and I had had a high impression of surgeons who had so served. Thirdly, it would afford more time with my wife as we traveled from one VA installation to another. By then her Alzheimer's disease was becoming more and more undeniable.

I had submitted my curriculum vitae, but then I neither heard nor thought any more about it until suddenly one day in 1986, I was informed that I had indeed been appointed and that I should start on January 1, 1987.

This was not possible, for I had not had time to inform the University and get my affairs in order over there. (The University and the VA Hospital were close beside each other.)

The VA said that I must begin by July 1, 1987, or another person would have to be appointed to prevent the money from reverting to other purposes. This represented a reasonable compromise and I began plans accordingly.

The financial disclosure process involved an incredible amount of detail and considerable accounting expense. The second year I tried to get all the material together myself, but in a telephone call from Washington the general counsel said, "Dr. Hardy, for heavens sake, hire an accountant!"

I was to be based in our own VA Hospital, and much renovation was employed to provide me with a private office, a second office and the secretary's office. There were French Impressionist paintings on the walls! I was the first VA Distinguished Physician that our VA Hospital had ever had.

So, I was ensconced in these most imposing quarters. But what was I supposed to do?

I called the general counsel in Washington and he replied, "Doctor, just do good for the VA."

Left to my own devices, I set about "doing good for the VA." First, I was expected to participate in the clinical and teaching activities in our own VA Hospital which consisted of making teaching patient rounds, giving a weekly 20 minute talk on one of the 40 topics I had prepared from the ongoing revision of the second edition of my *Hardy's Textbook of Surgery*. Since as editor I read each contributor's typed manuscript, then his galley proof and finally his page proof, I knew a lot about many

Moscow, 1971. JDH with Russian children who had had heart operations. Reproduced by permission of the University of Pennsylvania Press. (Memoirs)

things in most of the surgical specialties. And with the wealth of pertinent slides that I had assembled over the years, I announced through a VA system newsletter that I was available as a Visiting Professor. It may be seen from the illustration that these visits extended from the east coast to the west coast, but were concentrated in the south and mid-west. I tried to go to hospitals that probably had had few visitors. (The Duke Medical Center VA Hospital didn't need more speakers, I was sure.)

These visits to the different hospitals were a pleasure and rewarding—because they were truly appreciated. Even after my tour of duty was over, I received letters that my visit was the high point of the year. I usually stayed for three full days at the hospital visited. I did not operate, but I discussed the "unknown" cases that were presented (zebras, they were called). I made patient rounds and gave several of my 40 canned talks.

One of the hospitals in Missouri was truly way out in the interior boondocks, and as I was leaving, I told the manager that I would like to ask just one question. But before I could ask my question he beat me to it, "Everybody wants to know how a VA Hospital was placed in this lonely spot, and there is a story here. Mr. X, a citizen of this county, was in Harry Truman's outfit (artillery?) in WWI. And he had supported Harry in every political campaign through the years.

When Truman became president, he asked Mr. X what he wanted and he replied, Mr. President, I want just one thing, a VA Hospital in my county."

"You've got it!" Harry said.

I was eligible to serve a second three-year term, but by that time my wife's health condition required that she be at home, and I wanted to be with her.

One is reluctant to list several special honors, especially after noting the presidencies of a number of surgical societies elsewhere in this volume. But the ones below surely deserve special mention:

- The James D. Hardy Clinical Sciences Building
- The James D. Hardy Chair of Surgery (to be occupied by future chairmen of the Department of Surgery)
- The James D. Hardy Lectureship (to be delivered each spring by a surgeon selected by the current chairman)
- The James D. Hardy Library in the Department of Surgery
- The Matas Lectureship and Medal, The New Orleans medical schools, especially Tulane
- Moscow – Two medals, one for transplantation of the first lung in man and one for transplanting the first heart in man.

The dedication of the James D. Hardy Clinical Sciences Building. Left to right: Louise Sams (Weezie) Hardy, Bettie Winn Hardy, JDH, Katherine Hardy Little, and Louise Roeska-Hardy

*Dedication of the James D. Hardy Library in the Department of
Surgery Left: William W. Turner, Jr., M.D., Chairman of the
Department of Surgery Middle: James D. Hardy, M.D.
Right: A. Wallace Conerly, M.D., Dean and Vice-Chancellor,
University of Mississippi Medical Center*

Professor Vichnevsky: (Again)

The toast: "Professor Hardy, a lot of water has passed
under the bridge since you transplanted the first heart in
man but remember this: No words can ever be taken from
a poem, or notes from a song."

- PERU – THE ORDER OF THE SUN. I was called urgently
to assist in an operation on President Velasco for a leaking
abdominal aortic aneurysm. He went into shock while I
was en route, and the vascular surgery talent in Lima had
been mobilized to operate. There were several
postoperative problems that might have been avoided,
but the most immediately threatening was severe

373

ischemia of his right leg. His overall condition was so precarious that I elected to do only a fasciotomy on the right lower leg. The color of the leg improved but in the future it would be necessary to improve blood flow to the right leg.

Some months later I was invited to the Peruvian embassy in Washington to receive the Order of the Sun, the highest award that can be bestowed on a non-Peruvian. It was a most imposing occasion, with a reception, television and the Ambassador's and my acceptance remarks recorded. My name was then entered into the handsome volume which contained the others who had received the Order of the Sun. Weezie and our four daughters were present for the ceremony.

HONORARY MEMBERSHIPS:
- The Royal College of Surgeons, London (Honorary Member)
- The French Academy of Medicine (Honorary Member)
- The French Association of Surgery (Honorary Member)
- Philadelphia Academy of Surgery (Honorary Member)

James D. Hardy, M.D. Retirement portrait, 1987.

CHAPTER 17

୧୭

*The Family Unit and Some Advice for Life**

"The Family Is The Laboratory for Life"

MARRIAGE. The family unit is the major central experience of most peoples' lives. Marriage can involve the partners in a host of both emotional, legal, and financial considerations—and this holds true regardless of whether or not the marriage survives. Almost one-half of first marriages in the United States will end in divorce. For this reason many facets of this legal commitment deserve pre-marital consideration.

TAKE TIME TO KNOW EACH OTHER. All too often infatuation is mistaken for love, and after marriage the couple may find that they hardly know each other.

AGE. For a young woman to marry a man several decades older can pose serious problems. First, the desire for sex may vary widely and cause serious problems. Second, the young wife may become increasingly frustrated when she would like to go out dancing but the husband just wants to stay home.

*James D. Hardy, M.D., Jackson, Mississippi, and
Louise Roeska-Hardy, Dr., Phil., Jugenheim, Germany*

CHILDREN. The young wife wants to have her children before she reaches the age at which the incidence of Down's syndrome in the offspring is increased. The older male may have children from a previous marriage and does not want the financial and emotional responsibility involved with a new set of children. Too, there is some evidence that anomalies may be increased in the offspring of an older man.

SAME SOCIAL BACKGROUND. For one or the other to have had limited education can prove to be an embarrassment when the two's relatives come together.

SHARED VALUES. It has been said that hopefully the couple will be looking in the same direction.

DIFFERENT RELIGIONS. This difference could make problems. For instance, when a Protestant marries a Catholic, he may be pressed to agree that children will become Catholic. Moreover, on Sundays the husband and wife are separated while he goes to his church and she goes to hers.

MONEY MATTERS. Know about the intended spouse's spending habits. Any debts? A gambler? A closet alcoholic? Case report: A friend married a charming and effective man, only to find out much later that he was a closet alcoholic. He would go six months or a year free of alcohol, but one day he would drink just one drink. He then lost control and went on a binge for a week. During this time, he would buy all sorts of items—TV, new car, or whatever and have these delivered to his home. His wife was distraught as this continued for years. She finally consulted her minister and got a divorce. As noted previously, in such circumstances a joint checking account can prove disastrous.

Your spouse's bad credit may disqualify you from getting a joint mortgage or car loan. Creditors may seize jointly owned assets to satisfy your spouse's debts.

Such financial problems can lead to divorce.

INCOME AND MONEY CONTROL. This consideration has many factors. Individual or joint checking bank accounts? If the wife works and makes much more than the husband, his pride may be in jeopardy. If the wife does not work, she needs to have an allowance for herself and an allotment for the home expenses. If these sums are liberal within the total monthly income, much good will is gained. A joint checking account has, on the face of it, distinct merit, but there is the risk of overdrafts and stiff bank penalties. By and large, we think it best that one person be responsible for the major checking account.

RESPECT. Many consider respect the most important requisite for a successful marriage. A myriad of possibilities exist that over time will affect the admiration of one partner for the other.

LOYALTY. Loyalty is to be prized in all human endeavors, and especially in marriage. Happiness can be the reward for the husband or wife who knows he or she has solid loyalty from the spouse, that he or she has signed on for the trip. And this type of commitment will permeate the knowing children. Although we do not have the data at hand, our observations of friends has appeared to show that the children of divorced parents are more likely to divorce, themselves, after their marriages.

MARRY ONLY FOR LOVE IF FEASIBLE? However, in some countries the marriage is often arranged by parents, and such marriages do usually become successful.

INFIDELITY. Infidelity produces a wound that never heals.

CHILDREN. With his children a man becomes placed, in both society and posterity. They present a fresh new slate on which the parents are privileged to write. How well the parents do this will influence the child for much of his or her life thereafter, even to adulthood and beyond.

NURTURE YOUR FAMILY. Try to spend time alone with each family member. And remember, the most important thing a man can do for his children is to love their mother. The time devoted to the family is the best investment he will ever make. To quote Professor Charles Dubost of Paris who performed the first successful resection of an aortic aneurysm in the abdomen, "Jim, in the end, it is only the family that counts"—this as he prepared to visit his son in Singapore.

RESPONSIBILITY. Train children to take responsibility commensurate with their age.

EDUCATION. Here we refer to formal education, for significant education begins at birth. By and large, the choice between public and private schools will be decided by the child's location, the quality of the public schools, and the level of the family finances.

One should make an effort to get to know the children's teachers. Get involved and thus serve as a role model for your child.

For college, the great difference between the costs of a major public university and a major private university can prove to be the deciding factor. For superior high school graduates a wide variety of scholarships are available, but almost any graduating high school student can get some college tuition assistance. The guiding principle is to give your children the best education you can afford.

THE CHILDREN'S ALLOWANCE. When children are young, the weekly "spending the allowance time" can provide togetherness during which money values, decision making, respect for property, and honesty can be taught. The performance of chores can (may) be tied to a part of the allowance, but we feel that the larger portion of the allowance should be given without strings attached. The amount of the allowance will depend on the finances of the family, but the child should not be "spoiled" by being given everything he or she might want. Not only does excessive giving distort the child's sense of values; it also does not prepare the child for the financial realities of adult life. An only child is especially at risk.

When children are older, buying them a few shares of common stock may interest them early not only in investing but also in reading the newspaper, with the daily interest in local, national, and world affairs.

THE PRIMARY CARE GIVER. Be sure to make certain that the primary child care person (usually the mother) can get away from the routine of caring for the children and do something for herself that she enjoys so that she can in turn enjoy the children.

Likewise, establish a regular time to be alone with your spouse. Tell the children that mama and daddy want to spend some time alone. Even small children can learn that others deserve their "own time".

VACATION. The single person has great flexibility in choosing when and where to vacation. But the family with children has fewer options. However, there is much to be gained by family vacations. It usually involves a trip from the home environment. The father (and mother) are free from their work and other time commitments, and they are able to effect special bonding with the children that will be lasting. For example, the authors' favorite vacation site has been Destin, Florida, for over forty years, and even the Hardy grandchildren do not consider a vacation complete without spending some part of it in Destin.

DIVORCE. Heartache and a host of other considerations surround divorce, whether it is amicable or not. And the presence of children complicates matters still further. The many causes of divorce are beyond the scope (and knowledge) of this volume. However, if there are children, every possible effort should be made to save the marriage until the children are grown. For there is one fact that we do know. In most instances children do less well following divorce of their parents. We have seen, first hand, that children can "go to pot" after a bitterly contested divorce.

But if there must be a divorce, the children should be a first consideration. Clear lines as to what visitation rules are to be established are necessary and they should be followed. The opposing lawyers are not obligated to the children; their obligation is to get the best possible deal for their respective clients. The bitterly contested divorce places the children in an emotional wilderness. Their standard of living is usually diminished, with the educational and social limitations that this imposes.

PETS. Pets are important "members" of many or perhaps most homes, especially when there are children. Dogs are good companions in a great many ways and usually they reflect unmitigated loyalty toward their master. Having a pet not only delights the child but it gives training in the care which having a pet requires.

But pets come at a price. They require food, vaccinations, and veterinary service. If kept in the house, the animals may damage floors and carpets and still other furniture. If readily available, an obedience school will render the inside dog more easily managed. Liability insurance may be prudent if passersby on the street are injured.

However, pets are important and to most owners they are usually worth the price.

FAMILY FINANCE. Good finance is a basic component of family strength.

GENERAL GUIDES:

Be frugal. Spend wisely and with purpose. "Comfort without ostentation." Minor or major disasters will come to most families. These include major illness, severe injury to the breadwinner, divorce, death of a spouse, business failure, or the "pink slip".

Insurance. Life insurance on the major provider is essential. Likewise, health insurance should be given a priority. Automobile insurance is mandatory in many or most states and general insurance covering the house and contents is highly desirable.

The Females. The female members of the family should be given financial instruction along with the male members.

The older children should familiarize themselves with their elderly parents' financial resources, against the time when the children have to take care of them.

INVESTMENTS.

General Guidelines. Remember, no one else is as interested in the welfare of your money as you are. You must keep an eye on all major investments, whether in a trust fund or other management. Diversification is essential to financial safety. This holds with stocks, bonds, real estate, or other. To have all eggs in one basket can be disastrous.

Financial Planners. To the beginner a financial planner can be helpful, but research among your friends before selecting one. Many or even the majority of financial planners eventually turn out to be insurance or stock salesmen.

• Over the long haul common stocks (mutual funds) can show a better return than bank certificates. But federally backed bank certificates provide solid safety, greatly comforting when the stock market is down.

• Always keep a cushion of bank passbook deposit for unforeseen emergencies.

• Bonds require expertise beyond the ken of most initial investors.

• Real estate has been the source of many of the great U.S. fortunes. But it has the drawback of requiring a substantial financial outlay which for long periods may be nonproductive. Also, whereas stock or bonds can usually be sold promptly in an emergency, commercial or raw real estate may take many months, even years, to sell.

Trust Funds. For those who for one reason or another cannot manage their own finances, a trust fund can be useful. However, if the owner of the fund completely abandons his monitoring of his fund he does it at his peril. The biggest risk with some funds are the fund officers.

In closing, remember that a salesman must sell you something to make a living. His commission for selling one stock may be different than for another. The broker will not usually recommend a timely sell: To do so might impair his relationship with that company.

Taxes. Taxes must be paid. All applicable income must be reported. Failure to report all income can constitute a felony and the risk of imprisonment.

Keep all records of all income, all applicable expenditures, and all deductions. Good records are all important when you are audited by the various bureaus of internal revenue. Keep these records for at least three years.

THE DOCTOR AND THE FAMILY.

One of the first requirements upon moving to a new town or city is to find a competent and readily available doctor. This should usually be a general practitioner, who can refer to appropriate specialists if necessary. Such a physician can be located by consulting satisfied friends or by calling the county medical association. But however the physician is located and will accept still another patient, this physician should become "my doctor" and become knowledgeable regarding all members of the family.

Most modern physicians are well trained and up to date regarding important advances in medical knowledge. In the absence of a general practitioner, a general internist will serve.

For major emergencies, the emergency room of the nearest major hospital must be considered. If there is a university hospital in the area, competent medical care in all specialties is usually available.

The Doctor's Dilemma. What and how much to tell the patient of his fatal illness and how much to tell the family. It is justifiable to leave the patient the hope that therapeutic measures may to a degree be successful in the treatment of the widespread cancer, but the family must be told the precise situation. The patient must be made aware that he or she must put his affairs in order.

SAVING YOUR OWN HEALTH.

Do not smoke. Long term smoking not only causes mouth or lung cancer; it also causes numerous other conditions that include the heart and arteries throughout the body.

Avoid obesity and weight gain. Don't get fat. There are numerous deleterious effects, but a prominent one is the Type II obesity diabetes. Another is hypertension.

Alcohol in moderation. Chronic major alcohol intake can cause cancer of the mouth and esophagus, pancreatitis, and hepatic cirrhosis.

Lower cholesterol intake.

Fit exercise into your day. It has been shown that brisk walking for at least thirty minutes provides almost the same benefits as vigorous competitive exercise.

Get enough rest— mental and physical: Sleep.

WHAT TO TAKE TO THE HOSPITAL. Sooner or later the majority of Americans experience some period of hospitalization.

The most common needs are:
- Multiple pajamas or nightgowns, multiple sets of underclothes, bathrobe, socks or stockings.
- Toilet articles: for shaving with males and for

facial care with women.
- Reading materials.
- Writing paper and pen for notes.
- A few dollars for newspapers and magazines.
- Leave major valuables at home.
- Take health insurance policies.
- Arrange transportation.

DEATH IN THE FAMILY. The universality of death requires forethought and planning.

First, every adult should make a will to ensure that his or her wishes are carried out. And this will should be revised as a spouse and children come along. The will should in most instances be made by an appropriate attorney, and it should be stored in a safe place, as for example in a safety box in a bank.

When terminal illness is clearly at hand, the question will often arise as to whether or not tube or long term intravenous feeding is to be instituted. Families can be sharply and even bitterly divided over this problem. However, several studies have shown that tube feeding for the terminally ill does not prolong life and it often causes the patient major discomfort.

The death of a child or a beloved spouse can and will often cause profound sadness that may eventuate in clinically significant depression that requires professional counseling while time brings healing.

But the most immediate requirements are:
  -Select a funeral home.
  -Burial or cremation?
  -Select a burial plot.

Select a casket. (Beware of salesmen who recommend an unnecessarily expensive casket.)

Send notice and obituary to the newspapers with the desired recipients of the memorial contributions ("in lieu of flowers"?)

The Will and the Estate. Virtually all estates of significant value must be subjected to probate in many or most states. This process can be best managed through a lawyer who has special expertise in this field and knowledge of the laws of the given state.

SAVING TIME

Time is Like Money: Spend it Wisely

Intervals of Time. Each day provides an opportunity for a new beginning. Or, to quote our radio personality, Farmer Jim Neal, "Wake up, 'everybody, it's a brand new day. Ain't never been used yet." Honor Sir William Osler's daylight compartments.

Structure: The Day, the Week, the Month. When Margaret Thatcher was asked what she missed most from the office of prime minister, she is reported to have said it was the absence of the weekly structure: the cabinet meeting one day, the defense of her government in the house of commons another day, etc.

Getting Started. The first requirement of getting a task or job done is to start. Routine can help. A "leading in" choice may pave the way for the attack on the major task. Or, one can begin by starting around the edges, as with taking some examinations. Get out the materials and block out the time. Some writers drink coffee, and others sharpen pencils. With a piece of writing, it can be helpful to read what you have already written.

Do it Now. It will impress the boss. If you don't do it now it may be hard to get back to it later. And it has to be remembered. If possible, finish it at one sitting. For it will be more difficult when you return and events may make it difficult to get back to it (e.g., the physician and the new emergency).

The Notebook. Always have a notebook at hand for memory of tasks to be done and to capture useful thoughts.

Have a List of Priorities: for yourself and your associates.

Plan with your long term objectives in mind.

Learn to use little pieces of time.

Keep possibilities in your notebook.

Let The Essentials Come Last – This philosophy acknowledges the likelihood that the essentials will prevail before the deadline.

For Large Projects: Organize, communicate, and coordinate multiple elements. Set the firm deadline by which each element is to be completed.

In the home. For night lighting floor lamps can be superior to ceiling lights in that they are reachable for every member of the family to change the bulbs without finding a stepladder.

SAVING MONEY

A Firm Principle: Begin saving systematically early in life. Even as a young boy or girl, regular saving of a part of the allowance or money from another source, can develop into a sizeable amount over the years. The girl can do house tasks or chores for her mother and the boy can mow lawns or deliver papers. On the farm, the boy can sell produce from his own garden, drive tractors, and raise chickens. Other possibilities exist. The money derived from working gives the youngster a realistic sense of values in many directions. And it prepares him or her for life. When an adult, pay yourself first at the first of the month. Or even better, have this saving amount deducted automatically.

Do not mentally "categorize" unexpected money or income. Treat it exactly the same way you treat your regular income –carefully.

And keep the big picture in mind even when making "insignificant" purchases. It all adds up. What are your short term and long term objectives in life?

Do not borrow money for something you don't need.

The Risk of Borrowing Money (or other business) within the family. Failure to receive repayment promptly can impair interpersonal relationships. Failure to pay can reveal a private investment that has failed. At some times the recipient comes to think of the loan as a gift, and the giver is annoyed, but reluctant to ask for repayment.

The Risk of Credit Cards. The payment of a bill with a credit card seems less expensive than when cold cash has to be planked down. And this holds special risk for the person who holds multiple credit cards. The loss or theft of a wallet or purse containing many credit cards can result in the expensive loss of both time and money.

Look for Bargains But Only for What You Need. Avoid bargains across town except for major purchases. The cost of the automobile will offset the saving of the bargain.

Check the Newspaper "Want" Ads. And use the classified section for your own sales. It is no longer considered "tacky" to advertise discreetly and the current authors have saved many thousands of dollars in this way.

Household Maintenance Rules.

If you take it out, put it back.

If you use it up, replace or fill it up again.

If you open it, close it.

If you wear it, hang it up.

If you make a mess, clean it up.

Make Do. With imagination, many opportunities will arise to substitute for the broken or worn item. For instance, this is especially important on a large farm, when a new replacement may be fifty or one hundred miles away.

SHOPPING.

The Grocery Store. Make a list at home and stick to it. Check the refrigerator and pantry before going. Beware of impulse buying at the check-out counter.

Shopping for Clothes. Make a list of the clothes you need and stick to it. Beware of sales. Conservative colors. Buy quality. Remember that the number of times you wear a piece of clothing determines how expensive it is in the long run. A more expensive item worn for several years is a better buy than something inexpensive that doesn't last. Buy quality in coats. An inexpensive scarf, if worn and unflattering, is a waste of money. Take care to mend clothes and sew on buttons before a minor repair becomes a major effort. Buy two pairs of socks of the same color. Saves time when dressing.

If you pile clothes around the room, have one designated chair to catch the clothes. Periodically clean up the chair.

Major Purchases. Cash or credit? Shop around and get three bids. A close friend, a building contractor, stoutly maintained that the inscription he wanted on his tombstone was "He always got three bids." Research the large item. Check with friends and consult *Consumer Reports*.

The Automobile. New or Used? Cash or credit, or rent? There is much pleasure in having a new car, but its book value drops precipitously once the car has been driven even a short distance from the show room. A good used car, backed by a reputable dealer, will serve satisfactorily for most purposes. But for long distance and night driving, the security provided by a new and fully reliable car must be preferred when feasible.

A well maintained new car may begin to exhibit significant defects at four or five years. Then, this "new" car may become the second car and the purchase of a new car must be considered. Maintain the correct pressures in the tires. Automobile insurance is mandatory in many or most states.

Home Office Supplies. (Generally tax deductible). A copier is virtually indispensable as a time saver. A small one conserves home space. A computer is almost mandatory for storing records and the manifold other uses it provides.

For records, make a copy of any significant record, identify it, date it, and record what action was taken. Place names on photographs and where and when taken. Keep major documents such as the will in a bank safety deposit box. Use staples instead of paper clips which can be displaced.

Entertaining. Home or restaurant? The intimacy of a

small candlelight supper in the home may be selected. However, if a large group is to be in the home, it can be catered to allow the host and hostess to greet and visit with the guests.

• How much do you want to spend? If catered, get three bids unless the caterer is well known to you. Get a fixed price in advance.

• Place the flowers before a mirror.

• Polish silver and shiny surfaces.

Tipping at the restaurant: 15 to 20 percent of the bill if not included in the bill. If the tip is included in the bill (as it usually is in Europe), a few coins will suffice.

The Dwelling: Home or Apartment? An apartment would often be cheaper, but much satisfaction is derived from owning one's home. Too, until one buys a home, the other members of the community may not see permanence and may not accord the newcomer full acceptance as a member of the community establishment. The wife can plant bulbs with confidence she will see them bloom in the spring. Having the home also affords children a sense of solidarity, of place. Home ownership is a major stabilizing force in any community.

Work Ethic and Leadership
"Each Job is a Portrait of the Person who Did It"
General Considerations.

Punctuality. Chronic lateness will not be tolerated.

Motivation. Do the task like you are being paid for it, whether you are or not.

Do it Now. This will gratify your employer and it clears the day for other things.

Appearance. Put your best foot forward. Personal

grooming. Subdued colors with proper color codes. Have shoes shined and a recent haircut. Almost any young person can be attractive with good grooming. All this impresses not only the prospective employer: It also contributes to the wearer's self-esteem and confidence. Good grooming reflects respect not only for the hosts but for oneself as well.

Teeth. Attractive teeth convey a very positive impression.

Many years ago the senior author once sat beside a lady on the plane who had a major role in selecting new hostesses (now "flight attendants") for Delta Air Lines. It developed that the author's mother had taught her Latin in college. She said that the young lady's teeth were very important; but that if she had all the other positive attributes required, Delta could assist her in rendering her teeth attractive.

Dress, speech, and table manners place one in society. Avoid coarse or vulgar language and eschew profanity.

Attitude. If you must do a task (as in the military), do it pleasantly and well—and thus get full credit.

Work Structure. Develop a daily, weekly, and monthly work structure where feasible.

Excellence. Strive constantly to achieve maximum efficiency and excellence throughout your career.

Respect. Show respect for your co-workers. It will encourage them and it may be returned to you.

Guidance. Always remember who you are and what or whom you represent.

Cooperation. To get along, go along (within moral limits). But morality will be the ultimate reality.

Gossip. Do not gossip about colleagues. First, it may injure the target person, and, second, it may get back to you and impair your own standing with colleagues.

Loyalty. Every leader treasures loyalty on the part of his or her subordinates. He will see to it that a fully loyal employee thrives in the organization. Do not undercut your superior. Carried to extremes, it can result in administrative distrust, loss of the loyalty on the part of the leader, and even a citation for insubordination. And remember, the loss of one job can impair career momentum. The rolling stone gathers little moss.

PREPARE FOR LEADERSHIP

Public Speaking. Practice public speaking—club, church, business meetings, etc. The objective here is to stand and speak often enough to diminish the nervousness that commonly accompanies the need to speak to large groups of people. Remember the dicta: Speaking makes a ready man, writing makes an exact man, and reading makes a full man. Sensitivity and perception are essential to success in any field.

How to Give a Good Talk: Prepare carefully if time permits. Record ideas for months ahead. (The best way to give a good extemporaneous speech is to have an outline in each pocket!) Winston Churchill was said to develop bon mot remarks at home, against the time when they might be used in the House of Commons. Look upon the opportunity to address a large audience as a splendid opportunity. Many careers are made by seizing such opportunities successfully.

• Do not shave with a new blade immediately before a major address.

• As for the speech itself, several do's and don'ts are germane. Dress conservatively. Go to the lecture hall thirty minutes or, better, an hour before your talk is scheduled. Note the size and contour of the hall. Let the moderator know that you are present. If pertinent, slides and/or movie should be taken to the projectionist. Make sure the slides are in order. Sit near or on the front row. Ten minutes before your talk remind yourself that you are finally the next speaker. This will often activate the secretion of adrenaline, which will have subsided by the time you reach the podium. Know your audience. Do not exceed your allotted time. To do so is unfair to the next speakers and it irritates the audience.

• Expect, anticipate, and welcome questions from the audience (two of which you may have planted with friends). An active discussion period contributes to the rounded, fulsome aura of the address. Too, the discussion period can permit the speaker to make points that he did not have time for during his main address.

• Talk the address with slides or read it? It takes a lot more experience and poise to talk than to read. Both methods are effective but the talked address gives the speaker more contact with the audience. And, indeed, one of the British surgical societies informs the speaker beforehand that reading the remarks is not permitted.

• For the beginner, practice speaking to the mirror or to the spouse can be very useful.

How to Run a Board Meeting. Circulate the agenda prior to the meeting. Agree on the duration of the meeting.

• Prepare personally.

• If nominating, nominate first. This may discourage

further nominations. If supporting a proposal, before the vote, it may be well to speak last, taking into account the points raised by the previous speakers. Declaim vigorously to persuade the swing voters, for the pros and the cons probably will have decided already. Firm and steady persistence can move mountains.

Arbitration. Give each side time to withdraw, reflect, and then re-propose.

Written agreements. Always draw up written agreements before a major project is begun. This can preserve friendships and give credit where credit is due. For any publication of the results and conclusions, record who is to be the first author, the second author, etc.

How to Write a Business Letter: A Few Remarks. First, does the writer have a personal relationship with the recipient? What is the personage of the recipient? In general, the salutation should be mister if the recipient is older or is not known personally by the young sender. Err on the side of the last name rather than the first name if there is any doubt. And one should not address a much older and prominent man by his first name. For women, Mrs. is the preferable salutation of respect. In parts of Europe the mature woman still not married may elect to be addressed as Mrs.

Similarly, the closure of the business letter should reflect respect. Whether the closure is "Sincerely" or "Sincerely yours" will depend on the circumstances, but when in doubt it is safer to use the "Sincerely yours."

Rest assured that some recipients will be put off by an inappropriate salutation or closure, though they would never mention it.

A sealed letter carries more weight than an unsealed letter. And a stamped and mailed letter can be most welcome to a shut-in who now gets little first-class mail.

Recommendations. Can impact a busy person's time. Fortunately, the majority of persons requesting are pretty sure of getting a positive recommendation. However, some cannot honestly be given a strong recommendation and a dilemma arises. Therein lie three possibilities: (a) Tell the supplicant that one cannot recommend him or her, and no one wants to do that. Or, (b) a bland recommendation ("damn with faint praise"), or (c) recommend everyone with high praise. The "c" group recommendations eventually become known as worthless.

Delegate. Persons with less experience can perform many or most of the necessary tasks satisfactorily.

Departmental Audits. No organization through which significant amounts of money pass is immune from the risk of financial irregularities, most commonly some form of embezzlement. The responsible officer who ignores this possibility may eventually lose his own position.

Lawsuits. Occur almost everywhere in the United States and the person without liability insurance is at serious risk, especially if rumored to be wealthy ("deep pockets"). The insurance company will usually have a lawyer, but the defendant is wise to have his own lawyer. Lawyers' fees can vary widely for the same work (as do doctors'), and the charges of each lawyer consulted should be known at the outset (shop around).

Challenges. Face up to unpleasant problems promptly and do it first.

Achieve Continued Growth. Go to the meetings in

your field and keep abreast of advances. Example: A middle aged surgeon had trained originally at a major U.S. clinic. But after he entered practice, he did not feel the need for continued study and attendance at medical meetings. So, new operations came along and some of those he knew became obsolete. His practice had dwindled to a less than "make the ends meet" level. With impressive courage, he borrowed money, pulled up roots and with his family took cancer training in New York. Thereafter he went to Florida and became successful again.

The Local Hazards of Being Nationally Famous. We all like to be recognized nationally but it comes at a price. One may be named to more and more national committees, each requiring plane travel away from his home base. However, excessive absence will be noted, and a change may be made.

The Road to The Presidency. Being a good secretary (dependability) commonly leads to the presidency.

Enjoy Your Work. This can represent the greatest strength through the inevitable vicissitudes of life.

Achieving Immortality. Some measure of immortality is available to everyone. Make a contribution. TEACH: Children, colleagues, friends, and everyone who comes your way.

THE HEART AND MIND
Courtesies, Integrity, Self-Esteem, and Self-Renewal
Courtesies
General Principles
- Be pleasant.
- Be on time.
- Accept compliments with grace. Just say thank you.

• When you are meeting a person, go forward, state your name and shake hands.

• With house guests: Ask "How long can you stay?" Instead of "When are you leaving?"

• When visiting the sick, perhaps take a small present and make the visit brief. (It is tiring for the patient to entertain you.) But a brief visit conveys more than the telephone call with the "let me know if I can do anything." (But the call is also appreciated.)

• Make courtesy calls when you arrive and when you depart from a neighborhood or organization. You may meet them again, somewhere, sometime, as in the military.

• Offer congratulations in public, for this enlarges the dimensions of the congratulations. But make criticism in private. Remember, sticks and stones can break the bones but words can break the heart.

• Rehearse names before going to a meeting.

• When giving a dinner party, a glass of sherry and tiny biography cards to strangers who will sit together promotes welcome conviviality.

• In general, religion and politics can be risky topics and are usually best avoided.

• To remember a name, it is safe to ask where the person was born, how he or she came to live in this town. Try to associate the name with objects and relatives. Use the name several times and write it down as soon as possible. Knowing the work he or she does is very helpful but it is awkward to ask unless the guest volunteers it. People are flattered when their names are remembered.

• **The Letter.** As noted earlier, when writing a letter bear in mind the person and personage of the recipient. The inclusion of a remembered fact known only by the sender and the recipient may be included appropriately and to advantage. The salutation and the closure should reflect the writer's respect or affection, etc. It is inappropriate to use the first name to a person barely known. On the envelope, use the full name with the middle initial.

With the closure, graded nuances are often imperative. Titrate the circumstances. For a legal document or business letter, use your full name on the former and "Sincerely yours" on the business letter.

Examples for closure:

> *Sincerely*
> *Sincerely yours*
> *Warm regards*
> *Very warm regards*
> *Best regards*
> *Warmest regards (or best wishes or very best wishes)*
> *Affectionately*
> *With affection*
> *Always with affection*
> *Love*
> *Love you*
> *I love you (to sweetheart, wife or children)*
> **... And still others**

Unfortunately, the word "love' has come to be used so carelessly and indiscriminately that it no longer imparts the meaning it once did (to our regret).

• Do not mail an angry letter immediately.

• **Meet the Speaker**. Go forward, state your name, shake hands and compliment the speaker. He or she will appreciate it.

- **The telephone presence** of both you and your secretary is very important—as is that at the other end. The caller can, and will, form either a positive impression or a negative impression of the officials and the firms at the other end of the line. An intuitive and literate secretary can be invaluable to her boss and the firm.

- **How to get off the telephone gracefully** (without excessive fibbing). Keep in mind a variety of time deadlines for the hours of the day.

- **Return phone calls** (and answer letters) promptly. A thank you note is essential. It at least lets the sender know you received the present.

- **Anniversaries.** To the extent possible, remember birthdays and graduations and attend weddings and funerals. If time does not permit, send cards or other messages. Remember, with funerals you are honoring not only the deceased but his or her living relatives as well.

- **When a telephone call is less than a letter.** During World War II, the wife longed for a letter, as she herself wrote every night. But only a call came about every six weeks, though he was stationed in the United States.

- **To have friends you must be one and especially in time of need.**

- When conveying an important matter to an associate, **do it in person** if possible, instead of a note or telephone call. Some are acutely offended if only the secretary is the conduit of major matters.

- **Allow others to be "right" often.**

- **Do not interrupt or finish sentences.**

- **Become a better listener.**

- **Promiscuous use of first names** on brief acquaintance is likely to offend. In South America, a

402

married woman must not be addressed by her first name on brief acquaintance.

INTEGRITY
Do it.

- **Develop and maintain a reputation for integrity.**
- **Keep promises.** If you say you will do something then do it—and do it well. But be careful about what you agree to do.
- **Treasure your reputation** in all directions and dimensions. It is worth more than gold.
- **Morality** is the ultimate reality. A man's true life is that accorded him in the thoughts of other men.
- **Always remember who you are and what you represent.**
- **Exhibit rock hard honesty**—a man of his word.
- **Use hyperbole sparingly** (e.g., in recommendations).
- **Cheating and lying.** Loss of intellectual virginity. Unfortunately, once caught in cheating or lying, the character deficiency is exposed. Complete trust will not be regained.
- **Humility** becomes almost everyone.
- **Telling jokes.** Are almost all jokes cruel to some race, religion, prejudice, politics, etc.?
- Again, loyalty in all its dimensions and directions, is essential to happy relationships.
- **Honor thy mentors.** If school teachers, they have established the prestige of your institution and enhanced the value of your diploma.

SELF-ESTEEM AND SELF-RENEWAL
The art of happiness lies in the avoidance
of unpleasant thoughts.

• The **more interests** one has, the greater the possibilities of avoiding boredom and depression.

• **A hideaway** (a get-away) on a lake, without a telephone, may afford the needed respite. They don't know who you are and they don't care.

• **Hobbies, brief vacation, gardening.**

• For **disappointments** or failure, hold on and give time the opportunity to heal.

• Have a place to which you can **imagine** you're there: e.g., Neustadt in Germany or a hillside in Wales, are mine for meditation.

• **Early morning pleasures**: Coffee, newspaper, a brisk walk. Have quiet time for reflection each morning.

• **Mental health** is like riding a bicycle, one must keep moving. Completing unfinished projects will enhance self-esteem. However, each individual has a different threshold for becoming depressed by the same set of factors. Most of teenagers and adults can remember temporary periods of depression prompted by loss of a love, loss of a job, or a host of other causes. However, the vast majority recover mental health and in good time. It is the neurotic personality, the worry wart, who is most likely to exhibit clinically significant depression. Such persons should avail themselves of professional counseling.

• **Giving** to others anonymously can rebound to happiness for the giver.

• **Church work** can be a positive antidote to depression, and it affords a complete break with daily business routine.

CHAPTER 18

The Hardy Family

A Gallant and Beloved Wife and Mother

Louise ("Weezie") Scott Sams Hardy

• Born 312 S. Candler St., Decatur, Georgia, May 20, 1920. Youngest of three siblings, "A happy child."

• Agnes Scott College (just across the street and founded by her forebears). A.B., 1941.

• Married July 1, 1949.

• Lived first in Philadelphia where her husband was in a thoracic residency and held a Damon Runyon cancer fellowship.

• Her family was her career:

• First child, Louise Scott Hardy, born July 29, 1950. Blue eyes and curly hair like her father.

• Second child, Julia Ann Hardy, born October 30, 1951, a replica of her mother. Third child, Bettie Winn Hardy, born June 26, 1953, and fourth child, Katherine Poynor Hardy, born April 19, 1955.

She went to high school five times, once for herself and four times with her children. Three of these children made Phi Beta Kappa. The fourth barely missed Phi Beta Kappa when the "bar was raised" abruptly, but she made the equally impressive Alpha Omega Alpha, the scholarship society of medical schools.

Weezie's parents: Hansford Sams and Louise Scott Sams

Weezie's community participation in Jackson included member of the Auxiliary of the Covenant Presbyterian Church, the book review group, the Antique Club, the Casual Club, Town Club, Research Club, University Women's Group, University Medical Center Women's Auxiliary, the Discussion Club and the International Friends. Weezie visited the PTA meetings, visited the children's classrooms and knew their teachers. She ferried pupils to class outings and one of her favorites was a little black boy six or seven. Leroy, utterly uninhibited, spouted his wisdom from the time he got into the car until they had returned.

THE DISCUSSION CLUB. Shortly after we took up housekeeping in Philadelphia, Weezie and I formed a discussion group amongst our friends, after the lead of Benjamin Franklin in earlier years. These meetings were pleasant but not adequately informative for the several hours of the evening that they consumed. I was discouraged. And one night not long before Weezie and I

Home. Reproduced by permission of the University of Pennsylvania Press. (Memoirs)

left Philadelphia for Memphis, the last departing guest stuck her head back through the door and said, "Folks, it won't work if you drink."

Forward to Jackson. There Dr. Michael Newton, Chairman of Obstetrics and Gynecology, and his wife Dr. Niles Newton agreed to address the prospect of a Discussion Group, again. The format would include dessert but no alcohol, and the topic for discussion would be chosen and run by the host and hostess. The meetings were to be in the homes of the members and to be rotated monthly for ten months of the year. Some hosts elected to bring in a speaker, but Weezie and I adhered to the original philosophy that the objective would be true discussion and not lectures.

This Club was organized around 1955 and it continues today forty-six years later. Some of the original members have died, or moved away, or simply dropped out, but the basic corpus of the club membership has been maintained by inviting enthusiastic new members. The membership roster has usually been maintained at about twenty-five, but the monthly attendance has been on the order of about twenty or so. Weezie and I chose a wide variety of topics over the years, but I will cite only two. The first was during the segregation struggles of the 1960's. I had invited Doctor Felix Ominsky, a "Freedom Rider" from Chicago, who had been in the Mississippi Delta. I felt that our membership, largely segregationists, should hear the other side. Dr. Ominsky arrived wearing a black tam, a long golden chain with an emblem at the bottom, a black beard, and sandals. I welcomed him in, but the lady pouring the coffee almost dropped the cup! I don't recall what specific title was used, but after my opening remarks I asked Dr. Ominsky, seated by the Steinway grand piano, if he had any remarks thus far. Removing the pipe from his mouth, he noted that all doctors got rich and built a fine home like this! (The genteel audience gasped at such a break in etiquette.)

From there on the exchange between Dr. Ominsky and the male members, which included several lawyers, became vigorous indeed.

Then the Doctor slipped out. But several members just wished they could see him again, to continue the exchanges. But, in good form, one attorney observed that even General Robert E. Lee had worn a beard.

But now I had dug myself into a hole. Should I say nothing more? Or should I "tell all" on the spot? I elected the second choice. Rapping on the piano to get the attention of the thoroughly "activated" audience, I said, "Folks, Dr. Ominsky is my chief resident in surgery. He *is* from Chicago and he *has* been in the Delta—drawing blood from volunteers at our state penitentiary."

408

Mother "Nubbin" and the four "nubbinoids." Left to right: Julia, Bettie, Katherine, and Louise Hardy. Reproduced by Permission of the University of Pennsylvania Press. (Memoirs)

The second program I'll mention was undertaken after polling several couples. I had come across a book, approximately "*How Smart is Your Pet?*", published by the University of Chicago Press, as I recall. I asked if those polled would prefer this topic or "the resurgence of tuberculosis." (I was certain that my bird dog, Tennessee, would prove to be the smartest pet.) But without exception, the voters chose tuberculosis. I engaged the Mississippi state tuberculosis control officer for a brief current status report and invited a University Medical Center bacteriologist to set up a microscope in the back room and assist each guest in seeing what tuberculosis bacilli looked like. I then set up a recording of *Traviata* in the front room and of *La Boheme* in the back room. When all the guests were seated in the front room, both operas were abruptly snapped off, then I tapped the lectern and asked, "May we arise and honor the late departed."

409

Everyone did. I then tapped again and said, "The heroines of Verdi's *Traviata* and of Puccini's *La Boheme* have just died of tuberculosis. Tuberculosis has been a scourge of mankind for thousands of years."

THE INTERNATIONAL FRIENDS. As our department proceeded with transplantation research, we had an increasing number of applications for research participation and training in this field. Most of these applicants were from foreign countries, notably from Japan and Turkey but also from Great Britain and other western world countries as well. In general, the men spoke English well enough, but the wives were stuck in their apartments with small children and little chance to get out.

Weezie and others conceived the idea of establishing an International Friends organization which would meet monthly, invite these wives from foreign countries, provide for the care of the children too young to be in school, and put on an attractive program for them. This project was quite successful.

Incidentally, there was always the risk that the male applicant's English might not be adequate to permit effective participation in our research programs. But one Japanese applicant's English was exceptionally good, so we took him. To our dismay, when he arrived in Jackson with his young wife, he could speak virtually no English. His young wife, a pharmacologist, had written his application material for him!

"I SLAPPED LOUISE" (Weezie's personality). Weezie had a gentle personality and she affirmed soon after she became pregnant with her first child that we must never strike the child, that corporeal punishment had never been employed in her family.

My answer: "We'll see."

Then one day I came home from the hospital to find her at the door in tears. "What can be the matter?" I asked.

To this: "I slapped Louise!" (now about four years old).

I comforted the wounded mother: "Doubtless richly deserved."

Weezie never complained, and her ancestral breeding maintained the social amenities to the very end of her life.

I could rarely get out of the hospital before noon on Saturday, and so I eschewed golf, and tennis was delayed until they were big enough to learn and play.

But we did a lot of things together:
- dinner together each night
- tussling with the four on the floor
- gardening: Each girl had her row marked with the brightly colored seed packet on a stick.
- swimming at the River Hills Club
- the Memphis and Jackson Zoos. The girls loved a penguin at Memphis, but when we read in the paper that he had died we said nothing.
- walking together
- and going to spend the allowance on Saturday afternoon. The objective here was to give Weezie some time to herself, to bond with the girls, money values, honesty, respect for others' property, and practice in making decisions.

We all attended the Covenant Presbyterian Church together, where Weezie and I were among the initial members and where I served as an Elder for six years.

FAMILY VACATIONS. Beginning shortly after we had moved from Memphis to Jackson, Destin, on the Florida

411

Going to spend the allowance.
Left to right: Bettie Winn Hardy, Louise Hardy, Katherine
Hardy, and Julia Hardy, JDH in back.
Reproduced by Permission of the University of Pennsylvania
Press. (Memoirs)

412

*Destin, Florida,
circa 1990.*

*Destin, Florida, circa 1990.
Left to right: Louise Roeska-Hardy, James D. Hardy,
Louise S. Hardy, Bettie Winn Hardy, Katherine H. Little*

413

panhandle, became our favorite vacation site and it remains so to this day, forty-five years later. Even our grandchildren consider any summer vacation incomplete that does not include the visit to Destin.

BREAKING THE SET. September 19, 1968, represented a major departure in the life of our little family. This was the day we drove Louise to Atlanta and to Agnes Scott College in nearby Decatur. It was poignant in many ways, for Louise represented the third successive generation "Louise Scott" who had attended this all-girls college founded by her maternal great-grandfather. A businessman, he had believed that daughters should have a college education as sons did.

Just as we had finished loading the station wagon, the other three girls began to sing to Louise a little tune which was popular at that time and went *"And now you're going away."* At first we all joined in but presently it dawned on us that she really was going away, and we all fell silent.

For reasons not fathomable to me, I remained depressed for some weeks thereafter. No other departure, whether to college or marriage, ever pulled so strongly at my heartstrings. In retrospect I believe it was because this was the first breaking of the set of our little family, which had been close in Jackson because we were new there, often besieged politically, and had relatively few close friends. In succession, Julia went to Vanderbilt, Bettie to Southern Methodist University (SMU) in Dallas and Katherine to Vanderbilt.

1970. THE CARNIVAL BALL. Under the auspices of the women's Junior League, this was the premier social event of the Jackson season. By custom the king was elected secretly by members of the Junior League, as was the queen. The king was a mature and indeed at times almost an elderly man, whereas the queen was always a young lady, usually in college or just out of college. The king was generally some person prominent in civic affairs in one direction or another.

Before the 1970 Ball, several University personnel had in 1969 asked me if it was true that I was going to be named king. I had not been approached, but it suggested that my name had been considered, and inadvertently disclosed by some League "leakee."

But on September 11, 1969, about 9:30 p.m. I was called by the president of the League and she requested a meeting with me. I asked, "Now?" and she said "Yes, now." So she and two other members came that night to my home and informed me that I had been elected king for the 1970 Ball. My designation would be King Echo—a nymph in Greek mythology who pined for Narcissus until nothing was left of her but her voice.[1]

My queen was the lovely Miss Isabel (Ibby) Lutken. The Ball was held on Saturday, January 31, 1970, at 8:15 p.m.

It was a splendid event—the secrecy, colors and pageantry. My ladies were delighted. The University Medical Center allowed me to take the several thousand dollars paid for my regalia as a practice expense. I treasured the royal robes, the sword and crown for many years, but in 2000 I elected to donate them to the Junior League of Jackson, where they remain on display.

JOHANN SEBASTIAN BACH ("BACH"). I had cast about for a special Christmas present for Weezie when I recalled

[1] Webster's New Collegiate Dictionary, G. & C. Merriam Company, Springfield, Massachusetts, U.S.A., 1979.

415

King and Queen of the Carnival Ball,
James D. Hardy and Isabel Lutkin
Jackson, MS, 1970.
Reproduced by permission of the University
of Pennsylvania Press. (Memoirs)

that over the years she had expressed a liking for schnauzers. So, I asked our veterinarian where I could find a puppy that was to be weaned just before Christmas. He gave me the name and telephone number of a breeder in Columbus, Mississippi. I called him but all of his litter were already spoken for, but he said that a schnauzer breeder right here in Jackson had a new litter, a Mr. Jacobs. I called this breeder and as we chatted about price and timing he suddenly asked, "Aren't you Dr. Hardy?"

I replied that I was and he said, "Dr. Hardy, I'm a medical student in your quiz section!"

He urged me to come promptly and make my choice. The most captivating puppy was a female, but I wanted to avoid pregnancies. I chose the largest male, for Mr. Jacobs said that the larger the puppy at birth, the more likely he was to survive childhood. Mr. Jacobs told me to come over on Christmas morning, with a ticking alarm clock, a towel, and a warm hot water bottle in a box. The puppy would think he was with his mother and would not bark.

I secretly took the puppy home and wrapped the box in Christmas paper and placed it under the tree. I had left one corner of the wrapping open, for ventilation.

The daughters knew what was in the box and, as I passed out the presents, they kept saying to give Mamma her present. This I finally did and, on seeing my corner ventilation, she said, "And I see that you wrapped it yourself!"

She put her hand down into the box and exclaimed, "It is a furry toy."

But then the "toy" moved and she saw that it was a schnauzer puppy. She was totally delighted. She chose the name Johann Sebastian Bach, with "Bach" for short. The two were inseparable for the fifteen years he lived.

THE HARDY FAMILY
*Front Row: Louise Roeska-Hardy, Susanne Roeska, David
Little, Katherine Hardy Little, Katherine Louise Little (in lap),
Anne Hardy Story, Bettie W. Hardy, and Elizabeth Story.
Back Row: Daniel Roeska, Louie Little, Weezie Hardy, JDH,
Mark Story. Below: Karl-Otto Roeska and Julia Ann Hardy
Circa 1991*

DEATH OF A TWIN. After finishing medical school in
Philadelphia, Julian had returned to do his internship and
residency training at the Hillman Hospital in
Birmingham, where a new four-year medical school was
soon to be established. He married Marion Doughty of
Tuscaloosa, whom he had met when he and I were
freshmen in college at the University of Alabama.
Thereafter they had lived in Birmingham where he
conducted his private practice of obstetrics and
gynecology successfully. He had been recognized in
numerous ways, including the presidency of the Jefferson
County Medical Society. We saw each other perhaps not
more than twice a year, but we always felt immediate

intimacy of thought and confident reliance upon each other's trust.

One night, apparently by sheer coincidence, his son Pat and daughter Anne called me in Jackson to say that they were deeply worried about their father. They said that he did not act like himself and that they thought he was sick, though he maintained that he was not and saw no need to get a check-up. I had known that he, a longtime smoker, had had a bronchitis or something, but I had thought he was generally well. Taking the plane to Birmingham the next morning, and a taxi from the airport to his home in the Mountain Brook area, I found him alone at home, lying in bed and staring soberly at the ceiling. This simply was not Julian! Always very active, he clearly was not well.

He mentioned a recent chest X-ray. I asked him to get up and get dressed, and suggested we go over to his hospital and see the chest X-rays that his internist colleague had taken. Though they were more or less perfunctory, I saw a lesion in the right lower lung field, and Julian remarked that he had been very tired lately. He also told me, now, that he'd had angina pectoris on several occasions.

He agreed to see a cardiologist at the University of Alabama Hospital and cardiac catheterization and coronary angiography disclosed a severe stenosis of the left main coronary artery, which could prove immediately fatal if total occlusion should occur.

Coronary bypass was performed and he was awake and alert by early afternoon.

But about a week later his wife called me to say that she was worried about him, though his doctors did not seem to be concerned.

I rushed back to Birmingham, to find a most disturbing state of affairs. Julian had fever of about 103°F, a rapid pulse and his nostrils flared with each breath indicating air (oxygen) hunger. It was a Sunday but I managed to contact the resident, who said that Julian was not cooperating and that they were considering bringing in a psychiatrist!

I said that Julian was a very sick man and that he certainly did not need a psychiatrist.

In sum, he died suddenly some days later from (another?) massive pulmonary embolus.

ILLNESSES IN THE JAMES D. HARDY FAMILY SEXTET. Our family had the usual run of less than truly major illnesses and operations. Louise had an appendectomy and Bettie, now in Dallas, had an exploratory laparotomy for what was feared to be ovarian cancer but proved to be the benign endometriosis. The major "illnesses" were those of Weezie and myself.

My year of the Presidency of the American College of Surgeons began in October, 1980. It was continually eventful, but added to the professional considerations was a possible personal problem. Some months after I began my tenure as President, while standing in my office gazing out the window one Saturday morning as I prepared to thumb through some unread surgical journals, I had abrupt blurring of vision in my left eye, with a feeling of faintness. I quickly sat down in a chair and the attack passed off in a few moments.

Having routinely performed surgery on the four neck arteries to the brain, I knew at once that I might have had a cerebral transient ischemic attack (TIA)—a momentary blockage of a small artery to some segment of the brain.

The Hardy Doctors at Katherine's wedding.
Left to right: Louise, Bettie, Katherine, Julia

I noted the possible import of this visional disturbance but did nothing about it. Then, again, on a cold night in January, 1981, I went down to the office to do some work, started to hang up my topcoat with my left arm as usual, and suddenly found it weak. There seemed

421

to be no loss of sensation in the hand. No pain. This too passed off within a few moments and there were no other symptoms then or thereafter. Nevertheless, the previous eye problem, plus the current arm weakness, could well presage a serious condition. I resolved to check it out. However, as I was just beginning my year as President of the College, it was not convenient or advisable, from a political standpoint if no other, to go into a hospital in the United States to have studies performed, including carotid arteriograms.

The Executive Committee of the International Society of Surgery required my travel to Basel, Switzerland, twice a year and the next meeting was less than a month away. I asked Dr. Robert D. Currier, Chairman of our Department of Neurology, to try to arrange carotid arteriography in London. It developed that he knew Sir Roger Bannister (the original four-minute miler but now a neurologist at the National Hospital for Neurological Diseases). Dr. Currier wrote to Dr. Bannister and alerted him to the fact that I would be in touch with him.

After giving Dr. Currier's letter time to reach London and be considered, I called Dr. Bannister. He assured me that he would be glad to take me as the private patient I wished to be. He went on to say, however, that he could not allow me to have the arteriograms one day and then fly on to Germany the next day. At the very least, I would have to plan to be in the hospital before the arteriogram and for two or preferably three days thereafter to be observed for any late complications.

He wanted to know why I did not have the arteriograms in the United States. I told him of my presidency, that there was hardly any hospital I would choose where I would not be known. He advised me not to delay management too long, lest a stroke occur, and he advised that I take aspirin daily.

My Automobile Wreck. At about 6:45 A.M. on December 4, 1981, I was driving down to the hospital, as I had countless times over the years. The next thing I knew I was asking one of our surgery interns, who was looking down at me on the examining table, what was going on.

He said, "Dr. Hardy, you have been in an automobile accident." It was a busy time of morning, when nurse shifts were changing, and one of our University nurses happened to be just at the site adjacent to the St. Dominic's Hospital. She and a young physician both said that another driver had cut suddenly in front of me, against the light, and I had hit him broadside. This was corroborated by the police. It was said that I had got out of my badly damaged Mercedes, and announced that I did not need to go to a hospital. Of all of this I had no memory and never did have. The neurologists call this a traumatic regressive amnesia.

In any case, I proved to have fractures in both hands and a fracture of the right patella. Head X-rays and a CAT scan disclosed no skull or brain damage, though my head had hit the windshield. (At that time I was not routinely wearing a seatbelt.) A marked slowing of my heart rate developed (my chest had struck the steering wheel), and for a day or so serious consideration was given to the insertion of a pacemaker for heart block, at least temporarily. The heart monitor was strapped on but with the gradual increase in the heart rate, the need for a pacemaker receded.

The care I received from our nurses was superb. I had known they were good, but seeing them through the eyes of the patient, I was even more impressed and was grateful.

The first priority was to take care of the fractures. Our orthopedists had already managed these lesions, though it was necessary to wear casts on the hands and right leg for some weeks thereafter. The severe headaches were not as debilitating as the onset of truly extreme nausea and vomiting. This was probably due to temporarily increased intracranial pressure (in the "tight bony box"). But this gradually responded to anti-vertigo medication.

Carotid Artery Surgery. Arteriograms had now shown "ulceration" in both carotid arteries but the right one was especially affected and all my neurologic symptoms had been on the left, as would be expected.

Where to have the operation? My preference was to have the operation in our own hospital, but I was not satisfied with the anesthesia currently available and I decided to go elsewhere. After considerable reflection I chose Dr. Jesse E. Thompson at Baylor Hospital in Dallas. Since we had two daughters at Parkland Hospital, Weezie would have moral support and a place to stay.

The operation was eminently successful and I drove back to Jackson on the fourth postoperative day.

Several years later I had the left side operated upon in our own hospital.

My Heart Problems. I began to have angina pectoris and coronary arteriograms disclosed marked stenosis of the left anterior descending coronary artery and some moderate stenosis in the right coronary artery. Over the 1980's and well into the 1990's Dr. Patrick Lehan and his associates performed balloon dilatation for these stenoses four times. But finally, in January, 1999, severe renewed anginal pain made coronary bypass mandatory. Dr. Bobby Heath, our Chief of Cardiac Surgery, performed five bypasses over a period of almost three hours on the heart-lung machine. The result was excellent and I remain asymptomatic over three years later. (Sadly, Dr. Heath was drowned while scuba diving in the Bahamas.)

However, I discovered some side effects of prolonged cardiopulmonary bypass, few of which my own patients had rarely mentioned. First, I had clearly lost some elements of memory. For example, I continued to see Dr. L. Mac. on the wall as a former visiting professor. I could hardly believe that he had been in Jackson and I not know it. Finally, I just had to know when he had been here, that I must have been out of town. He replied that I had indeed been present and had treated him like a king. But with this jogging of my memory, I still had no recollection and none to this day.

The long pump run had changed my tastes, vision, smell, and minor motor activities. Specifically, my taste for coffee and sweets was greatly diminished. As for visual changes, when I looked out of a clear window there were geometrical designs on the pane.

Most of these changes gradually receded, but it left me wondering what else I might have forgotten.

LOUISE HARDY'S ILLNESSES.

Right Colectomy. Weezie had splendid resistance to the common cold and other respiratory tract diseases.

But one day when we were driving and hit a bump in the road, she felt deep pain in the right lower quadrant of her abdomen. We got an X-ray of her abdomen, and Dr.

Robert Sloan, Head of Radiology, called me down to see it. At some "prehistoric" time, Weezie had swallowed a straight pin and it had now penetrated the wall of the appendix to produce localized abscess formation.

This was only a week or so before Louise's marriage. Dr. William O. Barnett performed an exploratory laparotomy and found the expected inflammatory mass surrounding the appendiceal area. Since at Weezie's age cancer could not be excluded, a right colectomy was performed—uneventfully.

Alzheimer's Disease. By far, the most treacherous disease in the Hardy family appeared around 1981. It was hard to pinpoint but about this time, when she was about 65, she became depressed, couldn't sleep and lost weight. It was an insidious development, and I first thought it could represent the "empty nest" syndrome, for our youngest daughter Katherine, now Dr. Little, had married and left to intern at Parkland Hospital in Dallas.

But as time passed, I said to Weezie, "There's something wrong with you and we need to see a professional, psychiatrist or neurologist." Weezie was reluctant to see anyone at the University, for everyone there knew her, so I consulted a female psychiatrist practicing in Jackson. After preliminary assessment, Weezie was referred to the head of neurology at Tulane Medical School in New Orleans. We went down for several days and sleep tests and other possible causes of mental disturbance were excluded.

The conclusion there was that she did not have Alzheimer's disease and probably would never have it. But here I lost confidence in the examiners, on at least one point: Alzheimer's cannot be excluded short of a brain biopsy.

426

Weezie Hardy, circa 1981.

But our Jackson psychiatrist placed Weezie on a mood elevator and her depression was substantially improved. But her memory losses, though glacial in progress, continued inexorably.

It was like peeling an onion. Slowly, one by one, the things she'd learned over a lifetime were lost. She dearly

427

loved her little red Toyota but, after three accidents, all by inappropriate turning to the left against traffic, I had to sell her little car to preserve my own car insurance. She went to sleep while cooking something on the stove, and repairs cost $23,000. She began to wander and got lost at O'Hare Airport, in our own neighborhood looking for our dog (who was at home) and in the huge Galleria near the opera in Paris.

I had declined a second term as VA Distinguished Physician to be home with her, and we had a maid-sitter for most of the daylight hours. But it was a trip to our internist that finally brought matters to a head. I had placed her just inside the St. Dominic Hospital's back door, and told her not to move while I placed the car in a nearby parking space.

But when I returned she was gone! I had everybody looking for her, unsuccessfully, until I had a sudden idea: I told the police service to radio that she was wearing a white dress with large black polka dots. Very soon, a guard called from the back of a parking lot on the other side of the hospital. Rushing to her, I asked, "Weezie, what did you think you were doing?" She answered matter-of-factly, "I was going home." It almost broke my heart.

The reader of course cannot know the poignant memories this brought to mind but they stretched back to the Christmas before we married. I had come down to Charleston from Philadelphia and had driven us to Decatur, Georgia. I had not been specifically invited to stay at her parents' home. Though I expected to be invited, I also suspected that they would love to have their "baby" daughter alone with them one last time as a Sams.

In this uncertain state of affairs, I had privately

planned to go to a hotel. And Weezie asked me, "Aren't you going home?" (to Alabama). But I had no intention of not seeing her during Christmas. I said to her, "Weezie, don't you understand, home for *me* is where *you* are."

And then for some years after we'd married, when she said home she meant Decatur, Georgia. Then, one day, she said "home" and meant our home. And I fully knew, deeply for the first time, that I was forever responsible for the welfare of this girl who had left her happy home to become a Hardy.

I said to her, as we stood there in the hospital parking lot, "Come on, Angel, I'll take you home." And there came to mind the sad words of the song "I'll take you home again, Kathleen."

But this was the end of an era and we accompanied her a day or so later to St. Catherine's new Alzheimer's building. She lived there for about two years, for we had already "bought into" an apartment in the main building several years before. I visited her every day and she remained "happy" and involved in the many activities provided the patients. Above all, she loved jigsaw puzzles and played with them endlessly.

She had long since not known the names of her children, but she did recognize them as good friends. She knew me almost all the time, but sometimes I was not sure she was taking in what I was saying. So, two days before she died, I had asked her, "Weezie, what is my name?"

"James Daniel Hardy," she answered instantly. Then I asked, "Weezie tell me you love me."

And she said without hesitation, "I love you."

And these were the last words she ever spoke.

She died in her sleep in the early morning hours of

October 14, 2000. Even at 80, she had never lost her instinctive social graces and she was gallant to the very end.

CHAPTER 19

Appendix

CURRICULUM VITAE

BETTIE W. HARDY, B.S., M.A., Ph.D.
Born June 26, 1953, Memphis
Married Spouse: Mark Story
Children: Elizabeth and Anne

Current Position:
Clinical psychologist in private practice
1984- Clinical Assistant Professor of Psychiatry,
present Department of Psychiatry, University of Texas
Southwestern Medical Center

Education:
1975 B.S. Southern Methodist University,
major field of study - Psychology
Phi Beta Kappa
1976 M.A. Southern Methodist University, major field of study - General
Experimental Psychology

1982   PhD. in Clinical Psychology, University of Texas
            Southwestern Medical Center at Dallas

Work Experience:

1982-1983   Instructor in Psychology, Department of Psychiatry,
            University of Texas Southwestern Medical School

1982-1984   Chief Psychologist, Pediatric Inpatient
            Psychiatry Unit and Pediatric Psychiatry Consultation Service,
            Children's Medical Center at Dallas

1995-2001   Staff psychologist, Family Life Center, Dallas, Texas

1983-1995   Director, University of Texas Southwestern, Medical Center
            Eating Disorders Clinic

1984-1995   Associate Director of SMU Mental Health ServicePublications:

Articles: Thirteen, to include:

Dickstein, E.B. and Hardy, B.W.   Self-esteem, autonomy and
    moral behavior in college men and women. Journal of
    Genetic Psychology, 134:51-55, 1979.

Hardy, B.W., Waller, D.A., and Orsulak, P.J.   Bulimia and monoamin oxidase
    inhibitors: A predictor study. *Texas Medicine*, 81:39-42, 1985.

Waller, D.A., Chipman, J.J., Hardy, B.W., Hightower, M.S.,
    North, A.J., Williams, S.B., and Babick, A.J. Measuring
    diabetes-specific family support and its relation to
    metabolic control: A preliminary report. *Journal of the
    American Academy of Child Psychiatry*, 25:415-418, 1986.

Waller, D.A., Kiser, R.S., Hardy, B.W., Fuchs, I., Parkin-Feigenbaum, L., and
    Uauy, R. Eating behavior and plasma beta-endorphin in bulimia. *The
    American Journal of Clinical Nutrition*, 44:20-23, 1986.

Hardy, B.W., McIntyre, C.W., Brown, A.S., and North, A.J. Visual
    and auditory coding confusability in students with and
    without learning disabilities. *Journal of Learning Disabilities*,
    22:646-651, 1989.

Hardy, B.W., Waller, D.A. Bulimia and opioids: Eating Disorder
    or substance abuse? In Johnson, W.G. (ed.) *Advances in*

Eating Disorders, Volume 2, JAI Press, Greenwich, CT, 1989, pp. 43-65.

Community Service

Elder, Highland Park Presbyterian Church, Highland Park, Texas

CURRICULUM VITAE

JULIA A. HARDY, B.A., M.D.
Born October 30, 1951, Memphis
Vanderbilt University, B.A. and Phi Beta Kappa
Harvard, M.D.

PRACTICE AND STAFF POSITIONS

7/81 -Present	Private Practice of Outpatient Psychiatry: Psychiatric Consultation and Psychotherapy, Ann Arbor, Michigan
9/81-9/82	Clinical Instructor, Emergency Services Department of Psychiatry, University of Michigan, Ann Arbor

TEACHING POSITIONS

9/75-5/76	Teaching Assistant, Harvard College, Natural Science: Physiology

RESIDENCY TRAINING & POSITIONS

7/80-7/81	Chief Resident, Department of Psychiatry, University of Michigan
7/80-7/81	Consultation Psychiatry, U. of Michigan

7/79-7/80	Outpatient Psychiatry, University of Michigan
7/78-7/79	Inpatient Psychiatry, Vanderbilt University
7/77-7/78	Internal Medicine, Parkland Memorial, Dallas

MEDICAL SCHOOL

9/73-5/77	Harvard Medical School, Boston, Massachusetts Honors: Upper Third of Class, Master of Ceremonies at Medical School Class Day, Chi Omega Honorary Scholarship, Boylston and Aesculapian Societies

RESEARCH

1976-77	Clinical Research Project: "The Effect of Diet on the Insulin Requirements of Juvenile Onset Diabetics," pilot study at Peter Bent Brigham Hospital and the Joslin Clinic
1973	Research in Hypovolemic Shock in Dogs, Department of Surgery, U. of Mississippi

BOARD CERTIFICATION

American Board of Psychiatry and Neurology:

5/83	Part I passed in top quartile
6/84	Part II (Orals) Completed

PUBLIC EDUCATION PRESENTATIONS

2/96	"The Psychological Side of Creativity," Ann Arbor Women Painter's Winter Program

PUBLICATIONS

Zollman, W., Culpepper, R.D., Turner, M.D., and Hardy, J.A., "Hemorrhagic Shock in Dogs," *American Journal of Surgery*, 131:298-305, 1976.

Hardy, J.D., Hardy, J.A., et.al., "Fluid Replacement and Monitoring:" *Annals of Surgery*, 180:162-166, 1974.

AWARDS

1999	First Place, Ann Arbor Women Painters
1996	First Place, Toledo, PAA Exhibit
1995	First Place, Physicians as Artists

DEGREE PROGRAMS

1973   B.A., Vanderbilt University, Magna Cum Laude
1977   M.D., Harvard Medical School
1979-1981   Psychiatric Resident and Chief Resident,
            University of Michigan.

Curriculum Vitae

KATHERINE H. LITTLE, B.A., M.D., F.A.C.P.
Born April 19, 1955, Memphis
Married Spouse: Louie Edward Little, Jr.
Children: David Hardy Little and Katherine Louise
Little

CURRENT POSITION:
Director of the John S. Fordtran, M.D. Diagnostic
Center for Digestive Diseases since 1986
Baylor University Medical Center, Dallas, TX

EDUCATION:

Undergraduate: Vanderbilt University in Nashville, Tennessee;
                 major field of study – Psychology/Mathematics;
                 dates attended – 8/73 to 5/77; graduated with a
                 Bachelor of Arts degree, Magna Cum Laude.

Graduate: a) University of Mississippi Medical School in Jackson, Mississippi;
               dates attended – 8/77 to 6/81; graduated with a Doctor of
               Medicine degree, Cum Laude.

            b) University of Texas – Southwestern Medical

School in Dallas, Texas; internship and residency in
Internal Medicine; dates attended – 7/81 to 7/84.

c) University of Texas – Southwestern Medical
School in Dallas, Texas; fellowship in
Gastroenterology; dates attended – 7/74 to 7/86.

BOARD STATUS:

1) Board certified in Internal Medicine 9/84.

2) Board certified in Gastroenterology 11/87.

HONORS/AWARDS:

Graduated Magna Cum Laude from Vanderbilt University; graduated
Cum Laude from the University of Mississippi Medical School,
member of AOA, member of Phi Kappa Phi (scholastic honorary
society); received Surgery Award in 1980 for the highest academic
average in surgery at the University of Mississippi Medical School;
selected "Outstanding Hospital Based Attending" by Baylor Medical
Center medicine housestaff, 1989.

ORGANIZATIONS:

Fellow of the American College of Physicians; member of the
American Gastroenterological Association; member of Dallas County
Medical Society; member of the Christian Medical Association.

PUBLICATIONS: Thirteen, to include:

Hardy, J.D., Hardy (Little), K.P., and Turner, M.D.: "Massive Ringer's Lactate
Infusion: Comparison with Dextrose 5% and Whole Blood." *Annals of Surgery*,
1974, 182: 644-649.

Little, K.H., Lee, E.L., and Frenkel, E.P.: "Cranial Nerve Deficits Secondary to
Amyloidosis of Plasma Cell Dyscrasia Type." *Southern Medical Journal*, 1986;
79: 677-681.

Krejs, G.J., Little, K.H., Westergaard, H., Hamilton, J.K., Spady, D.K.,and Polter,
D.E.: "Laser Photocoagulation for the Treatment of Acute Peptic Ulcer
Bleeding." *New England Journal of Medicine*, 1987; 316: 1618-1621.

Little, K.H., Schiller, L.R., Bilhartz,, L.E., and Fortran, J.S.: "Treatment of Severe
Steatorrhea with Ox Bile in an Ileectomy Patient with Residual Colon."

Digestive Disease and Science, 1992; 37: 929-933.

Hogenauer, C., Meyer, R.L., Netto, G.J., Bell, D., Little, K.H., Ferries, L., Santa Anna, C.A., Porter, J.L., Fordtran, J.S.: "Malabsorption Due to Cholecystokinin Deficiency in a Patient with Autoimmune Polyglandular Syndrome Type I." *The New England Journal of Medicine,* 2001; 344: 270-274.

CURRICULUM VITAE

LOUISE SCOTT ROESKA-HADY, B.A., M.A., Dr. Phil.
Born Philadelphia, Pennsylvania, July 29, 1950
Married. Spouse: Karlotto Roeska
Children: Daniel Phillip and Susanne Louise Scott

Education

1972	B.A. with honor, Agnes Scott College major: philosophy minor: Greek Phi Beta Kappa President of Mortar Board
1975	M.A. *magna cum laude* Graduate School of Philosophy, University of North Carolina-Chapel Hill
1985	Dr. phil. *magna cum laude* in philosophy, J.W. Goethe-Universität, Frankfurt am Main, Germany

Current Position

Lecturer, Institut für Philosophie, J. W. Goethe-Universität, Frankfurt am Main, Germany

Fellowships, Grants and Honors

National Endowment for the Humanities summer fellow, "Folk

Psychology vs. Simulation Theory: How Minds Understand Minds" summer 1999

Wiedereinstiegsstependium des Landes Hessen 1993-94

Visiting lecturer, Universität Berne, Switzerland

Sibley Visiting Professor in Philosophy, Agnes Scott College, Decatur, GA 1995

fellow, Kulturwissenschaftliches Institut, Nordrhein-Westphalia 2001-2002

Teaching

lecturer in philosophy, J.W. Goethe-Universität, Frankfurt am Main, Germany 1985 -

interdisciplinary lecturer, Technische Universität Darmstadt, Germany 1988 – 1993

lecturer in philosophy, Universität Heidelberg 1993

lecturer in philosophy, Universität Mainz 2001

Professional activities

associate and lecturer, Forum fur Philosophie, Frankfurt am Main, Germany 1993-

consulting board, Dialectica, a professeional philosophy journal 1994-1998

director of the interdisciplinary study group 'Philosophie und Medizin', Forum for Philosophie 1988-1990

Professional memberships

American Philosophical Association,

Allgemeine Gesellschaft fur Philosophie Deutschland,

Gesellschaft fur Analytische Philosophie,

Society for Philosophy and Psychology

Publications: nineteen, to include:

Book:

Die Bedeutung in naturlichen Sprachen, Frankfurt am Main: Athenaum 1988.

Book Chapters:

1994 „Internalism, Externalism and Donald Davidson's Concept of the Mental" in: *Language, Mind, Epistemology. On Donald Davidson's Philosophy*, (Dordrecht: Kluwer Academic Publishers 1994): 255-297

2000 „Idealism and the, I' of Self-Ascription" in: *Indexicality and Idealism*, A. Ofsti, Truls Wyller (eds.), (Paderborn: Mentis Verlag 2000): 53-68.

2001 "Zuschreibungen und Personenverstehen" in: *Dresdener Hefte für Philosophie* Bd. II.

2001 "Indexicality and Mental Concepts" in: *Indexicality and Idealism II*, A. Ofsti, T. Wyller (eds.), (Paderborn: Mentis Verlag 2001).

Articles:

1997 „Zuschreibungen und die Ontologie des Mentalen" in: *"Perspectives in Analytical Philosophy"* (Berlin/New York: Walter de Gruyter 1997): 137-143.

2000 "Self-Ascription and Simulation Theory" in: *Protosociology* Bd. 14.

2001 "Moore's Paradox and the Concept of Belief" in: *Argument und Analyse*, *Paderborn*: mentis 2001.

Community Service

chairman of the school governing body, Lichtenbergschule Gymnasium, Darmstadt, Germany 1999 -

BIOGRAPHY OF
JAMES DANIEL HARDY, B.A., M.S. (Chem.), M.D., D.Sc. (Hon.)

Born: May 14, 1918, Birmingham, Alabama
Married: Louise Scott Sams, Decatur, Georgia, 1949, B.A.
Children: Louise Scott Hardy Roeska (Ph.D., Philosophy), Julia Ann Hardy, M.D., Bettie Winn Hardy Story (Ph.D., Clinical Psychology), Katherine Poynor Hardy Little, M.D.
Religious Affiliation: Presbyterian

Medical School: University of Pennsylvania (Philadelphia) – M.D., 1942   1938-42

Postgraduate Training: Hospital of the University of Pennsylvania: General surgery (certified) and thoracic surgery (certified)

Teaching: University of Mississippi Medical Center, School of Medicine (Jackson) Professor and Chairman, Department of Surgery and Surgeon-in-Chief, Hospital of the University of Mississippi   1955-87

Military Service: U. S. Army, 81st Field Hospital, USA, England, France, Germany 1944-46

Membership and Honors:
> American Board of Surgery (Vice Chairman, 1969-70)
> American College of Surgeons (President, 1980)
> American Surgical Association (President, 1975)
> International Society of Surgery (President, 1985-87)
> International Surgical Group (Founder Member)
> Society for Surgery of the Alimentary Tract (Founder Member)
>   (President, 1969-70)
> Society of University Surgeons (President, 1961)
> Society of Surgical Chairmen (President, 1976-78)
> Académie Nationale de Médecine (Honorary Member)
> Association Francaise de Chirurgie (Honorary Member)
> The Royal College of Surgeons, London (Honorary Member)
> Distinguished VA Physician, 1987-1990

Editorial Boards: Editor-in-Chief, *World Journal of Surgery*, 1981 (plus others)

National Committees:
  Surgery Study Section, National Institutes of Health   1958-62
  American Board of Surgery (Vice-Chairman, 1969-70)   1964-70
  Anesthesiology Training Grant Committee of the National Institutes of
    Health   1966-69

Visiting Professorships (34) and **Special Lectureships** (42)

Bibliography: 23 books and over 500 journal articles and book chapters

Publications of special interest:
1. Hardy et al. "Lung homotransplantation in man. Report of the initial case." J.A.M.A. 1963.
2. Hardy et al. "Heart transplantation in man. Developmental studies and report of a case." J.A.M.A. 1964.
3. Hardy et al. "High ureteral injuries; management by autotransplantation of the kidney." J.A.M.A. 1963.

Surgeons Who Had Their Training With Dr. Hardy

Ralph E. Abraham
Jerry R. Adkins
Pandeli Anas
James N. Anderson
Orlando J. Andy, Jr.
V. John Bagnato
Ralph V. Bailey
Stephen K. Ball
Jerry W. Bane
Kirk J. Banquer
Jare L. Barkley
Don W. Berry
Thomas K. Billups
William A. Billups
John B. Blalock, Jr.
James E. Booth
Fredricka M. Borland
John W. Bowlin
John W. Brahan
Shelby K. Brantley
Gray C. Buck III
Jeffrey P. Budden
Janis C. Burns
David E. Byrne
Robert S. Caldwell
David B. Carner
Clinton Moore Cavett
Carlos M. Chavez
Ernesto Ching
Frank B. Collins
William H. Coltharp
John J. Cook
Gary W. Cox
Harris Vann Craig
Mark H. Craig
G. Giltz Croley II
Russell Cummings, Jr.
Martin L Dalton, Jr.

John O. Dampeer Jr.
Stephen F. Davidson
David J. Davis
J. T. Davis, Jr.
Vincent C. DeGuzman
Robin K. Dhillon
Ralph H. Didlake
Philip D. Doolittle
Richard S Doyle
Laurence R. Dry
Mercedes K.C. Dullum
Robert L. Elliott
William C. Elston
Henry Pat Ewing
Leo A. Farmer
Edgar L. Feinberg II
H. Greg Fiser, Jr.
C. Thomas Fitts
Robert W. "Casey" Fitts
Hugh Agnew Gamble II
William C. Garre
M. Victoria Gerken
William J. Gibson, Jr.
W. Douglas Godfrey
Byron E. Green, Jr.
James C. Griffin, Jr.
James L. Hagan
Alexander J. Haick, Jr.
Jimmy Lynn Hamilton
Jeffrey K. Hannon
William J. Hardin
Lewis E. Hatten
Mark G. Hausmann
Allan H. Haydon
Stephen Henry Haynes
Bobby J. Heath
Susan E. Henry
Charles A. Herbst, Jr.

Benton M. Hilbun
Glyn Roy Hilbun
Jeremiah H. Holleman, Jr.
C. Wayne Holley
Allen U. Hollis
John E. Hoopes
Donald A. Hopkins
Hector S. Howard, Jr.
James J. Hudgins
Don G. Hunt
Steven A. Isbell
R. Blair Jackson
Henry McLean Jarmon
Mamoon Jarrah
Gerry L. Jeffcoat
Walter R. Jones, Jr.
Thomas L. Kilgore
Larry H. Killebrew
Richard I. Kirkland
Lawrence H. Knott, Jr.
Albert Michael Koury
Fred D. Kurrus
Cary Jake Lambert, Jr.
David A. Langford
Christopher L. Leach
Edward F. Levine
Anita K. Lindsey
C. Foster Lowe
Martin H. McMullan
Jasper L. McPhail
John M. McRae, Jr.
Albert L. Meena
Joseph Metcalf IV
Marc E. Mitchell
David O. Moore
Jerry D. Moore
Michael E. Moses, Jr.
Patricia C. Moynihan

Issa Muasher
William A. Neely
Barry D. Newsom
William E. Noblin III
Andrew J. Olinde
Robert I. Oliver
William Owen, Jr.
Harvey I. Pass
Ami S. Percy
John T. Perry
Anthony B. Petro
Charles G. Pigott
E. Leonard Posey III
Seshadri Raju
Jack L. Ratliff
Thomas E. Reeve III
Daniel Q. Richardson
C. Swayze Rigby
Edward E. Rigdon
Robert C. Robbins
Oliver Gordon Robinson, Jr.
Sam L. Robinson

W. Thomas Robinson
Jorge A. Rodriguez
Walter Thomas Rueff
Fred W. Rushton
William L. Safley
Suhayl Saleh
H. Randall Schmidt
John H. Selby, Jr.
Keith P. Smith
James P. Spell
Thomas V. Stanley, Jr.
H. Jerry Stone
Akio Suzuki
Stephen William Tartt
Robert S. Tarver
Richard B. Terry
William O. Bobo
Thompson
William C. Tompkins, Jr.
Frank H. Tucker, Jr.
Margaret Louise Turkleson
William H. Turney

Joseph Edwin Varner, Jr.
Harry S. Vorhaben, Jr.
George R. Walker, Jr.
James W. Walker
William H. Wallace
Peter Allan Ward
Robert L. Warner, Jr.
Edward Taliaferro Warren
Dov Weissburg
Ray L. Wesson
Jacqueline G. White
Robert D. Williams
Steven C. Williams
Thomas K. Williams, Jr.
William T. Williams
Johnnie W. Williamson
Jesse L. Wofford
Richard L. Yelverton
Richard L. Yelverton, Jr.
Charles Wallace Zollman

TEACHERS WHO HAVE BEEN IMPORTANT TO ME

Grammar School
Julia Ann Poynor Hardy

Highschool
Rispah Dudley
- Home Room
- Geography
Lillian Barksdale
- Civics
- History
Hazel Coke
- French
- Latin
Miss Lennie (?) Walker
- Math
Miss Utterback
- English
Miss Zelinski
- Choral music and band
Coach Sudduth
- Football

University of Alabama
Wanda Cade
- Freshman English
- English composition
George Palmer
- Atomic structure
Dr. J.L. Kassner, Jr.
- Quantitative analysis
Wooten and Quarles
- Physics
Henry Walker
- General biology
C.G.Breckenridge
- Mammalian anatomy

Jack Montgomery
- Organic chemistry
Herr Doktor Foster
- German
Helen Vickery
- Psychology
Berwind P. Kaufmann
- Genetics
Carleton Butler
- Director of Military band,
    football band, and concert orchestra
"Uncle" Tom Garner
- Director of the Glee Club

PENN MEDICAL SCHOOL
Freshman Year
Mary Hogue
- Histology
George De Renyi
- Embryology
David L. Drabkin
- Chemistry
Henry C. Bassett
- Physiology
Joseph Doupe
- Physiology
Henry F. Smythe, Jr.
- Chemistry
- Physiology
Henry Lee Spangler
- Anatomy
Sophomore Year
Mudd
- Bacteriology
Krumbahr
- Pathology

Coman
- Pathology
McCutcheon
- Pathology
Carl Schmidt
- Pharmacology
Robert Dripps
- Pharmacology
Comroe (J.)
- Pharmacology
Parcels
- Laboratory
Comroe (B.)
- Medicine
Junior Year
Arthur Phillips
- Outpatient Clinic
O.H. Perry Pepper
- Medicine
Charles Wolferth
- Cardiology
Francis Wood
- Cardiology
Richard Kern
- Infectious diseases and allergy
Edward Rose
- Endocrinology
T. Grier Miller
- Gastroenterology
Francis Lukens
- Research Medicine
Isaac Starr
- Research Medicine
I.S. Ravdin
- Surgery
Jonathan E. Rhoads
- Surgery
Elridge Eliason
- Surgery

Julian Johnson
- Surgery
Harold Zintel
- Surgery
Henry Royster
- Surgery
Dr. Ivy
- Orthopedics
Carl Bachman
- Obstetrics
Franklin Payne
- Gynecology
Joseph Stokes
- Pediatrics
Elizabeth Rose
- Pediatrics
Francis Adler
- Ophthalmology
Harold Scheie
- Ophthalmology
Dr. Schenk
- ENT
Col. Hitchhins
- Public Health and R.O.T.C.
Stecker
- Psychiatry

INDEX